TIME AND CHANCE
An Autobiography

TIME AND CHANCE

An Autobiography

Peter Townsend

COLLINS
St. James's Place, London
1978

William Collins Sons & Co Ltd
London · Glasgow · Sydney · Auckland
Toronto · Johannesburg

First published 1978
© Peter Townsend 1978
ISBN 0 00 211857 2
Set in Monotype Baskerville
Made and Printed in Great Britain by
W & J Mackay Limited, Chatham

To Marie-Luce and all my children

Contents

Illustrations

Again I saw that under the sun the race is not
to the swift, nor the battle to the strong, nor
bread to the wise, nor riches to the intelligent,
nor favour to the men of skill; but time and chance
happen to them all.

Ecclesiastes 9, 11

Prologue

No one ever said a truer word than Molière's Arnolphe when he remarked to his ward: 'The world, my dear Agnes, is a strange thing.'

I still marvel, sixty-odd years after I came into this world, at the way it has so strangely reshaped my life. Many have been the strokes of fortune – and misfortune – to which I owe this change. The key one, since it was so curiously related to subsequent events, occurred on 11 July 1940. That day I woke up just after first light and, rolling off the bed where I had lain sprawled in a shallow and all too short sleep, lifted the tent flap and peered out: low fog and drizzle. It was my turn for the dawn patrol.

An hour later, suspended on the end of my parachute, I was being wafted down towards the sea half a mile below. My aircraft had been badly hit, but by some miracle the blinding orange-coloured explosion in the cockpit had not blown my guts out. I had jumped for my life, counted one – two – three, and pulled the rip-cord.

Hanging there between sky and sea, I still clutched the rip-cord in my right hand. I carefully tied it to the dangling cable of my microphone; I would keep it as a souvenir when I got home. But perhaps after all I never should get home, for I still had to fall into the sea and I had no inflatable dinghy, only my 'Mae West' to keep me afloat. I might never be picked up. 'One of our pilots is missing', the BBC bulletin would say, leaving a last vestige of hope. However, in all that watery desert, there happened to be one small ship in sight – incidentally, miles off course. It was the second stroke of luck of that morning. The ship was some distance away when I splashed down into the sea, but it lowered a boat and not long afterwards I was hauled aboard.

The rip-cord which opened my parachute that morning opened also the way to a life which no man in my boots would normally have dreamed of. The destiny that was reserved for me was marked by three main events, all of which occurred also in July, on dates close to my escape that morning of the 11th.

A year later, on 17 July 1941, I married a girl whom I had known but a few weeks, a tragic mistake for us both, for it ended, like thousands of war-time marriages, in the divorce courts.

Then, on 14 July, thirteen years after that combat in which I had been trying, not very successfully, to defend England, I was expelled from the country. The reason for my exile was a pressing one: the world was speculating on whether the Queen of England's sister and I would marry.

The third event would eventually mean more to me than both the others: eight days before my early morning escape in 1940, an infant girl had celebrated her first birthday in Brussels, on the other side of the sea into which I had just fallen. Nineteen years later, she became my second wife, and, with her help, I have been able to build a new life on the ruins left by those two other shattering events.

What strikes me when I look at that rip-cord today is that this totally undistinguished object, a squarish, chromium-plated ring attached to a short length of steel cable, could have had such a bearing on my future. But for it, my life would have ended there and then and I should have disappeared unnoticed to join my ancestors.

CHAPTER I

Burmese beginnings

My ancestors, if they happened to be looking as their descendant was descending into the narrow sea off the east coast of England, might have found the episode inappropriate. For they were men of the West, worthies of Devon whose shores and granite cliffs resound with the thunder of the long Atlantic swell. Westward Ho! and across the oceans to the ends of the earth. That is the Devon tradition. Yet it was not until the mid-nineteenth century, when my grandfather married a girl from a sea-faring family, that my own family began to venture forth across the seas. Until then my ancestors had lived out their lives as squires or parsons in sleepy places with strange, sweet-sounding names like White-stone and Farway, Tedburn St Mary and St Mary Down, Ottery St Mary, Mohun's Ottery, Buckland Toussaints and Bovey Tracey.

My father was the son of Stephen, a doctor, and Mary Wooldridge, who came from a seafaring Cornish family. Mary doubtless kindled the flames of romance and adventure in my grandfather's heart. Instead of spending his life trotting on an old cob round a Devonshire parish visiting the sick, Stephen took the boat with Mary to India. There, as surgeon-general, he trotted alongside General 'Bobs' Roberts, hero of Kabul and Kandahar. General Stephen, now sporting the showy insignia of his rank, was a tall, substantial man and General Roberts, so I am told, had him ride beside him not especially for his company, but to draw the enemy's fire!

My father was born in 1864, at a time when Britain was the richest country in the world. New public schools were springing up everywhere and it was not surprising that my father should be sent to one which bore the stamp of the East India Company, Haileybury. He was a quiet, likeable person. Though not made for greatness, he lacked neither brains nor character and played as hard as he worked. His name is enshrined as a member of the 1881 rugby team in a gallery in the chapel precincts – sport and religion enjoyed, of course, equal status in an English public school, producing between them the muscular christianity needed of the men who ruled the Empire.

The Royal Military College, Sandhurst, taught my father the elements of soldiering, but he was never destined for a military career. He shared, however, his father's taste for adventure east of Suez and it was to India that he headed in the mid-eighties.

Hardly had he joined the Bengal Staff Corps than there occurred an event which changed his life. The Bombay-Burma Corporation had been caught poaching teak from the royal reserves of Thibaw, King of Burma. Thibaw imposed a fine and, encouraged by the French, made it hefty enough to ruin the Bombay-Burma. Queen Victoria despatched General Harry Prendergast and ten thousand of her soldiers to invest Thibaw's immense, moated palace at Mandalay. Thibaw wisely gave in without a serious fight; Victoria, Queen of foggy, far-away England, became overnight Queen of the Golden Land, a few degrees north of the equator. My father was one of the men sent to Burma to exercise the Queen's writ. He was not yet twenty-three.

Men like my father lived lonely lives in outlandish places. They were forbidden to marry until they reached their thirties. They administered vast territories practically from the back of a horse; their power, within its limits, was absolute but rarely abused. They were picked men, devoted to improving the lot of the 'natives', often too zealously for the latters' liking. With very little in the way of naked force at their disposal they relied on tact and persuasion. On one important occasion my father, in his lonely outpost, feared that, while the community celebrated, the 'bad hats' (as the Burmese themselves call the local under-world) would have a field-day. When the great day came he arrested them all and told them, 'Gentlemen, you are invited to be the guests of the King Emperor'. Whereupon he locked them up, fed them well and, the celebrations over, released them. All thanked him for His Majesty's hospitality.

My father moved rapidly up the ladder. He loved the Burmese; more, he realised, that some of them loved the British. It was nearly twenty years after he arrived there that he married. He was by then forty-two. My mother had come all the way from her home, Hartford Hall, in Cheshire. It is today a three-star hotel where, in the oak-beamed 16th century state-room, one may dance to 'live music'. I am sure that she would have been philosophical about this, for she lived with the times and never grew old. She was a great romantic, as ready for a walk in the woods as to sail or fly to the other side of the world in search of something new, unexpected, exciting.

This is what she found when, at the age of twenty-two and the end of a four-weeks' sea voyage, she arrived in the Golden Land. Notwithstanding the strict surveillance of her uncle, Harry Todd-Taylor, she was swept off her feet by my father, twenty years her senior, and led to the altar. As she once told me, she knew nothing, not even how babies were made. She herself made seven, all of whom adored and admired her. So did it matter all that much that her sexual education was nil? I believe that the fact that she had learned the basic values, how to 'behave' as the English say, was in the end what mattered most.

My parents were married in Meiktila, near Mandalay. The send-off after the ceremony was so noisy that the horses drawing the bridal carriage bolted. My father, being a good horseman, climbed with some agility (he had won the gym prize at Sand-hurst) on to the box of the careering vehicle where, top hat cocked over one eye and coat-tails flying, he took the reins from the terrified *syce* and coaxed the horses back to a steady trot.

The newly-weds honeymooned in Maymyo, its mellifluous name being a compound of Burmese and English: 'The place of May', the English colonel who laid out that cool little summer capital in the hills not far from Mandalay. Traversed by broad streets and winding lanes, planted with pine and eucalyptus and silver oak, it was a haven of rest for the English *thakins*. My parents returned at the beginning of every year, in the hot weather. It must have been there that they conceived me – I like to think so, anyway, for I love the sweet sound of Maymyo and its romantic old-world atmosphere.

They will tell you in Maymyo that all the red brick buildings were built by the English: the barracks, the garrison church, Saint Mary's Church and the rambling buildings of Saint Michael's School. Then there are all those red-brick Victorian villas still standing serenely in their spacious and well-kept grounds. In which of them did my parents stay? Fernside? East Ridge? Lily Cottage? The names are still on the garden gates. It was in one of those houses that my own life began.

Towards the end of his career my father, Commissioner of the Pegu Division and a member of the Legislative Council, was one of the handful of Englishmen who ruled fifteen million Burmese. Though his house has been pulled down and replaced by flats, the site will always be my *chet myo*, as the Burmese call it: the place where one's umbilical cord is buried. And the Burmese believe that, as firmly as you were tied to your mother before birth, you are tied for life to your *chet myo*. I believe so too.

My father gave of his best to Burma, I nothing. Rather, Burma has given to me. I never knew my motherland as a child except through the tales my parents told, the household souvenirs and pictures in the family album that my father showed me as I sat on his knee. It was twenty-one years before I returned to the Golden Land. Again I went back and again. Sixty years after my first arrival in Rangoon I found myself one night in a little Burmese town in the hills. It was the time of the Water Festival, which ushers in the New Year and festive music floated on the warm air, mingling with laughter and applause from the *Pwe*, the open-air theatre. The new moon lay on her back and cuckoos kept calling to the stars. Alone in the dark I listened, entranced. I was in love with my motherland, a dreamland of mountains, broad rivers and golden plains, where giant trees bloom pink and gold and mauve and flaming scarlet, where hyacinths crowd the water's edge and orchids grow wild. The Burmese, be they wizened, sun-dried old ladies or lovely maidens; silent, saffron-robed monks or enchanting sloe-eyed children; are gentle, unhurried and smiling people. They treat you as if you were one of them – which in a mysterious, un-changeable way I am.

Of this I was quite ignorant when, with my mother and my three year-old sister Juliet, I sailed for England. On a previous return voyage my mother had taken Audrey, my eldest sister, and Philip, my second brother; Michael, the eldest, was born at Hartford. Our voyage was not without perils; World War I was on, the Germans were entrenched not far from Paris and U-boats infested the Bay of Biscay. The overland journey to a Channel port being the safest way to England, my mother and her two offspring were put ashore at Marseilles.

During the three-days' journey across France at war I fed adequately from my mother's breast. All she herself could find to take the edge off her hunger was a single banana. Her odyssey finally ended at Tavistock, in Devon. There she left her five children in the care of our redoubtable aunt Edith, and a dragon of a nanny, Miss Knowles. Then she returned for the third time to join my father in Burma. Such was the lot of Britain's empire-builders and their wives. Two years passed before my parents saw their family again; then, in 1917, my father retired and returned to England, at that time half-starved and on the verge of defeat.

My parents must have found the change a hard one. Burma, despite the responsibilities, the separations, the lack of modern amenities, had after all been bliss: a climate of sun and warm, torrential rain, glowing sunsets, purple, starry nights and dew on the lawn at dawn; a prodigious vegetation, an easy-going people full of colour and laughter; faithful servants, kind with children. Then, the day ended, there was polo and drinks in the velvet twilight on the verandah. And of course my father was a man of authority, a *pukka sahib*. Now at Tavistock he was nobody – except to us, his children.

For us he was a father whom we respected, because his age and his quietness filled us with a certain awe, yet one whom we genuinely loved because of his goodness and his unconcealed affection for us. My mother, so much younger, was more approachable; yet she inspired a healthy fear in a way my father never did. With her blue and piercing eyes she could drill the life out of you.

So there at Whitchurch, near Tavistock, with the Golden Land behind them, my parents turned to the arduous task of educating their six children. They never failed us. Our education, though it impoverished them, brought us great riches.

CHAPTER 2

A Devon Childhood:
Westward Ho!

Cross House was our home at Whitchurch; its stone walls, washed a light pink as is often the way in Devon, harmonised pleasantly with the grey slates of its long gabled roof. A charming house, already a century or so old, it was solid, mature and comfortably contained our large family. Cross House has changed with the times – into two houses – but the original building has lost none of its allure.

During my parents' absence our aunt Edith took over as mistress of the house. She walked with a peculiar, purposeful gait, propelling herself with an elegant ebony walking stick. She wore a black velvet band around her neck which I took to be a permanent fixture, like the metal rings worn by those long-necked Burmese ladies. With her husky, commanding voice she did not endear herself too readily to my elder brothers and sisters, but she was not unkind and, as grown-ups went, I could get along with her. I have always benefited from strong characters, hard and demanding if you like, but comprehending.

That was Edie. She would have us down to the drawing room to sit in front of the log fire and read us stories. I forget them all except the one about the brave dog which saved a wounded British soldier from the Germans. We looked at pictures of the Germans and the sight of them, in their *pickelhauber*, plus the constant threat of my nanny: 'Master Peter, if you're naughty I shall give you over to the Germans', instilled in me a lasting fear of the Teutonic race. If it was not the *pickelhauber* it was the black Maltese cross, which seemed to me an emblem of terror until, in World War II, I met hordes of them in the air. Then, inexplicably, my fear vanished.

Aunt Edie, her reading over, would allow us to play the gramophone which looked exactly like the one where the white terrier is listening to His Master's Voice – a stout wooden box with a fluted trumpet like an overgrown, exotic lily. The little dog inscribed on the sound box bounced up and down on our warped records. We played our favourites until the records were scratched and discordant – the *Chocolate Soldier* and the *Girl in the Train*. We disputed hotly, until silenced by aunt Edie, whether to play first the *Stars and Stripes* or *Turkish Patrol*.

Like most little boys I was greedy, consuming jam and honey and cream and cake in exorbitant quantities. I was not above stealing certain delights, raspberries for instance, of which there grew in our garden a sumptuous white variety. The raspberry canes provided good cover, so that I could gorge myself with impunity. But one day my mother, fixing me with her blue eyes asked 'Have you been stealing raspberries?' and for answer I blushed as deeply as the red variety. My mother was more concerned with extracting the truth than in punishing; I think she must already have started to repeat to me one of her favourite dicta: 'Honesty is the best policy.'

To compensate for the good things there was no lack of gastronomic horrors: evil-tasting margarine which we were forced to stomach because the butter ration was negligible; and a variety of puddings of which rice and tapioca revolted me most. Memories of these culinary atrocities go back to my high-chair days. I was allowed to leave the skin, under which I would push as much as possible of the nauseating mixture. But nothing escaped my mother's eye. 'Go on, eat it up, every bit of it.'

My nanny, Caroline Knowles, was a great walker. When I went back over the old ground at Tavistock I was amazed at the distances I had walked as a very small boy. On one of these walks we were trudging up the steep, short hill leading to the church when a coal waggon laden with bulging black sacks and drawn by an emaciated horse began the climb. The coalman, mouthing a torrent of oaths, lashed the wretched animal with the leather thong of his whip and I watched in horror as the old horse heaved and strained against its impossible load, faltered and then fell.

That coalman, red-rimmed eyes glaring out of his lean, black face, was the first fiend I had ever set eyes on. His cruelty shattered my cosy little world of jam and honey and cake and kisses. In time I was to discover that there were brutes like him the world over, riding or driving jaded, half-starved animals with flanks and quarters beaten into raw, festering flesh.

My next encounter was with a robust and apparently happy animal. Miss Knowles walked me to a field, fortunately not too far away, for the fields around Tavistock soon give way to the wide, wild spaces of Dartmoor. Arrived there, we stopped in front of a five-bar gate on the other side of which was an enormous red Devon bull with a copper ring in his nose. He stood there, very calm, while Miss Knowles lifted me up so that I could stroke the curly forelock which topped his massive forehead. The red bull was a model of complacency and affection, which is more than I can say of other bulls I have met in country fields, in the streets of Tarascon or, more often, in ghastly nightmares when they pursue me, gaining on me all the time as I flee with leaden, dragging legs.

There were cows in that field, too; red all over, as befits a Devon cow, and not nearly as friendly as Mr Bull, whom I always met at such close quarters that I failed to notice the most impressive part of his anatomy. That of the cows, which swung, swollen with milk, voluptuously, between their back legs, I was able to observe at leisure. So impressed was I that when I got home I took my big fluffy ball and, indifferent to its white and blue-coloured segments, stuck it between my legs and crawled to my mother's knee, announcing triumphantly 'I'm a cow'. 'Yes, darling,' was all she said, leaving me none the wiser about my first brush with sex.

Miss Knowles's favourite walk was to Tavistock, the best part of two miles. She only went there on Sundays – for the good reason that her young man blew the trumpet there in the Salvation Army band.

Sometimes we arrived before the appointed hour and then we would loiter on the iron bridge across the Tavy, a singing, swift-flowing little river which provided yet another source of terror. Standing on my toes, I could just peer over the iron railing into the dark, peat-stained waters gliding swiftly below, swirling among rocks, whirling into pools and plunging headlong and foaming over the weir. Looking down from the bridge, I felt hypnotised by the power of that torrent, as I did later when first I saw the Victoria Falls and the rapids on the Congo River, downstream from Kinshasa.

Come 3 o'clock, Miss Knowles, with my small hand in hers, would be watching, entranced, as her young man stood round with the sombre-uniformed soldiers and the snooded ladies of the Salvation Army, bravely blowing the chords of a few happy hymns. Then, after a polite exchange of greetings between the two, the time would come to plod home. Invariably, long before we reached Cross House, I began to feel the pressure, but never could there be any question of relieving myself, however discreetly, by the roadside. 'You must hold on,' commanded Miss Knowles. 'Only another half mile' – a long way for my short legs. I did not always make it, but I tried, for the command was 'Hold on'. Thus at a tender age I was impressed with the essential secret of life – and more, of survival: *Hold on.*

One day, my second brother Philip was involved in a drama. A marvellously handsome boy with a fine head of golden hair, he came crying to my mother with marks of violence on his fair young face. My mother confronted Miss Knowles who responded fiercely: 'I swear by Almighty God I never touched the child', and left next day. Philip at this time developed a stammer which hampered him cruelly all his life.

I was about five when we moved from Tavistock to Bideford, on Devon's Atlantic coast, spending a summer holiday on the way at Trebarwith, Cornwall – known of old, I suppose to King Arthur at nearby Tintagel. At Trebarwith, for the first time, I came face to face with the ocean. I was terrified by that first confrontation with such an immense mass of swollen, angry water, by the incessant roar of the Atlantic swell as it did battle with the red granite cliffs, invaded their dark caves and retreated in a disarray of spume and spray. And when I walked on Trebarwith strand and the huge green rollers uncoiled in an explosion of foam and splayed themselves across the sand I shrank back, afraid to let the sea touch me.

From the high cliff top, where I sometimes sat with my brothers, the sea below, though still immense and brooding, lost some of its terror. Watching there, I marvelled at the seagulls gliding effortlessly on the invisible air currents. How different was the element in which those sleek white birds were floating, impervious to the forces at play below. From my bird's eye view, below all looked dark and dreary and dangerous, but up above there was light and boundless space. I longed to be a bird.

One day about this time a small aeroplane appeared in the Cornish sky, the first I had ever seen. I envied the birds, but infinitely more I envied the man in that flying machine.

Our new home, Glen Garth, was a roomy house at the end of a cobbled lane at Northam, near Bideford in Devon. Glen Garth had not the charm and the clean lines of Cross House, but its solid grey stone walls and spacious rooms gave it a friendly, reassuring feel. The garden was the answer to a child's prayer, with its croquet lawn and tennis court and yet another lawn, where shrubs and trees and flowers grew in abundance, which sloped down into a little copse we called the wilderness. Birds nested in the tree tops. Five giant cedars rose out of that great garden – each one of us had our own to climb. Bunches of fat grapes hung in the vinery close to the house, too close to make surreptitious tasting an operation entirely without risk. There was a more relaxed atmosphere when we gathered in a distant corner of the garden near the potting shed, where pink roses clambered in rich confusion; there we picnicked off eggs boiled in a saucepan on the bonfire and potatoes roasted in its red-hot embers.

That garden was paradise for us children and for my father too, who tended it lovingly with the help of Padden the gardener, a warm-hearted old rascal. His uniform, which never seemed to vary, consisted of a dilapidated waistcoat worn over a sweat-soaked flannel shirt, open at the neck, round which was knotted a red and white-spotted kerchief. His threadbare trousers were of corduroy and hitched below the knee with string. In winter, he wore on his head a greasy old gor'blimey; in summer, a broad-brimmed straw hat which he would pull down over his blood-shot eyes as he reclined in the shade for forty winks after the midday meal. Each day he brought cold tea in a green bottle with beef sandwiches and a hunk of cheese wrapped up in another red and white handkerchief. And, when the season was right, a little bird cage; for Padden, in defiance of the law, liked to trap gold-finches and bull-finches on twigs smeared with bird-lime. He would slip the little bird into the cage and carry it off home, concealed under the red and white handkerchief. Padden initiated me in the basics of gardening; thanks to him I first felt the earth with my fingers, the good red Devon earth which, when it dried on my hands in summer, gave me goose-flesh and made me want to dig my fingers back again into the moist soil.

One day, as I toiled beside Padden, a wasp stung me on the leg and I gave a howl of pain. The old man did his best to calm me. Pulling up an onion, he cut it in half with his curved knife and rubbed it on my pink, swollen flesh. There is no antidote better than an onion for wasp stings. One day, at my home in France, a wasp got into my mouth and before I could spit it out stung me on the tongue. I remembered Padden and sucked an onion. His remedy again saved me.

Michael, my elder brother, began to take me under his wing. He was a rather naughty boy with a fierce and sometimes perverse defiance of authority, doing evil not for evil's sake, but because he enjoyed the risks involved. I needed Michael and have always needed people like him; I lacked his cool courage, mine only coming with the heat of action. Michael sharpened my appetite for adventure and taught me how to handle risks. I found in him a loyal and daring ally; I in turn became his willing accomplice.

Our new nanny, Constance, was a nice, if slightly prim girl, who managed, despite her gold pince-nez, to look rather pretty. I was not in the least displeased to share her room and sleep in a bed alongside hers. One night I woke up with a start; at the end of my bed stood a whitish, ethereal figure with what looked like a mortar-board on its head. I prodded my sleeping companion and whispered urgently, 'Connie, quick! There's a ghost at the end of my bed'. She only replied drowsily, 'Be quiet and go to sleep'. Which I did, the shadowy figure having vanished.

Glen Garth has changed even more than Cross House with the times. Those splendid trees, grander than ever, are still in the garden, but in their shade have burgeoned half a dozen modern villas. The old house, like the Tavistock one, has been divided into two. The owner of one half, Mrs Walter, told me, 'One day I was gardening there, just beyond the terrace, when I felt a hand on my shoulder. I looked up but there was nobody'. Perhaps my ghost was still around.

We were a close-knit, happy family; our distractions were of the simplest; our visitors rare. Of these, my mother's parents impressed me most, but in different ways.

My maternal grandmother was a formidable personage. Her eyes were of the same blue as my mother's but more challenging. She put the fear of God into me and when she stooped to kiss me I trembled, only to find that her cheek was as soft as satin, pink and glowing with affection. She was terrified of thunderstorms, panicking at the faintest flash of lightning. Thunderstorms terrified me too. They were a sign that God was in a rage, throwing the furniture around in Heaven, punishing the human race, striking down a random victim here and there. If God was so indiscriminate I failed to understand how he could at the same time be the sort of loving father that people made him out to be.

My grandfather, whom I took to be about God's age, was to my mind infinitely kinder and more lovable. He was an adorable old man with a flowing white moustache and a twinkle in his eyes. He was a great ornithologist, riding all over the country to observe the birds he loved on a beautiful green bicycle with a string saddle, like a net. He mounted in the fashion of elderly men, placing his left foot on the 'step' (an extension of the back-wheel axle) and lunging gracefully forward on to the saddle. One day, at breakfast, he told me, smiling: 'I'm going to tie a knot in my tie' – a dark green one of the finest Macclesfield silk. 'Do you know why?' 'No grandpa,' I replied, puzzled. 'To remember you,' he said.

Another visit that I appreciated was the one made, all too rarely for my liking, by 'Cousin Addie', my godmother and my mother's cousin. My mother would thoughtfully warn me in time so that I could pen a note to Cousin Addie, discreetly hinting that I needed money or coveted a particular toy. Cousin Addie responded generously; an extremely vivacious lady, she always put new heart into my mother when the strain of her large family got her down.

Addie Gaitskell's two sons, Arthur and Hugh, were favourites with our family and not least with me, who was not too young to appreciate their charm and the indulgence they showed for one so small. One or other would take me, standing on the step of his bicycle and clinging on to his shoulders, shuddering across the cobbles of Durrant Lane and down the hill beyond. It gave me my first sensation of speed and I was thrilled. Hugh's penchant for high-speed pedalling cost him a broken arm; he was in any case less gifted for sport than as an intellectual, which is not surprising in one who became the leader of the British Socialist Party. Arthur's gifts lay in other directions. He was a great romantic, too. Though he failed in turn to conquer the hearts of my two elder sisters, he carried the day with my sister Stephanie, whom he married.

Another friend of the family who, happily, called not too frequently, was the local physician, Doctor Toy. An amiable man was Doctor Toy, with his big head of fuzzy white hair and his pince-nez attached to a black silk ribbon. His was one of the few cars in the district, an open two-seater T-model Ford with a dickey seat behind. Doctor Toy was as practised a hand with his Tin Lizzie as he was with his stethoscope. After every stop he cranked up the motor again and drove off, perched high on the driving seat, with the steering wheel just under his chin. He carried with him a leather bag containing his instruments and certain medicines: formamint or permanganate of potash crystals for the throat; cinnamon, aspirin and quinine for colds and 'flu; tincture of iodine for cuts – it hurt more than the hurt itself; Gregory's powder, a poisonous-tasting mixture, for stomach upsets; and of course castor oil for little boys. With this rudimentary pharmacoepia Doctor Toy kept our family in excellent health.

Our distractions, as I said, were few. Sometimes my brothers and I took the short cut through the fields and by way of Limer's Lane down to Bideford, where the air smelt of mud and seaweed and was full of seagulls' cries. There we would loiter on the quay where brown-sailed fishing smacks were tied alongside and little skiffs reclined on the mud-banks at low water, waiting for the tide to lift them back into the River Torridge.

An old fisherman befriended us; he wore a patch over one eye, the other looking out very straight from a face which was wrinkled and weatherbeaten and permanently covered with grey stubble. We called him Bosky-eyed Bill. I took to him, despite his rough manner and fearsome appearance. One afternoon he rowed us in a skiff up to Weir Gifford. On the way back I took a stick and made a semblance of rowing; I thought it right to give Bill a hand. But my charity was wasted on the old sailor; the current, not he, was doing most of the work as we drifted downstream.

One famous morning we woke before sunrise and ran all the way down to Bideford shipyard to see a launching. Whether you are six, as I was, or sixty, a launching is a moving sight; the new ship, graceful and erect like a debutante, gliding serenely down the slipway to make her first curtsey to the sea while those who watch send up a prayer for 'those who go down to the sea in ships and have their business in great waters'.

I first went to school at Northam, a simple little school run by Miss Simmons. I learnt to read and write – and recite. Miss Simmons taught me my first lines of verse and I have never forgotten them – who could?

> All things bright and beautiful,
> All creatures great and small,
> All things wise and wonderful,
> The Lord God made them all.

Simple, but basic. Miss Simmons did not stop at our reciting those lines. We lifted up our small voices and sang them. That song of praise made us feel good, and I still feel good when I hum it. Besides, it makes me think of Miss Simmons who was a very kind and dear old lady.

I had another sailor friend, Mr Cole, with a pink face and a trim white beard. He had retired from the Navy to settle in

Northam and wore the dark blue uniform of the village postman, with a red pin-stripe down his trousers and a bucket hat. I was always waiting for Tommy Cole when he called; he took me by the hand and led me to school. To me, no nicer postman could have existed and I felt as safe with him as any one of the letters in his brown canvas post-bag. He taught me how to make sailing boats and in time I made some beautiful ones, sails and all. I sewed them myself and rigged them to the mast. I was quite a gifted sempster and my mother, to tease me, sometimes called me Lucy, which enraged me. Sewing after all is as much a man's job as a woman's: if we are to have equality of the sexes it should work both ways.

Another hand I sometimes held on the way to school was that of a beautiful girl called Rosemary. She was five, with a character as sweet as her gentle, laughing eyes and her lovely face. I loved her. Rosemary's house was nearer school than ours and we walked together hand in hand up the road to Northam, a quiet country road plied by horse-drawn carts and an occasional car. What saddened me when, half a century later, I went back to look for Rosemary's house was not so much the fact that it had disappeared as that a constant stream of noisy, smelly cars was speeding along the road where she and I had walked so peacefully. Rosemary passed out of my life, but I shall always remember her for the joy she gave me.

On the Northam road a child risked nothing, either from those afoot or driving. I had only one apprehension: a walk to the village meant running the gauntlet of the 'village boys'. Not that I feared that they would hurt me, but they teased me and sometimes asked me to play. This I could not dream of doing – for the unarguable reason that it was not 'done'. My family belonged to the 'gentry', a part – now almost extinct – of the English middle class. Though only six, I knew exactly where I stood in relation to the adjacent layers of society, the 'lower class' and the *nouveaux riches*. With the former I must be neither familiar nor condescending, but courteous, respectful of their sterling qualities. They were the backbone of England, the archers of Agincourt, the 'tars' of Trafalgar, the Tommies who stuck it out in the trenches. The second category, the *nouveaux riches*, though far better off than us, were what my mother called (harking back to Burma) a 'different *jat*', another sort. Their unforgivable failing was to be 'common'.

This is how in my family the division was made between the sheep and the goats: on the one side people who were 'common'; on the other, who were 'ladies' or 'gentlemen', to be found mostly among the 'gentry' and the upper classes. A 'nature's gentleman', though rare, was accepted as a possibility. The English may be the greatest snobs on earth, but this aspect of their snobbery is unique and laudable because it is based not on material but on moral values, on the importance of proper behaviour (no matter how eccentric).

I was made to believe that the village boys were beneath me because of their lack of manners and education. It took me many years before I began to feel free of the inhibitions planted in me from my earliest youth and to acknowledge that 'village boys' could turn out to be far better men than the highest born in the land.

My father, true to the family tradition, was a religious man; no doubt more so because his long years of loneliness in Burma had inclined him to live, like an oriental sage, a life of contemplation. Not that for him, a father who had to provide for his six children, it was all that simple. He took care personally of our religious education. We gathered about him in his study every Sunday morning, when he read the Bible to us and rehearsed us in the catechism and the ten commandments. Mine was no more than a listening brief – I was too young to understand the Bible's wisdom or the Church's dogma. But the atmosphere impressed me.

The Sunday morning session over, we would troop off with my father to Northam Church. I loved those walks to church with the air full of the joyful peal of bells. The first of them was cast in 1553, when Drake sailed away from Devon around the world in the Golden Hind.

We ring the Quick to church the Dead to grave

goes the inscription at the foot of the belfry, and warns:

> He that shall ring in hat or spur or overturn a bell
> Or by unskilful ringing mars a peal
> He shall pay sixpence for each single crime

Today those who seek the Lord in Northam Church are turned away with an apology: 'We are sorry, this church has to be kept locked'. Mr Hookway, who was mowing the graveyard, told me why: 'Vandalism'. He unlocked the door for me; it was over half a century since I had been inside. There was our pew and opposite the legend, 'This yele (aisle) was made in anno 1593'. One thing struck me: the vergers' long staffs, which had used to be topped with a golden cross, now looked like billiard cues. I asked Mr Hookway what had happened to those crosses. He repeated sadly: 'Vandalism'.

It was at Westward Ho! that I at last came to terms with the sea. It was there that I found the courage to dash out and meet the Atlantic rollers, hurl myself into them and glory in their power as they bowled me over and swept me inshore in a mass of boiling foam. I am glad that it happened there, in Bideford Bay, for it makes me feel that I have in my veins just a little of the salt that is in the veins of the men of Bideford, men of whom, fighting the Spaniards, the poet had sung:

> Men of Bideford in Devon
> And they laid them on the ballast down below
> And they bles't him in their pain
> That they were not left to Spain
> To the thumbscrew and the stake
> For the glory of the Lord.

Sailors and airmen know what it is to ride the storm and to drift blissfully on the calm. The dangers they face from the elements, the elation they feel, are of the same order.

The time came – I was then about seven – when we left our garden of Eden and moved east, halfway to London, to settle in the prim purlieus of bourgeois Bournemouth. My father's sole reason was to find better schooling for his large family. To turn his back on the west, where he belonged, was a wrench for him, as it was for us. Michael was the only one of us to continue in the tradition of the west, at the Royal Naval College, Dartmouth. Philip was soon to go Londonwards, to my father's old school, Haileybury. The girls and I were despatched to local schools.

We were heartbroken to leave the house, and worse, the garden we had loved so much. In the garden at Glen Garth my father left something of himself, something that he had created. In vain; for of all his love and labour there remains no trace today.

After us came Mr Derry, a business man from London. The people of Bideford have a name for London, 'Smoke', and Londoners they call foreigners; but nobody called Mr Derry a foreigner, and for good reason. For Mr Derry, Londoner though he might be, lavished all his love and much of his fortune on Glen Garth's garden. And Mr Derry's gardener's name was Friendship.

What a beautiful name, Friendship. And one which harmonised perfectly with Derry. 'There was an old Derry-down-Derry, who liked to make other folks merry.' That is what Mr Derry did in his own way, with the help of Mr Friendship. Between them they made the garden of Glen Garth so splendid that people came from miles around to admire it. Alas, when Mr Derry died, Glen Garth was sold for a song – to an astute businessman. Much of that glorious garden was devastated to accommodate the half dozen villas now sheltering beneath the cedars we used to climb as children.

Though, when I met him, Mr Friendship was very old, his face was pink and unlined and his eyes a pale, luminous blue. He sat there in the sunny parlour of his home in Cross Street, Northam, gazing fixedly through the window. Our reminiscing about Glen Garth had created an immediate bond between us and when the time came for me to leave, Mr Friendship took my hand and held it, unwilling to let it go. He looked me straight in my own blue eyes and I understood. During the war a German airman whom I had grievously wounded held my hand and riveted me with his eyes in exactly the same way. It was the gesture of a man who, feeling death very close, clung desperately to life, seeking courage for the long, lone journey ahead. But for all the chagrin that Mr Friendship may have felt, there was perfect certainty in his blue eyes. He was a gardener. Nobody understood better the cycle of life and death, the rhythm of decay and rebirth. At one point in our conversation Mr Friendship had murmured, almost absently, those lines:

> You are nearer to God in a garden
> Than anywhere else on earth.

Perhaps, as he gazed through the window and beyond, he was thinking of the garden he would plant in Paradise.

CHAPTER 3

Eastward Ho:
Bournemouth and to school

The Moors, Spur Hill Avenue, at Parkstone, a suburb of Bournemouth, was our new home. Bournemouth, with its tea-rooms and Winter Gardens, its piers and its municipal orchestra, struck a very different note to that of Bideford and Westward Ho! We had come to settle in a bourgeois stronghold, an environment with which we were not familiar, but to which we quickly adapted. The house was hideous, too high for the ground it stood on, with walls of bright red brick, lavishly adorned with drainpipes; a roof of asymmetric slopes and equally bright red tiles completed the disharmony.

After the richly planted acres of Glen Garth, our new garden was but a narrow plot, from whose mean, gravelly soil my father somehow managed to coax a harvest of fruit and flowers. Hop manure was apparently his secret, judging by the sacks of it which went to nourish that starving soil. Narrow as the garden was, it was hedged in with ignoble laurel and sickly-smelling privet. They had been rooted there for years before we came and were our regrettable heritage, but at least they protected us from the neighbours who pressed in upon us from either side.

For the laurel I found a use; a screw-cap jar stuffed with crumpled laurel leaves provided my 'killing bottle', the gas-chamber in which the butterflies I netted were put to death. God forgive me; it seemed no offence to capture and preserve those marvellous colours and designs. Once my captives, Red Admiral or Small Copper, Peacock, Painted Lady, Cabbage White or Azure Blue, had succumbed to the laurel's toxic fumes, it was with an intense pleasure that I impaled their thin bodies on my setting-board and pinned out their fragile wings. Butter-flies were a pure joy, with their pretty names and the non-chalant folly of their flight, their gorgeous colours and lovely

landing places – crimson buddleia and mauve veronica and all
the fine flowers of the garden.

The front garden, as we called the small area between the
house and the road, was a confusion of trees, bushes and climbing plants – most of them, oddly enough, of oriental origin:
jasmine, japonicas and bamboo – which struggled heroically in
that inhospitable occidental soil to embellish the façade of our
suburban home, mellowing the aggressive red of the bricks and
camouflaging the array of drainpipes.

No one dreamed of calling the back garden by such a name.
It was 'the garden' – just that – and in it my father made a
brave attempt to retrieve the disaster of the front garden. Most
of it consisted of a grass tennis court surrounded by netting
which was hoisted into position at the start of every season. A
bed of roses, another of flowering shrubs, a line of fruit trees:
that was all, and it was not even enough to justify the help of a
gardener – which was just as well, because my father could not
afford one; he needed every penny to pay for our education.

What a come-down, after luxuriating in the glories of Glen
Garth, to be confined to this flat, narrow plot of ungenerous
land. But thanks to my father's love and skill, the roses bloomed
unfailingly, filling the air with their scent, so that, long before
I listened to Juliet passionately entreating Romeo, I knew too
that no flower could smell so sweet. So deeply did I inhale the
scent of those roses, so profoundly did they pervade my senses,
that I can smell them still.

Enhancing their beauty, there fell upon them, of course, the
drops of dew that one sees in gardening catalogues. And swarms
of green, gleaming beetles – a pest, I suppose, though they
looked like emerald or jade – descended on them, bees and
butterflies too. And then there was the fragrant verbena which
hung on the wall, and pungent-smelling geraniums, pink and
white and scarlet. Only later, when World War II came, and
men were thinking out the best possible means of killing one another, did I learn that one of the deadliest gases smelt of
geraniums. I thought it would not be too bad to die with the
smell of geraniums in the air.

Finally, there was the clean, fresh smell of newly-mown grass.

We all worked diligently to maintain our lawn. Mowing was reserved to my father and brothers; I was not yet considered to possess the required skill. My task was the humblest one of all, weeding. I loved it. I felt like a knight of old, chivalrously rescuing the fair grass from the villainous dandelions and plantains, uprooting each one with my pronged tool and leaving their corpses strewn in my path. The roller provided a different, a more ponderous pleasure. It was heavy for me to push, but in the early morning, while the dew still lay, I would roll that lawn, sweeping away the dewy carpet which had been laid overnight from heaven, leaving behind me parallel lines of light and shaded green. It was hard but rewarding work; you could see the immediate result of your labour.

I was sent to a kindergarten run by Miss Lawrence, a middle-aged lady whose dark brown eyes looked at you straight out of a finely moulded face; her sallow skin had the luminous quality of wax and her hair, combed back from a high forehead, was raven black. But behind Miss Lawrence's sombre features there abounded warmth and comprehension.

One day I found myself alone in her study facing those black eyes which shone like fiery coals. Miss Lawrence sat at her desk, behind which stood a vase containing a spray of peacock feathers. She might have been a maharanee, I her humble servant and worse, one guilty of a flagrant offence. For – encouraged, I must say, by other horrid little boys – I had lifted the skirt of a little girl called Betty. I did this not because I was curious to discover what lay beneath – having sisters, I already knew – but simply to humiliate Betty, a rather pretentious little girl. I doubt whether I used this plea with Miss Lawrence, for I have never been clever at defending myself with repartee and specious arguments. But there was something about me which impressed my judge – my innocent look, perhaps. Miss Lawrence might have whipped me or expelled me or reported me to my parents for my serious breach of conduct. She simply said: 'You are a very naughty boy. Don't you ever dare to do it again.'

There did seem to be something about me which provoked women's tenderness and indulgence. Another who had a soft spot for me was Miss Reeves, a charming girl who was a mistress at Miss Lawrence's. She taught us how to calculate in tens and hundreds, using white and pink cotton reels which we fitted on to long metal spikes. She made us learn a rhyme – not one with a religious theme, like 'All things bright and beautiful', but with an imperial message to stir our loyal young hearts – we were formed almost from the cradle to serve the British Empire. I copied it out in a large round hand in a glossy red notebook (red, of course, for the empire which covered a quarter of the globe).

'Where are you going to all you Big Steamers?' it began, and then ran through the Empire's main ports of call.

Miss Reeves, who lived nearby, often took me to school on the carrier of her beautiful Rudge-Whitworth bicycle. Sitting there, holding her slim waist, I was far from insensible to the movement of her hips as she pedalled away. It was another thing with Miss Davies, more elderly but no less well disposed. Miss Davies wore false teeth, no doubt the reason for her dreadful halitosis. Sometimes she drove me to school in her little two-seater Wolseley; her breath was almost unbearable, even with the hood down.

Then there were our neighbours, the Miss Walters, Laura and Violet, elderly spinsters who doted on me. Laura was comfortable and plump and appeared to be permanently seated. She dispensed freely of her warmth and I enjoyed her immensely. Violet was spare of frame, tense and energetic. It was she who piloted the Miss Walters' astonishing car, a 'Trojan', whose coachwork, painted battleship grey, seemed as solid as armour plate. Its engine emitted clouds of blue smoke and was connected to the back wheels not by the usual transmission shaft, but by a massive chain. The wheels themselves were solid and spokeless, like the wheels of a Trojan chariot; the tyres were of solid rubber and so narrow that Miss Violet frequently found herself battling to free the car from the grooves of the local tramway system.

One day I was summoned alone to the Miss Walter's and there the sisters, all smiles and affection, made me a wonderful present: a beautiful set of carving chisels which had belonged to their late brother. It was a present that I treasured, for although

I never acquired sufficient skill to use those precision tools to their full advantage, I was able all the same to practise my favourite pastime, carpentry.

My religious education and that of my brothers and sisters continued under the aegis of my father. Daily, he said prayers with all of us kneeling on the floor around the breakfast table, our elbows leaning on the soft leather seat of our mahogany chairs. Whatever our feelings, we submitted unquestioningly to this ritual – all except Michael, whose dissident spirit burned ever more fiercely. Heaven help me if he were kneeling next to me. With his devilish green eyes and dead-pan smile, he would shoot me a glance which sent me into a fit of giggles and it was always I and never he who caught the resultant packet from my father.

On Sunday, we would gather as usual in my father's study, a squarish, cosy room which gave on to that ghastly front garden. The study was heated by an anthracite stove of glazed brown tiles. My father's pipes were propped in a wooden rack on the chimney piece. His massive armchair was upholstered in red leather, well worn and punctuated with little red buttons; the bookshelves were full of leather-bound volumes, and a sheet of morocco leather covered his mahogany writing-table on which reposed the various implements he used for writing and reading – a powerful magnifying glass included – and for pipe-smoking: a jar of spills for igniting the tobacco, another of feathers for cleaning the pipes.

Although I was always rather afraid when I went to my father's study, he would receive us with the utmost gentleness. On Sundays, seated in his armchair, he would hear our catechism. I had made progress since Glen Garth; it now fell to me to answer the first questions: 'What is your Name?' 'Peter Wooldridge' I would reply hesitatingly as if I hardly knew. 'Who gave you this Name?' The answer was a big mouthful for a boy of eight: 'My Godfathers and Godmothers in my Baptism wherein I was made a member of Christ, the child of God and an inheritor of the Kingdom of Heaven.' It seemed to open up immense possibilities, which were seriously dimmed by the following question: 'What did your Godfathers and God-mothers then for you?' I thought of Cousin Addie, the only one who had ever done anything for me, and then only when I dropped the most obvious hints. But back I came with the ritual answer, which I found appalling in its implications: 'They did promise . . . First, that I should renounce the devil and all his works, the pomps and vanity of this wicked world, and all the sinful lusts of the flesh.' It was a lot to ask of a little boy who had put his arms around Miss Reeves's slim waist and, without quite knowing why, had felt a tremor of pleasure.

Catechism over, we trekked a mile to St Luke's church, all of us dressed in our Sunday best and well washed behind the ears. I could not wish to see a man dress better than did my father; in his perfectly tailored blue suit and his bowler hat, a rose-bud in his buttonhole and his gold watch-chain making a graceful double-U across his waistcoat front, he looked ex-tremely handsome. A light tap on the barometer before leaving would tell him whether to take his fine Malacca cane or silk umbrella, tightly rolled in the superstitious belief that it would stay the bottles of heaven. Church was as much a social as a religious occasion and my parents carefully controlled the pace of their little platoon, according to whether they wished to meet or avoid other families churchward bound.

In the pew in front of ours sat Mr and Mrs Popplewell. Un-like the Tavistock bull, which I only saw from the front, Mr and Mrs Popplewell I only observed from behind, and their behinds were of such ample proportions that a chair's width was left between them to allow for overlap. Mrs Popplewell's hat fascinated me. A black straw affair, there dangled from it under my very nose – for Mrs Popplewell remained permanently seated – a fat bunch of imitation fruit: grapes, cherries and plump strawberries. They made my mouth water, I longed to pick a few of those juicy-looking berries.

A Hindu prince I got to know years later told me that he pitied Christians because their religion was so dreary and morbid. In many ways it is; yet at Saint Luke's, Christianity, and particularly the songs that I heard christians singing, came across to me in a way that filled my young heart with gladness.

First, the *Venite*: 'O come let us sing unto the Lord . . . in his hands are all the corners of the earth . . . the sea is his and he made it and his hands prepared the dry land.' I thought it marvellous that the Lord was such a great fellow and had put himself to so much trouble on our behalf. Then that exhilarating expostulation in the *Te Deum*: 'Thou art the King of Glory.' What a superb title – so much more succinct and meaningful than that other one, splendid too but difficult to remember: 'High and Mighty . . . King of Great Britain and his Dominions beyond the Seas.' The *Benedicite* rocked me with its immense outburst of joy and everyone and everybody blessing the Lord – Sun and Moon, Stars of Heaven, Showers and Dew, Winds, Fire and Heat, Frost and Cold, Lightnings and Clouds, Mountains and Hills, 'all ye Green Things upon the earth,' even Whales and Fowls and Beasts and Cattle – 'O let the Earth bless the Lord.' What a glorious song; the choir and the congregation of Saint-Luke's were transported by it, and so was I, in my piping voice.

I was frightened of death, black, purple, hushful, lily-scented death, and by everything that evoked it: coffins and catafalques and top-hatted undertakers and hearses and their black-plumed horses, widow's weeds and black mourning bands. I spent part of one sermon furtively reading the Burial Service: 'Man that is born of woman hath but a short time to live. He cometh up and is cut down like a flower.' Not an encouraging prospect for an eight year-old. So dreary in fact that even in those childhood days I found it impossible to live with; resolutely I turned away from this morbid idea of going down into a hole in the ground, to the worms, the wormwood and the gall. The only way I could divert my thoughts from the grim vision of death was to bless the Lord, as the Sun and the Moon and all the rest did, and to magnify him for ever.

I was afraid of the dark, too, because death in some form seemed to be lurking there. In the night ogres and giants, witches and monsters would come to haunt me; or the queen of *Alice in Wonderland* would scream, pointing at me, 'Off with his head', or a giant from *Jack and the Beanstalk* would start chanting 'Fee, fi fo fum! I smell the blood of an Englishman . . .' One day

I pulled down a book from one of my father's bookshelves. It was called *Fire and Sword in the Sudan*; one of the pictures made me recoil: limp bodies, heads lolling, were hanging from a row of gibbets; others, headless, lay around in pools of blood.

Massacres and mortal accidents added to the horrors which came to terrorise me in the night. Often I would cry out and then my father would come in his dressing-gown of white towelling. The sound of his voice and the feel of his hand would bring me back again from this realm of horror into my own world where there was nothing to fear.

Fifty years separated my father from me. I could feel he loved me, but never did he say so. I loved him too; he was good, and gentle and kind. But I could not tell him so either. If ever we found words to express such feelings, we never dared to use them; thus we never got to know one another.

My youngest son, Pierre, and I are separated by fifty years, too. There is a lot of love between Pierre and me and we don't mind saying so. I wish my father could have passed on to me what I can give to Pierre, and I wish I could have been the warm and generous companion to my father that Pierre is to me. Pierre makes me laugh when I remember the horrors which so terrified me when I was his age. Watching a particularly ghoulish TV thriller, full of corpses and coffins, I asked him 'You're sure this won't give you nightmares?' He replied jauntily, 'Don't worry. The only thing that gives me nightmares is eating too much.'

If my father's study was the holiest of holies it was not a sanctuary reserved only for our religious instruction. I spent many a relaxed hour there. My father would show me *Punch* – his bookshelves were packed with rows of leather-bound volumes dating back to the turn of the century. The drawings were exquisite in detail and form, and the jokes fit for a child in a cradle, let alone one sitting on his father's knee.

What most enthralled me was *The Story of the British Nation*, done up in several thick red volumes. It came across so vividly from the text and the pictures that I felt a deep, if vicarious, involvement, especially in the battles against our island's invaders and our foes across the sea. From all the long saga of

British resistance, from Boadicea to the Battle of Trafalgar, there stuck in my mind certain lines that my father read me. The first were from the Anglo-Saxon Chronicle of King Alfred, who thrashed the Danes about a thousand years ago:

> They gave them blows instead of shillings
> And the axe's weight instead of tribute . . .

And the next, Nelson's signal at Trafalgar:

> England expects every man will do his duty . . .

And so at my father's knee I first learned the right attitude to take towards would-be invaders.

My parents nurtured in their home the sunny nostalgia of the east. The drawing-room, whose bay window admitted, when available, the maximum of sunlight, was the natural repository for their simple souvenirs: a few aquatints of the Irrawaddy and Mandalay and the Shan Hills; a teak, ivory-tusked elephant and another of shining ebony; a river boat with eyes in the prow, and a glass-fronted cupboard filled with Chinese objects; tiny blue silk shoes, delicately embroidered, which had once contained the bound, stumbling feet of some elderly Chinese lady; porcelain bowls and spoons painted by hand.

Then there were friends, 'old Burma hands' as my parents called them, who talked of the old days and sipped tea, a fragrant blend from Assam, and glanced, maybe, at the family album with its shiny sepia prints of scenes which were for ever gone: picturesque landscapes and pagodas and my father's polo ponies, their bridles held by respectful *syces*; the proud-faced polo team and groups of bald, bewhiskered *sahibs* with their *memsahibs* sporting flowery and immensely broad-brimmed hats, and here and there a senior Burmese official, small and slim in national costume, tucked in between those bony, broad-framed white men who ruled the Golden Land.

The Burmese nostalgia even extended to me, when my mother transformed me into a Burmese boy, with sandals and a golden Shan silk *longyi* and a pink *gaung-baum* wrapped round my head, to go to fancy-dress parties. These I hated, because I was shy and shrank from rowdy gatherings full of shouting children, but it was a relief, instead of sweating it out disguised as Father Christmas or a country curate, to wear sandals and the soft, smooth silk of the Burmese dress.

I kept on good terms with the cook and the kitchen maid: while the kitchen was out of bounds, they could be persuaded to become the clandestine purveyors of the good things which came out of it. Kindness went a long way with these often lonely, bleak-faced ladies who spent most of their lives in other people's houses and seldom had one of their own. I was a keen if not particularly gifted cook myself, though my culinary creations were chiefly limited to toffee, shortbread and jam, for my personal consumption. At the same time, I made so light of laundering that my mother nicknamed me the Chinese washerman. It is proper that a man be able to cope alone with his personal chores, when so many saints – notably, in my time, Mahatma Gandhi – have done the same. Besides, the staff who performed these tasks were already a fast disappearing race; the more so in my parents' case since the time came when they could no longer afford domestic help.

For the decline, not to speak of the fall, of the British Empire was preceded by the decline of the humble and obedient servants who had so faithfully served it. The causes of their decline – as with the Empire – were largely economic. People like my father, having served the Empire, felt bound, through loyalty and pride, to raise their sons in the same tradition of imperial service. This meant giving them a costly education, paid for from their own pockets, which often impoverished the unfortunate parents. My parents saw us through. It cost them dearly, though in the end it was not they who fell into ruin, but the ugly house in which they had raised my brothers and me.

Half a life-time later I found the house derelict. 'The Moors' now stood in a parched and weed-ridden wilderness, a neglected graveyard in which my father's and our own efforts lay buried and forgotten. Only the laurel and the privet thrived still, as poor creatures find the means of doing – without love or care. As for the house, it was a mausoleum in which reposed our shattered dreams, the perished ideals with which we thought we could change the world and make it a better place. My brothers and I, like so many of our generation and generations before us, had been raised to go forth into the world, with our gentlemanly ways and our gleaming swords, to slay the tyrant and defend the oppressed. We faithfully did our duty. But we failed. 'The Moors' seemed to be the symbol of our failure.

CHAPTER 4

Wychwood

Every little bird must leave the nest; but not all little birds, nor, for that matter, little boys, are pushed out of it at such an early age as English boys who are sent to preparatory boarding schools. I was eight when I was weaned from my family and sent to swell the bevy of boys who formed the stock-in-trade of Mr Insley, headmaster of Wychwood School. To be honest, I would say of most of my teachers that they gave us more of themselves than they ever got out of us in terms of income. I still owe much to Wychwood; it was a sort of nursery garden where the seeds of manhood were planted in us.

But the start was difficult. The impression of being abandoned – surely the most miserable that exists – made me feel like Oliver Twist; I cried in my bed at night. Not that, like Oliver, I felt hungry. There was no lack of food, though some of it was so repulsive that it found its way not into our stomachs, but into envelopes we carried in our pockets for the purpose. The most redoubted dish of all was one that is described in Webster's *Third New International Dictionary* as 'a dessert made from gelatinous or starchy substances and milk, sweetened, flavoured and shaped like a mould' – in a word, *blancmange*. Considering the contempt in which the French hold *la cuisine anglaise* it is about time that they admitted that its worst horror is their own horrible *blancmange*.

Wychwood stood up proudly among the pines and heather and rhododrendrons on the high ground north of Bournemouth. The house was an imitation, in red brick, of a French château, complete with *tourelles*. Perhaps the château motif was inspired by the fact that Wychwood, built at the end of the romantic period, was the first Anglican private school in England to admit Roman Catholics. The influence of the Vatican did not, however, deter Wychwood's then headmaster from an illicit love-affair with the school matron, a liaison which led to tragic consequences. Matron was not above the temptations of the flesh. While nursing a little boy gravely ill with pneumonia, she left the bedside of her young patient for the bed of her lover. During the moments of ecstasy that she enjoyed in the headmaster's bed her little patient was agonising in his. He died, alone and uncomforted. Not long after, Matron, full of shame, died too. Thereafter her ghost came to haunt Wychwood, sitting on the stairs in the corridor just outside the little boy's death-chamber, weeping. It was eventually exorcised by a Roman priest.

Our own headmaster, Mr Insley, was kind but severe. We feared him. A massive man, he had a rubbery nose and invariably wore rubber-soled shoes. So when, after lights-out, Mr Insley came striding down the corridor, we were warned of his approach by the squeaking of his soles on the linoleum. I suspect now that he purposely wore rubber soles to warn us of the approach of Nemesis.

They saved me from a hiding one night. While school rules were imposed from on high, we ourselves were a tight little society with unwritten rules of our own. Lucas, the boy who slept next to me, had been found guilty of infringing them. I was appointed to execute the sentence – four strokes on Lucas's bottom.

It was some time after 'lights out', but summer, so all could see. We crept out of bed; I, the executioner, and Lucas, my submissive victim. As I stood poised to deliver the first stroke with my own red slipper, I heard the unmistakable squeak of rubber on linoleum. My reflexes were quicker than those of Lucas. As Mr Insley strode into the dormitory demanding: 'Lucas, what are you doing out of bed?' I was already back in my own, my heart thumping so loudly that I was afraid the headmaster would hear it. 'Bend over', he commanded Lucas and, replacing me as executioner, administered justice, with my own red slipper, on the unfortunate boy. I was troubled by my neighbour's misfortune and would readily have shared it, for this is what our code of honour demanded. But Lucas kept shouting: 'It was him, it was him!' trying to inculpate me. This was unworthy of our code and a reason for silence. Mr Insley evidently agreed, and I was spared.

Another who walked on rubber was Mr H. He was fat and swarthy and suave, from his slimy smile down to the squishy crêpe soles of his shiny brown shoes. Mr H. was a pederast; not that it worried us, for we had not the faintest idea what a pederast was. Nor did it strike us as unusual that Mr H. should always turn up, a willing helper, at our bi-weekly bath-time, when Matron scrubbed us from head to foot.

One evening, I was washed by Mr H.; he massaged the more inviting curves of my small body with his soapy hand, sliding it up deftly between my thighs until, in a slippery lather of soap-suds, he was fondling my private parts. It never occurred to me what Mr H. was up to. Nor to any of us; all we noticed was that he disappeared abruptly one day, soon after, and was never seen again.

Yes, pure and innocent we were. To us *sex* was Latin for *six* or, at a stretch, a word to differentiate male from female. TV did not exist; only radio programmes of unquestionable propriety were broadcast from London by 2LO. Sometimes we tried to tune into these on a home-made 'cat's-whisker' set, but the crackling in our earphones discouraged us. We were forbidden to read the daily newspapers. Of sex and homosex we neither knew nor cared. None of us disliked Mr. H. He was our history master and taught us well. It was a pity that he liked us the way he did and, at bath time, came clean off the rails. For little boys, with their heads full of dreams and inventions, with their exploring and their experimenting, their hurts and disappointments, need the sympathy of a man they can trust.

Wychwood did not lack such men. One was Mr Williams, a rather special brew of Mr Chips. Brew was the word – Mr Williams liked his beer and often reeked of it. He was our Latin master. His blue eyes, blood-shot and short-sighted, looked out, over-large, from behind the thick lenses of his gold-rimmed pince-nez, which he removed in order to read, bending down to within nose-length of the paper. A white, tobacco-stained moustache and ill-fitting false teeth added to his forlorn expression. Despite it, Mr Williams often laughed, in a loud guffaw, and then his upper teeth would detached themselves and crash down on to the lower ones, leaving the bare gums of his upper jaw exposed.

Mr Williams was not to be judged by his forbidding appearance. His heart was of gold and, though he frightened us with his sudden outbursts of temper, we found no fault in him. 'You fool, you!' he would shout when infuriated by our ignorance. When he shouted at me, I often felt frustrated and helpless, not because I did not know the answers – for I was one of his best pupils – but because I could not say them for shyness. I panicked at the sound of my own voice and remained tongue-tied. That was how I got to know the agony of being a stammerer.

When he was not teaching us Latin, Mr Williams would coach us at cricket, his major passion. It became mine too. On Wychwood's cricket field I learnt the most civilised and testing game in the world. Cricket is not a trial of strength; it is a test of character and a key, incidentally, to the English character. People who do not understand cricket will never understand the English.

An Englishman's life pattern is largely based on cricket; it provides him with a code of behaviour, a technique for survival and the ability to remain detached when all about him is tumult. The Test score takes priority over the most world-shattering political event. The greatest moments in cricket take place in silence, not to the frenzied shouting of the crowd. There is melody in cricket: one of the most beautiful books I ever read about it was written by Neville Cardus, music correspondent of the *Manchester Guardian*. It is a game for the gods, which is why the English pay it god-like reverence. Fly low over England any Saturday afternoon in summer: on every village green you look down on white-clad cricketers. Before them, centuries ago, it was the archers who besported themselves on that same green.

I lived for cricket, I went off alone to the county ground at Bournemouth, timidly paying a few pennies to enter, and then sitting in the crowd, a small, inconspicuous figure in grey shirt, flannel shorts and felt hat with silken cord of red and green, the Wychwood colours. I sat there, basking in the glory of my heroes: Phil Mead of Hampshire and the fast bowlers Newman

and Kennedy; Boyes, a slow left-hander, whose style I admired
so much that I taught myself to bowl left-handed like him. The
Australians came, with Ponsford, Oldfield, Macartney and
Grimmet, the wizard slow bowler; Yorkshire with their wily
bowler Wilfred Rhodes and Dolphin, their fat, efficient wicket-
keeper; Lancashire with the Tyldesley brothers; Jack Hobbs,
the super-star of Surrey; Roote of Worcestershire; White of
Somerset and all the rest of them.

Inspired by these great cricketers and guided by Mr Williams,
I won my colours in the Wychwood XI. I was granted the
privilege of wearing a white cap emblazoned with the school
crest. It was as good as a crown. I kept it stuck in my blazer
pocket, being far too shy to wear it.

If old Mr Williams was the kind of man that small boys take
to, so, in his own way, was Mr Longley. He knew no Latin, he
played no cricket and perhaps he could not even write very
well. But of his solid goodness Mr Longley gave us much. He
was the school carpenter. An ex-sailor, he had departed from
naval custom and grown a small moustache, waxed and pointed.
His slow, soft accent marked him as a west countryman. As
solid of stature as of heart, Mr Longley amply filled his blue
overalls, yet the strength in his square hands and short, tattooed
arms was as gentle as his speech. It was he who awoke my
senses to the scent of oak and pine and to the stench which rose
from his little black glue-pot when heated on the stove. I
discovered from him the knack of working different grains with
plane and chisel and saw, keeping faithfully to the straight line
I had marked out with my carpenter's pencil. Under his
practised eye I learned the respect that a workman owes to good
tools and materials and the value of patience and precision in
realising his designs.

Yet, for all my admiration for Mr Longley, I reacted to
carpentry with a distinct preference for curves rather than
straight lines. I was happier with a spoke-shave – that small two-
handled plane for rounding off angles and flat surfaces – shaping
by eye from a rectangular block of wood the graceful curves of a
model sailing-boat. To me it was obvious that the most lovely
shapes were curved, like hills and clouds, rivers and waves and

the world itself – not to speak of women, which at that age I had
no inclination to do any way.

One night Mr Longley's wife died. Strangely enough, when
told by Hughes, the head boy, I just laughed – not out of cruelty
or indifference to Mr Longley's grief: it was the grim expression
on the face of Hughes. Instinct and, perhaps a little, reason made
me rebel against the notion that death was the ultimate catastrophe which people seemed to take it for – despite the promises,
admittedly tenuous and lacking in tangible proof, of eternal life.

Miss Busby the gym mistress, exercised an iron control over
us. It was not her beauty that commended her to us, though to
the sentimentally minded, with her tight bob, blue serge gym-
dress which barely extended below her supple hips and black
tights moulded to well-muscled legs, she might have suggested a
stage version of Joan of Arc. Miss Busby put us through it, on
the parallel bars, the wall bars and the ropes; when we vaulted
the horse in quick succession, she caught us in mid-air, to break
our fall, as if we were chaff. Then she would command us to lie
on our backs on the floor, to relax from the finger tips, from the
toes. 'Two minutes of this,' she assured us, 'will do you more
good than a couple of hours sleep.' I still practise Miss Busby's
technique.

This remarkable lady also taught us to box, a sport from
which I shrank from the first: it hurt so much hitting the other
fellow. She was, too, a graceful, if over-energetic ballroom
dancer. I had my first lessons from her, pressed to her firm
bosom – it was she who did the pressing, for she danced as the
man. I felt her body but in the wrong places: she clasped my
chest to her stomach, flat and hard as a board. My cheek never
reached up to hers, but reposed on her bosom. She propelled me
swiftly round the floor in a two-step or tangoed me in a series of
sweeping chassées and cross-steps, while pretty Miss Hunkin at
the piano bobbed up and down or swayed according to the
rhythm, which ranged from *La Paloma* to *Whistling*, the *Blue
Danube* and *Yes, we have no bananas*. When it came to the
Charleston, Miss Hunkin gave us her own hotted-up version of
Yes sir, that's my baby, which set us stepping frenziedly in that
most gloriously crazy of all dances.

Our zest for dancing did not stop at the ballroom variety. We swung into the Lancers and Sir Roger de Coverley; we tripped the folkloric toe to country tunes like *Shepherds' Hay* and pirouetted gracefully in old-time sword dances. At one speech-day, I appeared dressed as a sailor and danced a hornpipe before an enraptured audience of parents.

The gymnasium was not only the scene of our gymnastics, our boxing and dancing. We said our daily prayers there every morning at nine, we acted plays and we sang, under the baton of the Reverend Mr Batley, who took Mr Insley's place as headmaster a year or so after I arrived. An old Harrovian – of about the same vintage as Winston Churchill – Mr Batley was no every-day parson. The Military Cross won, God best knows how, as an army chaplain, dangled from his surplice. His car, a dark blue Bentley, was hardly a clergyman's runabout. In his early fifties, he was still wiry, his aquiline nose jutting out of a baldish head. From his mouth protruded, permanently, an enormous pipe which, when he laughed, he was careful to clench between his false teeth, so that they remained firmly in place. It was a good trick, which Mr Williams would have done well to adopt, except that it produced showers of saliva.

Under Mr Batley's inspiration, singing became part of our life. Gladly we lifted up our voices and sang – psalms and hymns and songs of praise, as well as the rollicking, sentimental and patriotic kind which we took from the Harrow song-book, *Gaudeamus*. The Reverend Mr Batley M.C. took care that our repertoire included songs like *The British Grenadiers*, *Hearts of Oak* and *Rule Britannia*, that stirred our hearts and prepared us subtly but surely to answer, if need be, the message: 'England expects . . .'

Mr Batley brought along with him a second-in-command, Mr Calkin, a younger man with a fine brain, dynamic and enterprising. If there was always a pipe in Mr Batley's mouth, Mr Calkin was never without a cigarette in his; with his tongue he rolled it incessantly along his bottom lip from one side of his mouth to the other.

Mr Calkin spent hours reading to us in his rich, expressive

voice. He opened our eyes to the beauty of the English Bible, preferring the Old Testament to the New. We were not mere listeners to the prose and verse that Mr Calkin read to us, but learnt much of it by heart, so that today it remains graven in my memory. Of course, he regaled us with all the best stories, of Samson and his beautiful, wicked Delilah; of David and Goliath – David the youthful hero; David and Uriah – David the decadent hero who falls to the depths of shame and deceit; of Saul, with his clandestine visit to the witch of Endor; of the weakminded Ahab and Jezebel, his bitch of a wife – and poor Naboth, murdered for his vineyard; of the avenging Jehu, 'who driveth furiously'.

Mr Calkin's reading went far beyond the Bible; his feeling for fantasy was contagious. We rattled off 'The Jabberwocky' and other rhymes from *Alice*, and revelled in the *Bab Ballads*. For fun, Mr Calkin read to us Jerome K. Jerome and Edward Lear; for romance, adventure and heroics, Conrad and R. L. Stevenson and Rider Haggard with, for good measure, the *Iliad*, the *Lays of Ancient Rome* and old ballads like the *Inchcape Rock*. The *Adventures of Sherlock Holmes* and the *Innocence of Father Brown* allowed us to savour different techniques in the detection of crime; Edgar Allan Poe provided all we needed, and sometimes more, of the supernatural and the macabre.

But of all this wide diversity I enjoyed the Bible most. Not that I was particularly religious; it was the melody and rhythm of the language, the marvellous stories, the poetry and the imagery and, above all, the wisdom. In it there was a message which no other book succeeded in conveying so wholly, so convincingly, even to one so young. I felt that I could trust the Bible and ever since have felt that until you have got its message you have no inkling, whoever you are, of what life is really about.

Mr Calkin's efforts on our behalf were not entirely sedentary. He led us down to Bournemouth pier and put us aboard the *Skylark*. Across the bay we sailed to Studland, to swim and play among the dunes. There it was that I first experienced the sensuous feel of flight. I jumped from the top of a high dune, like a bird from a cliff-top, into space, hurtling, wingless, through the air, falling and falling till I flumped into the soft, warm sand far below. I would gladly have stayed and camped in those dunes, as the Wright brothers had done in the dunes of Kitty-hawk, Virginia, when barely twenty years earlier they became the first men to fly. I longed to launch myself into the air again and again, for sheer joy. But the time came to board the *Skylark* and chug back across the bay.

Mr Calkin helped us to make a huge relief map of Purbeck, with the contours sawn out of plywood and moulded over with putty, and the features painted in. Purbeck, to my mind, was a Land of Canaan, a Promised Land which could only be reached across a strip of water, wider and deeper than the Jordan, and traversed by the ferry at Sandbanks. My father forbade me to cross, fearing that I would wander too far. But, one day, I disobeyed him and bicycled away, across the ferry, far into the Purbeck Hills, returning at dusk. When my father asked 'Did you cross the ferry?' I replied without conviction: 'No.' My father did not say another word. He knew that I had lied and I knew that he knew. That hurt more than any other punishment could have.

Unexpectedly, the return to the Promised Land came the following spring, when all six of us (a seventh, Francis, having just arrived) were packed off to an adorable cottage, surrounded by a sea of bluebells and cowslips and primroses, with the air full of birds' songs. Two miles walk away, at Seacombe, we climbed down a chain fixed in the cliff face, long ago, by smugglers, and dived into the heaving swell. Then back, hand over hand, up the chain and across the fields to the Square and Compass, there to drink fizzy lemonade. Once, Michael had my glass filled with half a pint of rough Dorset cider. I drained it and afterwards lay sprawled on the grass, rather drunk, listening to the larks blithely trilling and the plovers' cries, with the clink of the hammers of Purbeck stone-cutters drifting on the breeze. I was ten.

Fifty years passed. I returned to the Square and Compass. The sound of the larks and plovers and the stone-cutters' hammers was still in the air. Sea-birds flocked on the cliffs and flew out across the glistening sea. Nothing seemed to have changed. Only I had. The landlord too, of course. The present one, Mr Newman, grandson of the man who served me cider fifty years back, now drew me another half-pint. Not far away, at the Bournemouth Education Committee's seminary at Langton Matravers, I found the relief map I had helped to make.

But of Wychwood school I found no trace, save the carpenter's shop, now a faded green, where I had worked with Mr Longley. The big house had been razed to the ground. A tall orange crane towered against the blue sky on the site where it once stood. The romantic château motif had been abandoned: the houses going up were advertised as 'luxuriously appointed Georgian style'. The cricket field, once hallowed ground, had now become a housing estate. Only at Wychwood Cottage, built for Mr Calkin on the slope below the cricket field, was tradition honoured: the grille over the back window, installed to save it from a hard-driven ball, was still in place.

CHAPTER 5

Haileybury

Wychwood had moulded me, rather than knocked me, into shape and filled me with ardent dreams for the future. Haileybury was to provide the toughening process, the technique of survival. It was a hard school.

I was still only twelve when I passed the entrance exam, taking second place. This put me in a class with boys much older than myself. They adopted me as a kind of mascot and were kind to me – which was not the case with my house-mates in Lawrence, my father's old house.

With his hand gently clasping the nape of my neck, my father propelled me towards the dormitory where he, in his time, and my brother Philip, in his, had slept for five years. My own five-year spell was beginning. I was a 'new guv'nor' and wore the prescribed dress: a blue suit and bowler hat. My father bid me goodbye – it would be three months before I saw him and my family again. I felt no desire to cry, only to steel myself for worse times which, I knew from Philip, were yet to come.

Lawrence was one of eleven houses, each of fifty boys who slept in one long dormitory. My pied-à-terre for the next five years would be a cubicle separated from the next one by a low, white partition. In half of this narrow space a modicum of privacy was possible when we dressed or undressed and the surrounding red curtains were drawn. The other half contained a bed covered with a red blanket.

At seven o'clock each morning, the school bell tolled, a dreadful, compelling sound which dragged us out of our sleep and sent us leaping out of bed to undress and run, half asleep and totally naked, at top speed, to the bathroom. Any hesitation or loitering on the way, and you were punished. Many were the boys who, waking with the most flamboyant symbol of their puberty arrogantly refusing to subside, rushed to the bathroom praying that it would do so before they arrived there. This enforced exhibitionism was an offence to our pudor and amour-propre.

If we accepted this embarrassment, we felt differently about the treatment meted out by the senior boys of the Dormitory Classroom. The 'D.C.' was the home of a dozen and a half first-year boys. Its floor was of bare boards. On one side of a large rectangular table, chipped and mutilated by preceding generations, was an upholstered bench, the 'soft-arse', reserved for the privileged bottoms of all but us new guv'nors, who were relegated to the 'hard-arse', a wooden bench opposite. Extra seating was provided by a few dilapidated Windsor chairs, most of them with the spokes of their back-rest missing. In one corner stood a chest-of-drawers where various cooking utensils were stored. At the far end of the room, rows of lockers, one for each of us, completed the rudimentary furnishings.

In these uncongenial surroundings, we were tortured with diabolical thoroughness. The first trial came three days after our arrival, with the 'new guv'nors' exam'. Each candidate was required to recite Kipling's poem *If*, from beginning to end. Well might it admonish you to

> . . . keep your head when all about you
> Are losing theirs and blaming it on you.

Blows rained down on us at each mistake we made. They were struck with tennis shoes on the hand. It hurt. Trick questions followed: 'How many masters are there?' Few of us knew that there was only one 'Master', the headmaster; the rest were 'beaks'. More blows. 'How many plots of grass are there in "quad"?' Four, you would have said, but you were wrong; there was another slender strip, making five. Again more blows. From the start I resolved to submit without resistance; the humiliation would harden, not diminish my own pride and my contempt for my torturers.

Another event was the obstacle race, the course leading us diving under the table and wriggling through the back of the backless Windsor chairs. At every available occasion our tormentors beat us with wet, knotted towels. The last obstacle was the chest-of-drawers, along which we had to do the 'splits'.

I was in the lead. I took the jump in fine style – a bit too fine, for at the end of the chest-of-drawers there protruded a long nail. It was Sunday and I wore my best blue suit; the nail ripped through the cloth and gashed my right thigh for six inches, leaving an ugly, bleeding wound. (The scar is still there.) In my cubicle I tried to staunch the bleeding. Jim Jordan came; he was the house servant, the 'Toby', a little man with broad shoulders, good and brave, who had been shot clean through the lungs from front to back in World War I and left for dead. He knew what it was to suffer and he was good to us. He wanted to tell the housemaster, Ashcroft, but I begged him not to; 'sneaking' was an unforgivable sin and anyway, the wound did not hurt me so much as the fact that the trousers of my new blue suit were torn.

I was beaten for trivial offences on six occasions. Once, realising my number was up, and to minimise the pain, I slipped a silk handkerchief – the recognised specific – into the seat of my trousers. After an interview with the head of the house, which ended with the command: 'Prepare the D.C.', I had to run down the length of the dormitory to do so. As I ran, I noticed my silk handkerchief (it was red and white, like the one that Padden, the gardener, wore) fluttering like a pennant from the bottom of one of my trouser-legs. That earned me an extra stroke.

The condemned prepared the D.C. It was like digging your own grave. You cleared all the furniture to one side – except two wooden chairs which you placed back to back, so as to allow your executioners a clear run at you of three or four paces. For the victim, a beating was a test of behaviour. You awaited your executioners; when they arrived and you received the command 'Bend over', you climbed the scaffold, in the noble tradition of the courageous host of martyrs, kneeling on one chair and bending over, so that your head touched the seat of the other. You gripped that seat with your hands and waited for the first of the executioners to come running in, then the second, the third and the fourth – the maximum allowed for a house prefects' beating. Then came the command: 'You may go', and you rose with all the dignity you could summon and, head held high, left the room – with the certainty, if you had not flinched, that you had successfully accomplished yet another exercise in survival.

The house was a community where the boys were the masters and the masters – the 'beaks' – stood aloof. Immediate and slavish compliance with the wishes of the older boys provided the only hope of survival. Two disfiguring diseases came to visit us during the winter season, when the big playing field 'Twenty-acre', which accommodated several games of rugger at a time, was often a soggy morass. *Tinea Cruris* – T.C., or just plain 'Crutch-rot', and 'Scrum-pox', were fungus diseases of the skin which, it was said, persisted so tenaciously in our day because the germs had been in the soil since the region was hit, in the Middle Ages, by the Black Death. A tall story perhaps; but these two pestilences caused as frequent if not as fatal ravages among us. The treatment, let alone the disease, branded you as unclean. Crutch-rot would only succumb to an ointment which burnt the testicles and the groin a livid purple-red. In the bathroom, the victim was isolated from his fellows; he only needed a bell to mark him as a leper. The facial sores caused by scrum-pox were daubed with silver nitrate, which left the sufferer's face covered with black, scabby blotches. Crutch-rot and scrum-pox created, for a season, a caste of untouchables.

At Haileybury, where life for us young ones was hard and sometimes cruel, there was no one to help us but ourselves. Yet, for all the cruelty, the callousness and the unloveliness, it did no good to cry out for pity. On the contrary, the grim conditions made me clench my teeth; I felt within me a growing determination to resist. Without knowing it I was being inoculated with the serum of survival. Survive your first two years at Haileybury and you could survive anything.

At the start of my second term, the summer term, a disaster befell me. We were summoned to 'New Guv'nors nets', where our prowess as cricketers was put to the test. Paralytic, as usual, with nerves, I made a poor showing and was rejected as a candidate for further coaching. I, who lived for cricket, who had won my colours in the first XI at Wychwood, had been rejected! I was mortified, nor could I count on anyone for sympathy. I felt disgusted with myself and with authority. I put cricket out of my mind. Never again did I want to handle bat or ball, or smell the divine aroma of linseed oil. I took to swimming. I swam so hard that I won cups for races and more cups for diving. I became a champion and gained my 'wings', badge of a small élite. They were sewn on to my blue 'bim-bags', the scanty slip we wore, not far from where a fig-leaf might have been more appropriate.

But wings suggested flying, and so I was in a way, when I dived like a bird through the air and into the water, both elements in which speeding bodies, aerofoils and hydrofoils, obey similar laws. Speed, or rather the sensation of speed, clean, cleaving, straight and silent, intoxicated me. I loved the water; its sensualism appealed to me, and swimming suited my temperament.

Unable to rely on myself when it came to a test of nerves, like going out to bat, I needed an additional impetus to get me going. Later, aeroplanes and race horses did the trick admirably – once in the cockpit or the saddle, they provided the impulsion which forced my unwilling reflexes to act. With swimming, the crack of the starter's pistol did the same. It cut through my taut nerves and torpedoed me into the water. The problem was akin to the stammering complex: if a stammerer could shout or sing or roar with laughter, out would come the reluctant words.

Following on the heels of my setback at cricket came another graver experience. I had been warned, of course, about 'older boys', but it never occurred to me that I should run into trouble in that area. I was innocent to the point of naivety, uncorrupted with every intention of remaining so. Yet, one day, Ashcroft, my housemaster, called me to his study. 'Sit down', he said. 'I have something very serious to say to you. It has been reported to me that you have been consorting with older boys.'

I was stunned. All the boys in my form were much older than me, anyway, and it seemed idiotic to make insinuations about their or my conduct. I burst into tears of anger and despair. It appeared that our drawing master was the author of this sinister report. I had taken him for a friend, he had helped me with the problems of perspective involved in drawing aeroplanes and ships. Perhaps he meant to do me a good turn, but I took him for a traitor and a purveyor of lies. I went on crying bitterly, screwing my handkerchief up in a ball, while Ashcroft continued, quite kindly, to lecture me. Then he let me go.

I wrote immediately to my father to tell him of my woe and that I could no longer stay at Haileybury. 'My life is ruined', I concluded.

There was no reason why my father, now well into his sixties, should suddenly take an interest in aeroplanes: on the contrary, if they were not exactly anathema to him, they represented a break with tradition. So it was, I believe, entirely because of his goodness to me – because he meant to prove to me that my life was not, as I thought, ruined, and because he must have noticed that I always looked up at the sound of a motor in the sky – that he took me to an air meeting at Bournemouth: a kind of aerial Derby Day, with its atmosphere of the fairground and the crowd pressing to the edge of the paddock-like enclosure, where the shining little thoroughbreds, all biplanes, waited to taxi to the start.

My father propelled me, his hand as usual on the nape of my neck, to one of the turning points. From there, I witnessed a spectacle which itself was a turning-point in my life. I watched, spellbound, as those little aeroplanes came boring down at full throttle on the chequered pylon, banking vertically so that I could see the pilot crouched behind the windscreen, his scarf trailing in the slipstream.

That sealed my passion for the air. Henceforth, hulls and sails gave way to the more voluptuous forms of wings and fuselages.

And it so happened that the pilot who turned lower and faster than any that day, was my future commander-in-chief, Sholto Douglas.

About this time, when I was thirteen, we moved from Bournemouth back to the West Country. Our new home was a 400 year-old cottage, once the village blacksmith's and his forge, now knocked into one. Crowcombe was our village, a tiny one beneath the rolling Quantock Hills in Somerset. We all breathed more freely now that we were back in the west, though my father was rather piqued that it was Somerset and not his native Devon.

For me the horizon widened. I loved the hills. I climbed to Hurley Beacon and lay there in the heather, listening to the coming and going of the bees in the warm air. Where I lay, I imagined that I was in an aeroplane looking down on the patchwork of fields and woods in the valley below. And looking up at the buzzards soaring and wheeling in circles, I felt certain that one day I should be like them. I wandered alone in the hills, running down the paths which led into those deep, narrow valleys called 'combes', to gather speed for the climb up the other side. I ran with sheer joy, as if I were flying. I rose at daybreak and, with an old hammer-gun, went back to the hill to hunt rabbits. Then I felt that the world belonged to me. Later, when I was a pilot and flew on the dawn patrol, I got the same feeling.

Back at school, I began gradually to emerge from hell. Moving on from the Dormitory Classroom to the House-room was a release from one ghetto to another, where conditions were less sordid and sadism was not on the daily menu. Moreover, our house-room, being wedged between the Master's house on one side and the library and the chapel on the other, was in a kind of silent zone, and that tended to restrain its senior inmates.

We congregated twice every day in 'chapel'. Under its high-domed roof we prayed briefly in the morning, and went back for more prayers and singing in the evening. At Haileybury, as at Wychwood, singing was part of our life, an uplifting and dynamic influence. It was in chapel that the school motto *Sursum Corda* – Lift up your hearts – came alive. We lifted up our hearts and our voices and sang, the five hundred of us, with all our youthful verve.

I, who would not dare utter a note in public, and would only sing in my bath with the tap running, found myself singing with full-throated, almost reckless assurance. Our faith was pretty formal, our theology practically nil. It was not the religious theme, but the mood that got us going. The praise-and-glory hymns are unfailing morale-raisers; the emotional ones stir you to the depths; and the crusading ones made you feel you could conquer the world. Christmas would be dull without carols; the triumphant Easter hymns justify the preceding tragedy. And at the end of a long summer's day we sang:

> The day thou gavest Lord is ended
> The darkness falls at thy behest

and went to bed with the surge of its words and music in our ears.

The din of the world can never, in my mind, muffle the words or silence the music of those hymns. They penetrated into the depths of my soul and there will they remain until I depart from this life.

My housemaster, Ashcroft, who had been gassed in World War I, was understandably a lover of fresh air. He inhaled the largest possible quantities of it when he went flying. Ashcroft loved flying. He knew too that I was longing to fly and, being a good and an understanding man, he fixed it for me one day, during my fourteenth summer.

He drove me to the R.A.F. base at Old Sarum, near Salisbury, where I presented my father's written permission for the venture. And venture it really was: flying was practically unknown to the general public, and to small schoolboys in particular. I signed a 'blood-chit' absolving the R.A.F. from responsibility in case of an accident. The 'blood-chit' gave me the fleeting thought that I might die; if so, it would be a hero's death.

From Old Sarum's grass field, I soared off the ground for the first time. Standing in the back cockpit of the Bristol Fighter – a World War I biplane – I watched the green grass and the golden fields of corn slipping away below, until we rose to a height where we seemed to be poised motionless. Looking out along the wings, I could not believe that we were flying through the air, were it not for the slipstream pressing like a cold, strong hand against my face, exhilarating me and taking my breath away.

That flight decided me: I would become a pilot.

The squadron-commander, Leigh Mallory, wished me luck 'if ever you think of joining the R.A.F.'. He did not know that my mind was made up, and I did not know that, eleven years later, I myself would be a squadron-commander under Leigh Mallory's command.

Ashcroft took me under his wing and I began to feel more secure. He fanned my enthusiasm for flying. He took me to North Weald, a nearby R.A.F. base, where I watched the little Siskin fighters gambolling in the sky. Then I met the pilots; they seemed to me like gods descended from heaven to earth. I flew again, thanks to Ashcroft, and yet again. It sounds banal, but in those days it was very rare for earthbound creatures to fly.

Ashcroft took me to see the finish of the King's Cup air race; years later, I would myself compete in this aerial classic, flying the Hurricane entered by Princess Margaret. I went alone, in an open, red double-decker bus, to Hendon to watch the R.A.F. display. I was so enthralled by the 'tied-together' aerobatics, by the old Virginia catapulted into the air and the parachutists clinging to the interplane struts as they took off for their daring act, that it was not until the end of that hot summer's day that I thought of eating the bar of chocolate in the pocket of my suit. It had melted into a brown, uneatable mess.

Another time, as I drove with Ashcroft to the Experimental Station at Martlesham, Suffolk, he asked me: 'What is your favourite English word?' I hadn't an idea. 'What is yours?' I asked him, and he replied: 'Maintenance'. He explained why, and now, fifty years later, I still agree with him. Maintenance is a pretty word when spoken and written; also, whatever it may concern, alive or inert, it connotes love, respect and continued, sustained care and effort.

At Martlesham I admired the latest experimental aircraft, including the slender, nimble little Hawker Fury, which I would one day pilot. At nearby Felixstowe, the Marine Experimental

Station, I enjoyed the unimaginable privilege of sitting in the cockpit and handling the controls of the Supermarine S.6B the ultimate winner of the Schneider Cup and setter, in 1931, of the world's speed record of 407 m.p.h. From the S.6B. with its Rolls-Royce 'R' engine was born the Merlin-engined Spitfire.

Along with my growing passion for flying came a consolidation on other fronts; I became captain of swimming, won a place in the rugby XV; and Ashcroft made me head of Lawrence house. The statutory exams passed, I became early entrenched in the VI Form, the top one, waiting until I was old enough to pass into the R.A.F. College. Maths and higher maths being essential subjects and my weakest, they caused me long and uneasy hours of sweated labour. I enjoyed writing and worshipped Shakespeare, though I had a perverse preference for the earthy Geoffrey Chaucer:

> My theme is always one and ever was:

> *Radix malorum est cupiditas.*

Six centuries have changed man's appearance, but not his heart.

I was no intellectual yet I was admitted to the Guild of Pallas Athenae, the select and secret society composed of VI Form intellectuals. When I read them my thesis on the History of Aviation, they hung on every word, so little was known of the subject outside aviation circles. Finally, I ascended to Elysium, the club restricted to a dozen of the élite. Elysium, the sunny paradise which had seemed so remote when contemplated from the sordid, sadistic hell of the Dormitory Classroom. It was good that I had held both ends of the stick. I could sympathise with those who now held the dirty end.

I passed fifth in the written exam for the R.A.F. college, gaining a cadetship which spared my father the fees – an important contribution to his sorely strained budget. However, it was a blow to him to learn that I had failed the medical exam. A kick on the head at rugger had apparently damaged a blood vessel in my head. Today I am not so sure. There was no doubt about the kick, but the diagnosis depended much on my own testimony. And, at this moment, there came to me a premonition – I am at a loss to explain it – that this was not the moment to leave Haileybury. It influenced my answers to the doctors' questions.

My rejection left me, on account of my father, with an uneasy conscience. I would have to re-sit the written exam; could I again win a cadetship? No one was more surprised than I when, at the next attempt, six months later, I passed fourth into the R.A.F. College. The doctors cleared me; so did my conscience. But the delay involved was to change the subsequent course of my life.

CHAPTER 6

Cranwell: fledgeling pilot

Like the Lincolnshire poacher, I was bound apprentice, as a
pilot, in that famous county – at the Royal Air Force College,
Cranwell. The Cadet Wing, formerly housed in dingy black
huts, had just moved into a splendid new building. Clean of line,
with a tower whose revolving beacon shone forth each night, it
was the inspiration of Sir Herbert Baker, architect (under
Lutyens) of New Delhi and of the dining hall at Haileybury.
That proud edifice gave prestige – badly needed – to the R.A.F.

It was autumn 1933. The Royal Air Force was just fifteen
years old. The Royal Navy – since the Armada, the sure shield
of Britain and her pride – and the crack regiments of the Army
could boast of centuries of hard-won glory. The Royal Air
Force, short of money and modern equipment – it had been
contemptuously nicknamed the Royal Ground Force and the
Cinderella Service – could boast of nothing, save a belief in its
destiny.

The R.A.F.'s impudent claim that priority should be given to
air defence rocked the sea-dogs and the Colonel Blimps. It was
unbearable that the old country should have to look for protection to pilots of the R.A.F., whom the old guard tended to
despise as the rag-tag and bob-tail of the country's youth, beyond
the fringe of respectable society, with their pub-crawling and
their noisy sports cars. Insurance companies exacted an extra
premium from these accident-prone young men.

As far as I was concerned, the R.A.F.'s role in a future war
could not have interested me less. Though Hitler had already
begun to build his secret Luftwaffe, war, on our side of the
Channel, seemed too remote even to consider. All I yearned for
was to fly, and the R.A.F. enjoyed, deservedly, the reputation
of being the best flying club in the world.

Flying had not yet emerged from the pioneering stage. It

offered the highest form of adventure; it was dangerous. 'I see in *The Times* there has been another R.A.F. crash,' my father would say – all too often, but with just enough indifference to avoid upsetting me.

There was, however – and this is what fired me – a positive, side to flying. It was still a new thing, unfamiliar, thrilling, and out of this world and it attracted young people, like myself, who thirsted for adventure along new and untrodden paths. It was only fourteen years since the British flyers Alcock and Brown had made the first-ever non-stop trans-Atlantic flight.

Alcock and Brown and Lindbergh were stars among a heroic galaxy which included Coste, Le Brix, Bellonte and Saint-Exupéry; del Prete, Ferrari and Balbo; Cobham and Kingsford Smith – a galaxy which was not without its heroines: Amelia Earhart, Amy Johnson, Jean Batten. They were the pioneers of the new air age, living, and alas, sometimes dying before my very eyes, at a time when the flame of youth happened to be burning at its fiercest in me and a few others – we were not all that many to be caught up in this skyward surge.

For flying meant breaking with the slothful pace and the safety of *terra firma*. It meant risking your neck. Precise data was too scanty and technology too imperfect to exclude all reasonable risk of engine or structural failure. Radio and meteorology and the aids to navigation were rudimentary and unreliable. To make up for these shortcomings, a pilot needed to possess a powerful mixture of faith and enthusiasm and senses keen enough to enable him to fly by the seat of his pants. Thus provided, we felt in us an immense urge to rise up into the sky in the wake of the pioneers, to free ourselves from the confines of earth and discover the exaltation of flying through the boundless realms of the air.

Early in September 1933, my instructor, Flight Lieutenant Poyntz Roberts, introduced me to the Avro Tutor, a little open-cockpit biplane powered with a 250 h.p. engine. My initiation in the art of flying had begun. Poyntz was a small, irascible man with a face as pink as a rose and an inexhaustible vocabulary of swear-words. The advice he gave me, laced with oaths, came straight out of the R.A.F. Training Manual. But he left me with two dicta of his own invention: Treat everybody else in the air as a bloody fool; handle your aeroplane as if she was your favourite girl.

After six hours of take-offs and landings, of diving, climbing, banking, gliding, side-slipping, spinning, rolling and looping we landed one afternoon in the middle of the vast sward of Cranwell's airfield. Poyntz climbed out of his cockpit and on to the wing below mine. 'She's all yours,' he shouted. 'Off you go'.

That day, 15 September 1933, I made my first solo. It was less than thirty years before that Orville Wright, the first man to fly, had made his – that is, the first powered, controlled, sustained flight. Not many more years after my first solo, men would be landing and taking off from the moon.

I was eighteen. For the next two years I submitted, gladly for the most part, to the intensive and variegated process which was to mould me as a pilot, an officer and a gentleman. Our education, largely academic, was generously dosed with sport and parade ground drill and spiced, all too slightly for our liking, with flying. I had some difficulty in reconciling flying – to my mind all grace and zest and poetry – with its technical and military aspects. Yet I soon discovered that there did exist a nice balance between the idealistic and the material. When I donned my blue uniform, of tunic, breeches and puttees (senior officers wore black riding-boots), my heart beat a little faster: cavalry of the air – I shared the pride of Colonel Calverley of the Dragoon Guards, in *Patience*:

> When I first put this uniform on
> I said, as I looked in the glass,
> 'It's one to a million
> That any civilian
> My figure and form will surpass . . .'

And I found it exhilarating to drill, with the precision of a guardsman, under the crisp orders of Sergeant Blandford, late of the Grenadiers, and to march briskly behind Drum-major Simms to the lilt of the *Lincolnshire Poacher* or *Colonel Bogey*.

I did not, I admit, take easily to my bird-like view of flying being reduced to the base, technical formulae of aerodynamics and engineering terms. Yet pleasant features began to appear out of the gloomy fog of technical theory and practice. The aeroplanes we flew were 'rigged' – like a sailing ship; a 'rigger' maintained the airframe in proper trim. Many contemporary aircraft had airframes of spruce, a wood that Mr Longley had taught me to appreciate. Our technical vocabulary included melodious names like longeron, fuselage and aileron, camber, dihedral, tailskid and undercarriage (undercart for short); joystick (which we always called the stick) was a sublime pseudonym for the control column; it evoked the essence of flying.

Airframes and wings were covered with taut fabric, and this enabled me to exercise a talent learnt in my childhood when, under the expert guidance of Tommy Coles, I sewed and rigged the sails of the ships he helped me to build. Now I was learning to sew the fabric of our aeroplanes, repairing a rip in wing or fuselage with a villainous curved needle, the kind that surgeons use, slapping over the seam a patch of new fabric which I daubed with red acetone dope, smelling deliciously of peardrops.

The incredible complexity of an aero-engine at first flummoxed me; but here again the terminology intrigued me to the point of enabling me to master a perplexing subject. An aeroengine is composed of a myriad of moving parts, from its fat pistons down to its minuscule contact-breakers. Within its entrails, squirming and oscillating, seething and heaving, are spiggots and splines and sprockets, rockers, poppets and pushrods, camshafts and crankshafts, big-ends and little-ends. It was the lure of these names that ultimately created an intimacy between me and my engine – plus the cold fact that my life depended on it. But when it came to choosing a subject for my mechanical thesis I selected from among fifty-odd highly technical themes one which was rarely discussed: the Flight of Birds. Never have I written about a more fascinating subject. I envisaged the use by man of a number of bird-like devices, among them the variable geometry wing. Had I possessed the genius of another flight-cadet, Frank Whittle*, ten years my senior, my life-pattern might have been different.

Our routine consisted of a relentless sequence of lectures, flying, sport and drill. We paraded every morning at 8 o'clock with rifle and bayonet. 'Get fell in, B Squadron!' Orders barked out by voices which often cracked under the strain galvanised us into synchronised response. Punishment was summarily meted out for the slightest infraction, a speck of dust on our uniform, a false or slovenly movement. But behind our stiffly military stance and our straight faces we enjoyed the comedy. 'Head up and look to the front, Mr Townsend!' – usage obliged our instructors to address us as 'Mr' when they would certainly have preferred to call us 'you idle little bastard'.

Behind all this stiff ceremonial hovered the wispy figure of Mr Blanchard. Blanchard was my batman, a frail, elderly little man invariably dressed in dark blue regulation serge and a green baize apron. The salient features of his pink face were a white moustache and a pair of gold-rimmed spectacles and these were crowned with a neat little cloth cap, which he wore as a permanent fixture.

Blanchard lived in a world where everything shone. He polished my buttons until they gleamed like gold; he burnished my boots and my bayonet scabbard until they took on the lustre of ebony. He was a totally devoted professional. Discreetly, he would run his eye over me as I left for parade; a loose button or the faintest smear of dirt on my uniform and he was immediately to the rescue with needle and cotton and cleaner. 'A lucky shot!' he would call the last-minute operation which would save me from three days' extra drill.

Outside the serio-comic atmosphere of drill and physical training, we were nurtured in a discipline which was stringent and just. The tone was set by the commandant himself, Air-Vice-Marshal Mitchell. Stocky, rubicund, jovial, 'Ginger Mitch' was an impressive figure. One day, he telephoned to Flight Cadet 'Queenie' Cairns, who was a frequent target for practical jokes.

* Sir Frank Whittle, father of the jet engine, had, when a flight-cadet, chosen as his subject for the mechanical thesis, 'Gas Turbines'. His paper was the basis of British jet engine development.

When Cairns heard a voice at the other end of the line saying: 'This is the commandant. I'd like to see you at 10 o'clock to-morrow morning,' he replied jauntily 'The commandant, eh? Well, balls to you!' and hung up. Shortly afterwards an orderly handed him a message: 'Report to the commandant at 10 a.m. to-morrow'.

Next morning Cairns stood stiffly before the Air-Vice-Marshal. 'Cairns', the latter asked him, 'when I called you yesterday you replied, if I am not mistaken, balls to you?' 'Yessir' replied the petrified Cairns. Ginger Mitch eyed him coldly. 'Well balls to you,' he snapped. 'Good morning'.

The R.A.F. at that time policed, at relatively low cost, the far-flung territories of the British Empire. We flight-cadets were initiated into the peculiar ways of soldiers and sailors, for most of the pilots who manned army-cooperation squadrons and 'flights' of the Fleet Air Arm then wore the pale blue uniform of the R.A.F. While the Army showed a haughty disdain for the possibilities – and the menace – of the air, the Royal Navy were still smarting under the R.A.F.'s efforts to usurp its place as Britain's shield. R.A.F. pilots afloat in aircraft carriers were impressed by the navy's efficiency in its own element, but they laughed irreverently at the navy's tendency to apply nautical practice to the air, a thinner medium than the sea in which machines moved faster, could not 'heave to' or 'make fast' and had an alarming tendency to sink when they lost forward speed. The sailors were chided for fitting bulky objects like compass binnacles and companion ways outboard in the slipstream; occasionally naval aircraft were said to be fitted with anchors and encrusted with barnacles. R.A.F. Fleet Air Arm pilots sang boisterously:

> We don't want to fly in a flying-boat,
> Row in a rowing-boat,
> Sail in a sailing-boat,
> We don't want to fish in a fishing-boat,
> We are the Fleet Air Arm.

R.A.F. pilots, back from a spell of service with the fleet,

brought with them stories which made us laugh immoderately. Flight-Lieutenant Beisiegel, who had served in the China Fleet and was now our instructor in Naval Cooperation, told us this one: the admiral, urgently needing to get some of his kit laundered, sent for the Chinese washerwoman. The Flagship signalled ashore: 'Admiral's woman urgently required aboard'. The shore station, as mystified as it was intrigued, flashed back: 'Message not understood. Repeat.' Back came the reply from the flagship: 'Insert washer between admiral and woman'.

As my first year of training ended, there came bad news about my father. He was seriously ill. I hurried back to Crowcombe and found myself, at nineteen, acting head of the family, my brother Michael being on the high seas and Philip with his regiment, the Gurkhas, on India's northwest frontier. My father was sinking steadily, while my mother kept watch by his side. She asked me if I would like to see him, but I refused. I knew he was dying and I could not raise the courage to look a dying man in the face, be he even my own father. I wanted to cherish the image of him alive, smiling, gardening, reading his *Times* or walking, debonair, to church on Sundays. Had he asked for me I should of course, have gone to him, but he never did.

I would not put it beyond my father voluntarily to have spared me the sight of him sinking towards the grave. He knew me well, my childhood terrors, my fearful thoughts and fancies, and he understood, I am sure, how I, a stripling pilot, shrank from looking death in the face. For an airman, death was always round the corner, and might show up at any moment. Until then, we preferred not to look its way. It was not until some forty years later, on the Golan Plateau in Palestine, that I looked a dead man in the eyes . . .

So my father died. He had enjoyed, I believe, the satisfaction of having raised his seven children in the best tradition, hard though it may have been on his purse and his health. These last few years of his life were the years of our marvellous youth. He followed approvingly our comings and goings, were they in the shaded combes and wind-swept beacons of our beloved Quantock Hills, the Himalayas, where Philip was encamped,

where Michael ploughed the ocean wave, or the rolling clouds
which were my own particular playground.

They came, the village sexton and the pall-bearers, to the
house, bringing with them a simple, old-fashioned bier – a hand-
barrow upon which they set my father's coffin. Through the
village they took him on his last journey to the church where, as
evening fell, they laid him before the altar. My family were in
disarray before the event of my father's death. My sisters were
tearful or speechless. I persuaded Audrey to come with me to
pay a last homage that evening, when peace filled the little
mediaeval church, with its narrow pews and oaken benches,
lavishly carved at their ends, where we had worshipped at my
father's side.

Beside our pew, in the aisle, a stone slab marked the vault of
the Sweeting family. Henry, the first of the Sweetings, had lain
there for two centuries and a half. We would shuffle over the
dead Sweetings on the way to the altar, there to receive bread
and wine in memory that Christ died for us. More tombstones
paved the other aisle; they paved the way, too, for the new-born
who were carried across those ancient dead to the font, there
to begin their life in Christ. The process was endless: life and
death, the ebb and flow of the tide, the passing seasons, the rise
and fall of the sap, the leaves and flowers which bud and burst
into colour and fade and fall.

They buried my father next day. The rector – dressed in
black – breeches, gaiters, frock coat with a top hat to crown his
cadaverous face – looked like Death itself. 'Man hath but a
short time to live . . .' he intoned in his rich, sonorous voice. I
led the little cortege down the aisle. The massive oak door
creaked open and we moved out into the sunlight where the
breeze and the birds and the scudding clouds brought a welcome
breath of life to the morbid scene. We filed past the ancient
stone cross, pitted by time and tempest, and the sturdy yew tree,
past the family vault of the Carews, who once owned land at
Crowcombe and still, in death, possessed this little parcel,
fenced off from the rest. Then we came to the grave, a heap of
fresh, moist earth beside it, gaping wide in the trim turf. As my
father was lowered into the red Somerset soil the gentlemen of

the parish and the worthies of the village inclined respectfully. The raucous chatter of the rooks and the bell's mournful tolling was in my ears as I advanced before these elderly, lugubrious gentlemen to scatter the first handful of the earth which was to seal my father off from this life.

I am glad that my father – and, later, my mother – were laid to rest in Crowcombe, for the village, as Bideford had done, entered into my soul. I felt a regular villager.

With my father at rest in the bosom of his beloved West Country, I again took to the air. At nineteen, I was fatherless – deeply saddened, but without a feeling of irreparable loss. I felt passionately alive, absorbed by my longing to fly. Yet deep within me something had broken.

Within a few days of my return to flying an ugly rash broke out on my arms. Little was then known of stress and the nervous and psychological origins of eczema (or indeed the latter's association with asthma). Though I lived for flying, it apparently created within me tensions of which I was not conscious. These, and the events of the recent days had evidently overstressed my nervous machinery. It was four years before it recovered. During that time my skin was to be ravaged by hideous sores. The doctors plied me with a variety of antiseptics, ranging from tar to an extract from a rare fish. Nothing availed; the cause of my affliction lay not on the surface but deep down in the complex chemistry of the body.

This was a time when I turned for encouragement to the Book of Job. In my distress I often thought of poor Job: 'So went Satan forth . . . and smote Job with sore boils from the sole of his foot to his crown.' I never had it as bad as Job but, through him, I discovered my favourite book in the Bible. Meanwhile I went about my duties with increased fervour, pretending to myself, though rarely with success, that my affliction did not exist. Paradoxically, flying, its root cause, was also the best palliative.

Now in my second year, my training on 'service type' aircraft began, and I was overjoyed at being designated as a fighter pilot. The single-seater fighter mentality suited my temperament of a 'loner'. The Bristol Bulldog had just replaced the Arm-strong Whitworth Siskin as the standard fighter. Powered with a 450 h.p. Bristol 'Jupiter' engine driving a two-bladed wooden propeller, the Bulldog had a top speed of 170 m.p.h. You sat her well forward in a shallow open cockpit, right up in line with the trailing edge of the top wing. The single-seater Bulldog felt good and looked it: she was tough yet coquettish and a viceless performer. Not so the dual version whose fuselage had been stretched to accommodate a second cockpit for the instructor – this shifted the centre of gravity aft and disturbed the airflow over the tail. 'Straight and level' the dual Bulldog was a pleasant ride; in a spin she was a bitch.

Spinning was the most regular, if not the most frequent, of all our exercises. A spin, if it occurred too low or was not properly handled, was a sure killer. Because of her vicious habits, it was forbidden to spin a dual Bulldog below 8,000 feet (2,500 metres). One day, my instructor Flying Officer McKenna, a burly, smiling man with a rolling gait, like a sailor, called cheerily through the Gosport speaking-tube 'Spin her to the left off a steep turn'. The Bulldog shied briskly into a spin – one turn, two and three. 'Bring her out' called McKenna. Stick forward, opposite rudder. No effect, save that the spin now became flat and dangerous.

We were sinking rapidly and I was conscious of an eerie hush, of the clatter of the engine's poppet valves and the reek of burning castor oil, the standard lubricant for this engine, of the propeller, in a slow tick-over, brushing the air, of the air rush-ing past my ears and through the bracing wires, making them whine, while the aircraft pitched and tossed in a sickening, circular movement, totally, hopelessly, out of control. 'I've got her!' yelled McKenna, now far from cheerful. Banging open the throttle lever, pumping the stick, kicking the rudder, he tried to rock the Bulldog back into flying position.

In vain. 'Get ready to jump,' shouted McKenna and I moved my hand to the quick-release of my fighting harness, praying to God that I should not have to pull it. With throttle, stick and rudder McKenna kept fighting the Bulldog. We were down to 2,000 feet when at last he brought her back to an even keel, with just enough height left to dive and pick up flying speed. His voice, now very quiet, came through the speaking tube: 'That was a near one. Now climb her up again and we'll do another'.

Accidents were not infrequent. One afternoon, three up-turned Siskins simultaneously adorned the otherwise barren airfield. Another afternoon, a group of us were drinking an afternoon 'cupper'. Flight-cadet Treasure got up and with a jaunty, 'Well boys, I'm off for a spot of aviation', walked out of the room. Twenty minutes later he was dead, leaving us, for days – and nights – to come, to fight off visions of fear.

Then there occurred a disaster which drove us into the deepest gloom. A mid-air collision killed two instructors and two cadets; bodies torn apart and mutilated were recovered from trees and neighbouring fields to be reassembled, as best they could be, for burial. There was not one of us who did not think, 'This could happen to me,' and tried not to believe it – thoughts which were drummed into us as we marched in the funeral cortège to the slow, sad measure of Chopin's haunting melody, thumped out by muffled drum, blaring trumpet and trombone. The sepulchral atmosphere was mitigated but a little by the 'lively music' prescribed by the drill manual for the return march back from the cemetery.

However, we bit by bit built up our defences against these depressing visions. We developed a peculiar sense of humour, a way of looking at things which, if macabre, suited our condition. Our jokes and rhymes and songs fortified our morale. Yes, flying was a dangerous trade. We who were learning it and accepting its risks were paid seven shillings a day. Half of this pittance was devoted to our food and laundering. Sixpence a day was deposited to our account. We received, net, three shillings a day. It never occurred to us as being too little, for we received, on top of it, an inestimable reward. We were learning to fly.

Some eighteen months had passed since my first solo and I was beginning to feel bored with the conventional ways of a col-legian and the dullness of life as a groundling pilot. I longed to fly more. So did we all, but some hid their impatience better. Try as I did to lend an attentive ear to our esteemed professors, my thoughts always wandered beyond the classroom to the sky.

My dwindling interest was quickly noticed. The assistant commandant, Philip Babington, summoned me to tea. I was his only guest and he lectured me as severely as tea-time talk would permit. But he was understanding. He called me a 'rebel', but not reproachfully. 'The world needs rebels' he said. I promised to mend my ways. I was promoted Under-Officer; there were only three of us and I was tipped for the Sword of Honour.

The thrill of winning a clean-fought race is one thing. But there is a weakness – or perhaps a strength – in my character which compels me to give way when I find myself caught up in the rush for a coveted place. The Sword of Honour was won – deservedly – by the man who wanted it most. That was not me, and I felt no pangs of regret.

I felt mortified, however, at not being entered for the Groves Flying Prize, but once again the psychosis of the cricket nets at Haileybury had prevailed. 'You are too sensitive', my flying instructor told me. 'You might put up a brilliant performance, or you might make a complete ass of yourself.' They were hard words to swallow, all the more so because they were true.

My apprenticeship in Lincolnshire culminated with a posting to No 1 Fighter Squadron, one of the R.A.F.'s three crack interceptor units. The verdict of Philip Babington on the 'rebel' he had once lectured over a cup of tea was flattering. 'Should make an excellent pilot . . . has more than the average ability and brains . . . more than he credits himself with . . . will do very well when he gets over his shyness . . .'

His shyness. This, apparently was the obstacle and Babington even mentioned, 'his reluctance to attempt anything which might make him noticeable'. It was an interesting remark, considering what was to befall me later.

CHAPTER 7

Fighter pilot

A month's leave gave me time to get used to the fact that I was now an officer in His Majesty's Royal Air Force. My commission, written in bold italics on stout linen parchment, was signed 'George Rex et Imperator'. I was charmed to the point of embarrassment by the cheery, intimate manner of my sovereign liege George V. '*To our trusty and well-beloved . . . greeting*' he began and continuing in the imperial plural, informed me that 'we' reposed especial trust and confidence in my Loyalty, Courage and good Conduct. I must carefully, and diligently discharge my duty, exercise and well discipline the inferior officers and airmen under my command and use my best endeavours to keep them in good order – a lot to ask of a twenty-year-old, had not the King-Emperor assured me that 'we' had commanded them to obey me. Thirty years later this famous document was eaten by our labrador Julie who, failing to digest the imperial message, became extremely ill.

I felt proud, yet when the day came, late in August 1935, for me to assume my duties with No. 1 Fighter Squadron at Tangmere in Sussex, I was so overcome with shyness that I waited till dusk before slipping into the camp unnoticed and creeping into bed. I had never worn my wings nor my thin pilot officer's stripes in public. Next morning, feeling awkward in my new uniform, I braved the breakfast table. Immediately the hospitality of the 'best flying club in the world' – the R.A.F. – was mine. 'Why didn't you let us know last night?' those pilots of the R.A.F.'s crack squadron asked me, the stripling in their midst. 'We'd have given you a party.'

A keen and sometimes reckless rivalry united rather than opposed No. 1 and its sister squadron No. 43. Both flew the nimble, silver, streamlined, Fury biplane. The Fury was sensual, thrilling, like a lovely girl, perfect in looks and manners;

slim, graceful, tender to the feel. She responded tactfully, generously to every demand and was never spiteful, as some aeroplanes – and girls – can be. Though feminine charm cannot be measured in terms of bust, waist and hips only, I give the Fury's basic data: she was driven by a Rolls-Royce Kestrel motor of 650 h.p. Her speed was just over 200 m.p.h. and she was armed with two Vickers machine guns which, by means of an interrupter gear, fired through a two-bladed wooden propeller. The gun-breeches projected into the cockpit, so that, when the guns fired, they splattered you with oil and gave you a rather heroic look.

Beside the right-hand gun hung a neat little tool-bag, whose most precious tool was specified as a 'plug, clearing, Vickers'. When a split cartridge jammed a gun, you gripped the stick between your legs, and with your Fury careering half out of control across the sky, fumbled in your tool bag, extracted the 'plug, clearing, Vickers' and stuck it into the breech of the jammed gun, wriggling it to and fro to clear the cartridge.

Our planes were proudly caparisoned with the squadron markings on the top wing and fuselage – flaming red triangles (as the press called them) for No. 1 and black chequer-boards for No. 43. If war came we would ride forth in our colours like knights of old to joust with the enemy. But not for a moment did the possibility of war occur to us, nor that we were potential killers. The public, admiring our cavortings in the sky, called us intrepid birdmen, dicing with death. We liked that; it made us laugh.

The airfield at Tangmere was a broad meadow. The slender spire of Chichester Cathedral pointed the way there; another landmark, more rustic, was the old windmill on the Downs to the north. In summertime the wheels of our Furies swished through the long grass as we landed; soon after my arrival they took a second crop of hay off the airfield and a herd of sheep was set to graze the herb. Slothful sheep and flying Furies were not meant to co-exist; both they and we had some alarming moments.

Aircraft hangars, with their massive bulk, do not normally fit easily into the rustic scene. Ours did, with their wooden beams

and uprights and their gently curving roofs. German prisoners
of war built them in 1917, and German airmen were later to
demolish them with their bombs. Meanwhile life at Tangmere
was peaceful, pastoral. I loved the place; it was my home from
home.

Fighting Area (our command) possessed but thirteen fighter
squadrons to defend Britain. (There were 52 when the Battle of
Britain began in 1940). We flew off to lunch with friends at
other fighter stations or away for the week-end, our suitcase
squeezed into the space where the oxygen bottle and the radio
set were normally housed – or simply strapped on to the lower
wing. The latter method was ruled out after a pilot – his name,
ironically, was Angel – killed himself while diving low over his
girl-friend's house to say hullo. With the added resistance of the
suitcase, Angel's wings simply folded.

Three of Fighting Area's squadrons, ourselves, 43 and 25,
were designated 'Interceptor Squadrons'. We were the élite
troops, the first to be thrown against the enemy in the event of
an attack, climbing steeply and rapidly to intercept the first
waves of bombers. Just how we were to find them, nobody
knew. Radio communication and direction-finding were still in
the folkloric stage, as witness our pleasantly bucolic call-signs
and the exercises we performed to perfect our positioning technique. We were 'Waxwing'; 43 were 'Wagtail'; the ground-
station was 'Woodpecker', always crying out for the position of
his feathered friends so that, after some delay, he could pass
them a new interception course. By which time the enemy
would be several miles away.

'Waxwing' and 'Wagtail' pilots knew their sector like the
back of their hand – naturally, since our pin-pointing exercises
sent us off in search of objects as small as duck-ponds, water-
troughs and odd-shaped telegraph poles. The Old Man of
Cerne Abbas provided the acid test. A huge figure cut out of a
chalk hill in Roman times, he was hard to spot. To prove you
had done so, you had only to mention a striking detail: the Old
Man sported an erected phallus several yards long.

Radio 'homing' was available, but fighter pilots more often
trusted their own instincts rather than the uncertain technique

of the ground station. Our favoured method was to 'Bradshaw', (so called after the railway time-table); you followed roads and railway-lines, flying low enough, when necessary, to read the name-boards of the stations.

At Tangmere, the black ball indicating 'no flying' was automatically hoisted when clouds covered the Downs. If the weather clamped down while you were north of the Downs, the standard approach to Tangmere was to fly 'on the deck' down the London-Arundel railway, through the Arundel Gap (in the hills), turn right to Barnham Junction and there, right again and count sixty. Unfailingly, Tangmere then loomed out of the murk. But our make-shift methods of navigation and interception, while always remaining part of a fighter-pilot's répertoire, were soon to be replaced by scientific ones. Some way from Tangmere, at Polegate, huge lattice masts were being erected – sinister sentinels in a forbidden zone. They were an unmentionable secret. Their name was radar.

We carefully preserved a non-professional atmosphere in the mess. Talking shop was *mal vu* and a fine was imposed on pilots 'shooting a line' with gestures which went above shoulder-level. The 'Line-book' recorded exceptional claims, of which the best-known R.A.F. classic went: 'There I was, on my back, in a cloud, with nothing on the clock.' We made fun of danger, of death even, and took care to prevent our profession from turning us into professional bores. We were not the army, nor the navy. We had precious few traditions and we knew it. We just lived, sometimes all too briefly, for the joy of living.

Our day's duty done, we immediately discarded our uniform. Once a month, we dressed up in our tight-fitting mess-kit of 'overalls' and 'bum-freezers' for a guest-night. After honour had been done to the guests and the royal toast had been drunk, squadron then pitted itself against squadron in a rowdy, good-natured debauch, which relaxed our nerves, tautened by weeks of flying. In an atmosphere charged with smoke and beer, we sang bawdy songs and recent hits, like Harry Roy's 'I blow through here and the music goes round and round' or Hutch's 'Get that old hunch again, champagne for lunch again. Back to those happy, happy days'. Hi cock o'lorum, mess rugger and billiard-fives put a bursting strain on the tight seams of our mess-kit. For the guests, irrespective of their station, gallant air marshals, crusty admirals, lord bishops or the local mayor or peer, there was a kind of crossing-the-line ceremony, only they had to cross the ceiling, on foot. The soles of their shoes were blackened and willing hands helped them up the wall and across the ceiling where, like Man Friday, they left their footmarks. Among the distinguished ceiling-walkers was the Bishop of Chichester.

During those orgies, two men remained calm: Macey and Hoskins, the white-coated barmen, as they passed to and fro through the swing doors of the anteroom, bringing fresh beer. I admired their detachment and envied them, impervious as they were to the din and the hubbub around them – in which I was a participant, not because I particularly enjoyed it, but because, being a young 'sprog', I could not stand aloof. Gay parties were not really my line and I shied away from the noise and clamour which are generally regarded as the criterion of fun. I liked my fun a different way, in quieter company, with people who kept their voices low and held their drink. But, those evenings, I downed the beer that Macey and Hoskins brought. We drank our fill, but rarely to excess. That was not possible on a drink bill limited to £5 a month and with the obligation, scrupulously respected, to be on the tarmac at 8.30 next morning, ready to fly.

In October 1935, the shadow of war fell, if ever so lightly, on Tangmere. Mussolini launched his invasion of Abyssinia; his son Bruno returned exultant from a raid against tribesmen armed with bows and arrows to describe how his bombs had exploded amidst that mass of black-skinned flesh, like scarlet flowers bursting into bloom. Reading this account, I felt sick, never imagining that it would one day fall to me to slay men.

Theodore MacEvoy was my squadron commander – no one attempted to call him Theodore, but just Mac. Though handi-capped by serious spinal trouble, Mac was one of the R.A.F.'s best pilots. Unable to turn in the cockpit, he wore a mirror on his wrist and in it he watched my station-keeping as he led me, wing-tip to wing-tip, through clear air and dense cloud.

Another Mac, MacDougal, 'Rip-cord Ralph', a charming joker in 43 Squadron, took me under his wing. He seemed to get a laugh out of my burning ambition to become an ace, which was as well, because he took the recklessness out of me and taught me, clandestinely, in some unfrequented corner of the sky, the ultimate finesse of formation flying – wing-tip touching and formation aerobatics, forbidden games which brooked no errors, but exacted the highest precision and concentration. Mac also taught me an aerial practical joke. You lowered your seat fully so that your head was no longer visible in the cockpit. Then, looking through the gun-inspection panel in the cockpit side, you sidled up beside some unsuspecting pilot, who, terrified at being pursued by an apparently pilotless aircraft, would panic and flee, with the phantom aircraft on his tail.

MacEvoy, as my squadron commander, taught me the serious stuff. He gave me generously of his superb skill and his sympathy. When I dived too low on the ground target near the airfield boundary, he called me into his office and, by way of a reprimand, showed me a sketch he had made of the local bus passing the airfield with my Fury level with the windows, from which the passengers were waving enthusiastically. MacEvoy smiled gravely: 'Not so low next time. It would be a pity to have to scrape up your remains off the deck.' I was soon able to redeem myself. As I zoomed away from the ground target, my Fury's nose pointed high to the heavens, the engine cut. Caught in the worst possible position, I could only bang the stick forward and, collecting just enough speed, curve round the airfield and land into wind.

Curiously enough, two more engine failures occurred soon afterwards, both well out to sea, but with enough height to glide back to Tangmere. Airmen, like sailors, tend to be superstitious. Never two without three, 'and that', I said to myself, 'is enough to last me for some time'. But another thing struck me: for the first time in my life, I felt aware of an invisible protecting hand – more than a guardian angel and less frivolous.

The Abyssinian crisis made Britain stir from her pipe-dream of peace eternal. The bases along her life-line to the Far East – Gibraltar, Malta, Suez, Aden, Colombo, Singapore – had to be reinforced, and this meant depriving her fighter defence of pilots. 43 Squadron prepared to fly on to the aircraft carrier *Furious* which had steam up to sail for the Middle East. Half of 1 Squadron's Furies were sent, with their pilots, to Suez. I begged Philip Babington, now Director of Postings, to let me join them, only to be reminded that my training as a fighter pilot was not yet complete. It eventually culminated at the Air Firing Range at Catfoss, in Lincolnshire. There, in what seemed to me to be the dreariest outpost of the British Empire, I spent my 21st birthday in a dingy hut, before a foully smoking stove, waiting for the chilly North Sea mist to clear.

CHAPTER 8

Asian adventure

At the outset of her marriage, my mother, with thousands of miles between her husband's post in Burma and her young family in England, had been torn alternately from one and the other. Now that my father's death had separated him from her for ever, the careers of her sons were to take them too from her. One after the other, the Empire claimed them. Michael was away for years at a time on the high seas or in some distant naval base; Philip on the north-west frontier of India. Now my summons came to leave. The long awaited telegram from the Air Ministry stated curtly: '*Posted to 36 Squadron Singapore*'. It was further than I had bargained for and 36 Squadron was a torpedo-bomber, not a fighter squadron. No matter, there was a threat of war and anyway I had had enough of the cosy life, kicking my heels at home, and of the cold and clammy mists of England. I was headed for adventure beyond the seas and I could not wait to be off.

At Southampton, the troop-ship *Neuralia* was alongside. My mother came with me to the foot of the gangway. She showed not a trace of emotion, though I knew it was there and for a moment felt uncomfortable. But so eager was I to be away that I gave it no thought – until years later, when I realised the pains that mothers bear for their children. My mother kissed me, warmly but without fuss, and just said: 'Well, off you go.'

The *Neuralia*, a rickety old coal-burner, steamed slowly eastwards. The great mass of Gibraltar loomed out of the rain and gloomy tidings came from the Spanish warship anchored alongside us: a dozen men had been executed on her quarter-deck that morning. Spain was on the verge of civil war; it was to claim a million Spanish lives, and provide an arena in which Hitler and Mussolini could practise for total war. Junkers 52's of the German Luftwaffe circled us as we set course for Malta.

We coaled at Port Said, ports and hatches sealed against the fine black dust. All day long, coolies, like an army of ants, as black as the coal they carried in a sack on their back, jogged up and down the gangways, filling the ship's bunkers. Then the *Neuralia* was washed down and we glided through the Canal into the Red Sea, past the barren rock of Aden, until we were a speck in the Indian Ocean, a dark, translucent blue, except where the flying fishes skimmed and left a passing trace of white.

One thing· pleased me above all else, during those lazy, pleasant days. My skin affliction had miraculously disappeared; not a weal nor a scar remained. I believed myself cured.

We came to Colombo and coaled again. Five days later, we were steaming through glassy waters, picking our way through the archipelago at the approach to Singapore.

Hardly berthed, we were brutally reminded of the risks peculiar to our role of torpedo-bombers. A crew of three had been lost at sea that very night. I suddenly felt far from home and wondered whether I should ever return.

Our Vickers Vildebeeste torpedo-bombers, square-winged and as ugly as their name, were for all that, splendid machines, full of character. Their single Bristol Pegasus motor, however, was our sole means of support as we flew over jungle and shark-infested sea. There was precious little else to fly over. We navigated by 'dead reckoning', that is by compass, map and a good deal of instinct. No radio was carried except, on exercises, by the flight commander; by means of a trailing aerial weighted at the end with lead beads, he could contact base in Morse. To us he signalled, and we to him, by a wave of the hand. Our eyes never left him. He was our shepherd and our surest chance of a safe return to the fold, though in the darkness of the night and in the violent storms which rent our tropical skies, the chances were diminished.

A torpedo attack was no picnic, even when the target was a friendly cruiser or a fat, black-funnelled P & O liner with a captive audience leaning over the rail to admire your prowess. From 8,000 feet, you winged over and plunged seawards, But, far from feeling like a heroic hell-driver, you nervously watched the airspeed needle climbing round the clock. 140 m.p.h. was our maximum permissible speed. Faster, and the Wildebeeste's tail would come off – an eventuality you were anxious to avoid as you spiralled down, throttled back, gunning the motor now and again to keep it warm. If you forgot this simple precaution as I did once (but only once), the motor would merely splutter rudely when you opened up again at dropping height – twenty five feet above the sea, which was often so glassy smooth that you misjudged the height. Too low, and the torpedo's splash gave an almighty thwack against your tailplane; too high, and it broke the surface like a leaping salmon, a pretty sight, but not one which earned you the congratulations of your commanding officer.

Our torpedo attacks were made miles from the coast. At night they were particularly dicey, for that narrow margin of twenty five feet between you and the sea had to be judged by the light of flares, which parachuted down from above and sometimes flickered out at the critical moment. After which, you scanned the dark sky to pick out your flight-commander's navigation lights, wheeling among the stars, and hitch on to them for a safe journey home.

I tremble now as I think of those perilous exploits, but at the time they were fun and I enjoyed them hugely – and not least the aftermath in the mess, the can of beer, the line-shooting and the laughter. And so, in the early hours, we shuffled off to bed, each of us grateful, though we never let on, that we had survived another night attack.

A few days after I resumed flying in Singapore, a personal disaster hit me. During the voyage I had believed that I was permanently cured of the sores on my arms. But now they broke out on my feet and the torture began again.

Otherwise, life at Singapore was serene and enjoyable. Day in, day out, the sun set at six, rose again at six the following morning. All of Singapore, ourselves included, rose with it. The mynahs began their chatter and Suan Kye, my Chinese boy, came shuffling down the corridor in his wooden sandals, slipping them off before sliding silently through the lattice door of my room. 'Morning', was all he would say, as he laid down a tray of tea and fruit and arranged my clothes.

Tamil coolies, chanting little songs, filed nonchalantly across the luminous skyline to work. Chinese fishermen wearing shady, conical hats, rowed furiously in long boats as they raced to the fishing grounds. Coolies, muscular men stripped to the waist and full-bosomed women dressed in coarse blue cloth, attacked the day's work.

The Chinese were intelligent, indefatigable workers, even the aged, squatting at some household chore, and the children, with their lissom bodies and bright smiles.

With Suan Kye I struck up a friendly understanding, limited though it was to a few words of pidgin English, a gesture here and there and smiles of approbation. Suan Kye understood everything. He was silent, discreet and honest – with me. Yet he would – for me – gladly steal a light-bulb from the room of one of my friends. I liked the music of his name and thought that, if ever I owned a yacht, I would call it *Suan Kye*.

Singapore's population was a *mélange* of races. The Chinese, numerically superior by far, provided the mind and the muscle. The English, a tiny minority, were the masters. Their social and business clubs – cricket, golf, yachting, racing, and swimming clubs – were exclusively English. Asians and Eurasians were barred from English life, not with ill-feeling, but simply because it wasn't done to mix with 'the natives'. This was the secret of the British Raj, wherever it might be installed; how a handful of British held sway over the hundreds of millions of His Imperial Majesty's subjects. The British simply did not mix with 'the natives', however rich or influential they may have been, however beautiful their wives and daughters.

In many ways it was a pity, because we missed so much by not mixing. Many of us wanted to; I often felt far more inclined to mix with 'the natives' than with the British; but such conduct would have been considered unbecoming to an officer and a gentleman. So my contacts were limited to simple people like Suan Kye.

Spy scares were not infrequent, and almost invariably the Japanese were involved. They were a tight, retiring community, for the most part masseurs, tailors, barbers and photographers, trades in which they were well placed to listen, record and report. My hair was cut by a Japanese, who massaged my head with cool, astringent bay rum, ending up with a little tap of his hand on the nape of my neck. A harder one, karate-fashion, and he could have broken it. It was a Japanese photographer who took our annual squadron photograph. Doubtless he took others, if only mental ones, on his way through the base, and sent them back to G.H.Q. in Tokyo.

What incredible naïveté the British display before their enemies. In Singapore we took the whole subject of Japanese spies as a huge joke. Yet Singapore was riddled with them and, within five years or so, the Japanese would be the masters in Singapore.

Then, there were the Sikhs. Sikhs guarded the airfield, bayonets fixed. When my turn came for orderly officer, I had to inspect their guardroom – after midnight. As I rode up in the dark on a motorbike, giant Sikhs sprang off the *charpoys* where they had been resting and fell in with shouted orders and the clatter of rifle butts on the asphalt. I, who was white and twenty-one, found myself facing a row of rigid, black bearded warriors. Meekly I inspected them; then, for a while, I would talk and joke with them, and they laughed huge, throaty, white-toothed laughs from out of their massive beards. I had the feeling that they took me less for a superior officer than a morsel of white meat, tender, appetising, good to kill and eat. I was not all that wrong. When the Japanese captured Singapore, many Sikhs, in a kind of Asian free-for-all, turned on their British officers and murdered them. I suppose, if I had been there, they would have murdered me, laughing as hugely as ever.

Finally, there were the Malays, the indigenous race who, to all appearances, were incapable of exerting themselves – which explains why they never got the best-paid jobs. Why should they? They lived in *kampongs*, charming villages in the shade of coconut groves. Fishing and coconuts were their livelihood: fishing, because it involved no effort – the fish, attracted by a light, got themselves caught automatically; coconuts, because it involved no effort either – a monkey on a string was sent up the

The author as a baby in September, 1915

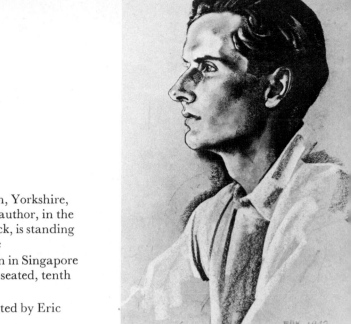

Above: At Church Fenton, Yorkshire, October 1940. The author, in the centre leaning on a stick, is standing in front of a Hurricane

Below: No 36 Squadron in Singapore 1939. The author is seated, tenth from right

Right: The author painted by Eric Kennington

EHK 1942

The author, aged twenty five, as commander of 85 Squadron in July 1940 at Martlesham. Next day he was shot down by a Dornier over the North Sea

tree and threw the coconuts down. All the Malays had to do was to get someone, probably a Chinese, to pick them up and take them to market. Malays liked being chauffeurs too; the job involved the minimum of work with the maximum of sleep and excellent facilities for gambling during the *tuan's* office hours.

Those days at Singapore, spiced though they were with the danger of flying, were days of *dolce far niente*. Our duties held us from 7 a.m. till 1.30, when our working day was ended. After lunch came the siesta, officially recommended 'because the climate thinned your blood'. Some of us who were not drowsy with Pimms or beer or too much *tiffin*, went sailing instead. With a friend, Ted Thornewill, I shared a boat, which we bought for almost nothing. Or we swam at the swimming club and ate delicious ice-cream called 'Eskimo Pie'. Then maybe a glass or two of black Munich beer, aboard a Norddeutscher liner, if one happened to be in port, or a *'stengah'* (a 'half' whisky-soda) after squash at the Tanglin Club, or a gin-sling at Raffles. Then, if we felt in the mood, we would go to the 'New World' or the 'Happy World', to dance sedately with slim Chinese hostesses, whose plump mothers or *amahs*, waiting by the ringside, would have made nonsense of any attempt at further fun. Finally home, with the windscreen folded flat, so that we could inhale to the full the balmy night air, laden though it might be, as we passed a Chinese village, with the stench of dying fish and human excreta.

We seldom went out with girls, because there were very few girls – white ones – to go out with. Once, when I had to stop a couple of nights at Kuala Lumpur because of engine trouble, the *memsahib* of a local *tuan besar* (in Malay: big chief) had me to her home. I met her daughter, a lovely girl. Boys and girls ripe for love could rarely have had such a chance so far east of Suez. But I was not ripe for love. My only love was my dear, ugly Vildebeeste, and it was with her that I spent the rest of my time in Kuala Lumpur.

One day a boat-load of young Germans came steaming into Singapore in the training cruiser *Emden*. The first German I ever met in my life was stark naked. We confronted each other under a shower in the Tanglin Club, alike as two peas in a pod – in our birthday suits. But back in uniform we were each in a different camp. That evening the Germans, our guests at dinner, raised their hands in the Nazi salute as the band played *Deutschland Über Alles*. They looked quite comic. Later, a toast was drunk: 'Germany and England will beat the world!'

Outside my ground-floor bedroom was an asphalt space where I parked my beautiful, blue, long-nosed M.G. (which consisted of the bits and pieces of two or three others, put together by an ingenious Chinese). One afternoon I was changing the right, rear tyre when something made me stop and walk over to my bedroom, ten yards away, to look for a rag. During the few seconds I was there I heard an aeroplane pass over the mess, approaching to land. A moment later I was back beside my car; the right rear mudguard was deeply gashed and on the ground beside it lay a string of lead beads, the kind that were attached to the end of a trailing aerial. The weighted aerial would have cut me in half like a piece of cheese, had not that kindly unseen hand pushed me out of the way just in time.

Adventure now awaited us: the squadron, with twelve aircraft, was to fly the 4,000 odd miles to Risalpur, on India's northwest frontier. Cruising at 100 m.p.h., it would take us five days' hard flying. Our aircraft were grounded during the month of October 1936, overhauled and packed with stores and equipment (which included a spare wheel bolted beneath the fuselage).

We were off on a fabulous but gruelling trip. Fastened for hours on end in a cramped, open cockpit, you shifted from one side of your bottom to the other, longing to be free of the straps which held you in. The Vildebeeste possessed no sanitary arrangements; you simply peed in the cockpit, though considerations of hygiene – and amour-propre – kept you agonising until your bladder was ready to burst.

At Alor Star, our first stopover, I spent the night under a mosquito net, in a sumptuous double bed, with a single mosquito. It was only in the small hours of the morning that the mosquito, sated with my blood, apparently passed out. So did I, but not for long. We took off at dawn. Four hours later, we landed at Victoria Point, a tiny grass field surrounded by shimmering palm trees. There we refuelled – from two gallon tins. Pilot and fitter sat on the top wing pouring fuel through a chamois leather and funnel into each tank. An empty tin, dropped by a clumsy coolie, tore a hole in the fabric of my bottom wing. Along came the Flight Sergeant and, with needle and thread, repaired the damage.

Next day we came to Rangoon. The golden, glinting spire of the Shwe Dagon pagoda rose through the blue haze and seemed to beckon me back to my birthplace, my *chet myo*. It was the first time that I had ever returned there.

My godmother, ebullient Cousin Addie, still lived in Rangoon. Ever a *fantaisiste*, she paraded me before her household staff – about a dozen, all told. 'You saw the giant birds fly over', she reminded them. 'This young man was riding on one. He comes to you like a god from heaven.' Addie's humble servants salaamed obediently, but were obviously unimpressed. I felt stiff and sheepish and utterly un-godlike.

We climbed away from Rangoon high above the inhospitable Andaman range, heading for Akyab, where we slipped in over the cemetery and landed. Lying there, the startled dead must have looked up and wondered. Some would have known my father who, before men flew, had exercised the imperial writ, as district commissioner, at Akyab.

What a glorious adventure I was living, for a boy of twenty-one. Risking my neck, to be sure, but behind leaders – Dick Keary, my flight-commander, and Peter Davies, my squadron-commander – who were, just as much as me, risking theirs. They were the only kind of leader I could follow; ones who took the same or greater risks than I.

Leaving the coast, we cut out across the Bay of Bengal, then groped our way down through the brown haze, across the myriad tributaries of the Ganges delta, and landed at Calcutta. Then we forged on, at about the same speed as a modern car on an auto-route, across ancient imperial India.

The fifth day of our odyssey brought us within sight of the Himalayas, looking like a mass of white cloud, tinted rose by the early sun. At our destination, Risalpur, we climbed stiffly down from our cockpits, exhausted. But the air was crisp and cool, and it smelt of wood smoke, like an autumn day in England.

From Risalpur we reconnoitered the Khyber Pass, the country of the fierce Pathan tribes, Wazirs and Afridis. Behind my Pegasus engine, I felt safer than if I were in an impregnable fortress. While at Risalpur, I went by train to visit my brother Philip at Abottabad. At every station two drinking fountains stood next to each other, one marked 'water for Hindus', the other 'water for Muslims'. The water of course was the same, a symbol of how the two communities, under British rule, lived peacefully side by side.

Philip and a few other British officers lived high up in the mountains in a community of Gurkhas, little men with shaven, shiny bullet-heads, broad smiles, slit-eyes and tough, squat bodies – formidable fighters who were never without their *kukri*, a shapely but murderous-looking knife. Philip's army billet was a cottage smothered in pink roses. Aside from the blue mountains, it was as if we were back in Somerset, and that, probably, was how Philip saw it. For, in the outposts of empire, the British created a home from home, with all the nostalgia and appurtenances of a house and garden in England, never ceasing to dream of the day when, at last, they would return. I had no such dreams. It was my wanderer's instinct, I suppose, which led me, like a gypsy, to move on, hopeful of finding a new oasis.

36 Squadron's return journey was grandiosely called a 'Colonial Development Flight'. After enjoying the fun and the flesh-pots of Delhi, we landed on the scorched grass of Dum-Dum airfield at Calcutta, refuelling from 4-gallon drums, heavy and hard to handle, pulling the covers over cockpit and engine and fastening the wings to pickets screwed into the unyielding earth. In a muck sweat, I repaired to my tent, dirty brown, cramped and stifling hot. There I thought back to the day, a year before, when I had sat shivering before a smoky stove at Catfoss, waiting for the mist to clear, the day of my twenty-first birthday. Today I celebrated my twenty-second with a glass of tepid beer, and a leech, fastened into my leg, gorging itself with my blood.

We flew on to discover new airstrips in Burma with mellifluous, romantic names: Cox's Bazaar, Sandoway, Kyaukpyu
and Pagoda Point. My flight-commander, Dick Keary, led
Dickie Longmore and me to Pagoda Point, at the mouth of the
Bassein River. Never had aircraft wheels touched its virgin
surface. Dick Keary was the first to violate it. Waiting my turn,
I circled low over the sea where giant rays heaved themselves
out of the water, flapping clumsily, trying to fly like me, but
falling back and churning up fountains of spray. I blessed the
Pegasus motor which kept me flying.

The Thai government invited us to Bangkok after which
we headed back to base. On 3 December we landed at Penang,
an enchanted island, where the scent of frangipani fills the air
and fishermen row past in the night, stirring the phosphorescent
sea into watery sparks and singing songs to the stars. There I
picked up a newspaper, the first I had seen for days, and in it
read, for the first time, of the Abdication Crisis. The King-
Emperor Edward VIII was about to renounce the throne for
the woman he loved. When, on 5 December, we landed at
Singapore, the crisis was nearing its climax. A week later a new
King-Emperor, George VI, was on the throne.

It was an event which riveted the world's attention – and one
of unpredictable consequence to me, years later. For the present
the new King-Emperor became the figure-head, the imperial
'We' to whom I owed allegiance.

CHAPTER 9

Preparing for war

Early in 1937, Singapore's defences, considered impregnable, were put to the test in a full-scale exercise. Flying-boat squadrons scouted the sea for the imaginary enemy (which no one now doubted would be the Japanese). We, in 36 Squadron, were despatched to torpedo imaginary enemy warships and transports, while the long-range batteries pounded them in an imaginary bombardment. As everyone now knows, the pundits were imagining all the wrong things. The enemy, when he came early in 1942, overran the defences from the rear. My old squadron was wiped out.

Possibly I would have perished with them, but for the plague which had afflicted me for four years and was reducing me to a physical and mental wreck. No doctor had yet found a remedy, but after a year in Singapore, I found, quite by accident, a doctor wiser than them all: Professor Young, head of the School of Tropical Medicine. We met at a dinner party; afterwards, in the warm Singaporean night, I unburdened myself to him. He examined me next day; yet all his tests and treatments were unavailing. Then, one morning he said to me, in his quiet voice: 'Stop thinking that you have the plague. The origin of your trouble is entirely nervous. Without your realising it, flying gets you over-strung, hence the skin lesions. There is only one thing for it: you must give up flying, go home and live like a cabbage for several months.'

I nearly cried. Give up flying, the one thing that I lived for! 'It's your only chance', said this kind, wise doctor. I departed, heavy-hearted, on the next homeward bound P & O liner, shutting myself in my cabin and playing Rossini's *Barber of Seville* most of the day – it lightened my sorrow. Within a few days, my skin was once again as smooth as a baby's bottom. A month later, I faced the R.A.F. doctors in London and showed them

Professor Young's report. They gaped at it, then at me. 'But you are perfectly well', they chorused, and rated me fit for flying duties.

It was incredible. I had been sent home, over 10,000 miles, to be cured of a four year-old illness provoked by flying. And here was the medical grand jury pronouncing that flying was just the thing to set me right. Why in heaven's name, then, had I been sent home?

My sole consolation, short-lived as it happened, was to be sent back to Tangmere, this time to 43 Squadron. It was a joy to be back in my home-from-home, thrilling to feel once more the Fury's zest and lightness, after the plodding paces of the Vildebeeste. A plague on the doctors and on the plague itself! I threw myself back into flying and, in no time, it was again on me.

I soon realised another depressing thing, as I tried, not very successfully, during the summer of 1937, to settle down at Tangmere. Dramatic changes had taken place since I left. The R.A.F., faced with the growing menace of the German Luft-waffe, was expanding fast. Gone were the halcyon days of 'the best flying club in the world'. Tangmere was now peopled by strange faces, different people with a different style. I resented this new generation of pilots who had answered the R.A.F.'s urgent appeal and found heaven-sent relief from boring civilian jobs.

My prejudices against them were ignoble, for they were soon to become the most generous-hearted friends, then, a little later, die, most of them, for England. But I was a purist and jealous of my calling. I had joined the R.A.F. solely because, since my earliest youth, I was fired with a desire to fly. I felt ill at ease among these parvenu pilots and they, not surprisingly, showed little enthusiasm for me. With my slender seniority, I had usurped the place of one of them, Fred Rosier, as flight-commander. But Fred had by far the best of it in the end; as Sir Frederick, he later became Commander-in-Chief of Fighter Command.

Worst blow of all, the holy ground of Tangmere, ever a fighter base, was now desecrated by a squadron of Coastal

Command – great types, brave as lions, but not fighter boys. My die-hard instincts were offended, and my sky looked very dark. Then, of a sudden, the clouds parted and down came a goddess, a blue-eyed, fair-skinned Danish goddess with an authentic goddess's name, Bodil. She took my hand and I fell in love for the first time – madly, but, alas, impossibly in love. Why in heaven did I have to fall in love with someone so lovable, yet whom I could so rarely see? For Bodil returned to her Viking lair and I was reduced to telephoning her, on Sunday evenings, from the red call-box in Chichester – seven shillings and eleven pence for three minutes of bliss; that was all I could afford. I dared not use the mess telephone for I wanted no one to know that I was 'broody'. Other pilots quickly notice a 'broody' pilot. He tends to keep a more respectable distance in formation, to avoid aerobatics, to keep his feet on the ground if the weather looks menacing. His imagination begins to work, a bad thing for a man who must take risks.

I spaced out my leave so that my visits to Denmark were as frequent as possible. When I was broke, I undertook the sick-making North Sea crossing second class, pacing the deck to avoid the nauseating smell of cooking. It was worth it, if only to fall into Bodil's arms on arriving at Copenhagen in the small hours of the morning. I saved every penny and sometimes flew Imperial Airways from Croydon. It cost about a month's pay. The Lockheed air-liner carried a dozen passengers and took four and a half hours, via Amsterdam and Hamburg, to reach Copenhagen. Separated as Bodil and I were, by time and distance, our love affair was a stronger than usual blend of heaven and hell. But it shone like a beacon through the darkness which now blackened my horizon, and continued to do so until the war unkindly severed our relationship.

Having served temporarily in a torpedo-bomber squadron, Coastal Command now claimed me as theirs, and the Air Ministry, forgetting that I had been trained and had served as a fighter pilot, treacherously posted me to an air navigation course at Manston, on the eastern tip of Kent. It could have been in Siberia, for all I cared; this was the crowning disaster – being deported, for life it seemed, from fighters.

Besides, I now realised that, in our training, the accent was not so much on flying as such, but on 'destroying the enemy'. Consciously, methodically, we were training for war. The prospect of having to kill was as real as it was revolting. I only wanted to fly. The risk of being killed while doing so did not deter me, but I rebelled against the thought of flying being used as a means to kill. It went against all that flying meant to me – the joy, swift and clean and sensual, of *living*. It might kill me. So be it. But I shrank from enjoying it as a means for killing others.

I turned to Philip Babington who had known me as a problem-child since Cranwell days, and told him that I wanted to quit the R.A.F., and why. He was sympathetic, but reasoned with me: the Axis Powers, Germany and Italy, would not stop at war in order to achieve their ambitions. It would be more sensible if I faced the possibility of war, however unpleasant, and stayed put. So I reported at the School of Air Navigation.

The Air Ministry finally sent me back to Tangmere, to the Coastal Command squadron at the end of the tarmac. It was the ultimate humiliation. Condemned to these lumbering twin-motored aircraft which staggered off the ground with a crew of four, I watched bitterly, enviously, as my friends in 43 Squadron gambolled in their Furies. I determined to escape. I still had the plague on me and, for once, I was glad. I wrote to the Air Ministry an incredibly naïve but categorical letter. I said that, flying as a passenger in a multi-place aircraft, I became so nervous that it made me ill; my skin complaint was still there to prove it. Unless I could return to single-seaters and receive proper medical treatment, I would resign.

That letter did the trick. Within a week I was transferred from the Coastal Squadron at one end of the tarmac to 43 Squadron at the other. At the touch of the wand, I was changed, from a navigator, back into a fighter pilot. And the doctors, apparently impressed by my threat to resign, sent me away on six months leave. Thus, a year after Professor Young had advised me to live like a cabbage, I was at last allowed to do so. I vegetated in the Quantock Hills.

In September 1938 I went back to 43 Squadron, back to

flying, and never again was my skin marred by another sore. The cure had worked. So glad was I to be delivered, as if by the Almighty, from my satanic affliction, that I felt like crying aloud with friend Job: 'I know that my Redeemer liveth'.

The signs of war were growing daily. In the Sudetenland province of Czechoslovakia, people were clamouring: '*Ein Volk, Ein Reich, Ein Fuehrer*'. And the Fuehrer turned his rage and threats against Czechoslovakia. Hardly had I taken to the air again with 43 Squadron, in September 1938, when the Munich crisis brought England to the verge of war.

At Tangmere, all was gloom. We were less depressed by Hitler's threats than by the fact that we were so poorly armed to meet them. The R.A.F.'s proud claim to be England's first line of defence now made us look, and feel, ridiculous. Our Furies were obsolete. The German Heinkel and Dornier bombers (not to speak of their Messerschmitt fighters) could easily out-strip us – which was of academic interest anyhow, for, if by some miracle we managed to get within range of them, our two puny Vickers guns would merely act as pinpricks.

On the 28 September, Londoners were being issued with gas-masks and digging trenches, a passive form of resistance against the Luftwaffe's expected 'knock-out blow'. We, in 43 Squadron, spent all that night in the hangar, making up ammunition bands for our guns and daubing our shining silver Furies with war-paint, brown and green. The added weight and skin-friction of this camouflage made them drag their heels even more.

Occasionally, we slipped back to the mess for a beer, only to find a funereal atmosphere, heavy with anxiety and despair. The older officers, who had already seen one war, sat round, their heads in their hands, praying that they would not see another. We young ones, too, prayed silently that we would not, this time, have to defend England.

With the departure to Munich of the British and French premiers, Chamberlain and Daladier, the suspense eased somewhat. Within 48 hours they had agreed to sacrifice Czechoslovakia to the Teutonic war-god. Chamberlain returned to

Croydon airport, waved a little white paper signed by Hitler, and talked in his frail voice of 'peace in our time'. He was hailed as a saviour. War was averted and the nation cheered gratefully.

At Tangmere we stood down. We did not cheer, but just heaved a sigh of relief.

The Air Ministry lost no time in administering the tonic needed to revive us – Hurricanes, the new '300 m.p.h.-plus' monoplane fighters. By mid-December we were fully equipped. We felt better, and braver. The Fury had been a lovely plaything; the Hurricane, with its powerful Merlin motor and its battery of eight machine-guns, was an engine of war.

Unfortunately, it quickly, and quite undeservedly, gained a bad reputation. It was not the sweet, soft thing that the Fury had been. It was far less tolerant of faulty handling and needed more room to recover. A mistake at low altitude could be fatal. Up and down the land, death stalked the fighter camps. Tangmere was not spared. One young pilot, flying too slow, slid out of a turn and crashed before our eyes. Another hit a tree while landing; we watched helpless, as he was burnt alive.

The death of one of our little band, the useless waste of a young life, greatly saddened us. But we had our own methods of restoring our morale. In the early hours of that morning, in the mess, we mourned our lost comrade in our own peculiar way, which smacked somewhat of the ritual of primitive tribesmen. Fred Rosier took his violin and to the tune of the can-can from *Orpheus in the Underworld*, we danced hilariously round the mess. Thus immunised against the gloom of the final rites, we laid our comrade to rest in Tangmere's peaceful graveyard, where so many other pilots slept. Then we went back to our Hurricanes and climbed again into the sky, revelling in their mighty, exhilarating power.

A complete change of mind and heart had by now come over me. I relished every moment of flying, now that it no longer afflicted me with the plague. My pacifism of the previous year had evaporated; I was becoming rather bellicose – at least as bloody-minded as every other Englishman felt towards the swaggering, bullying Germans. And, in the growingly tense atmosphere, I was discovering that those parvenu pilots I had once so resented were really the warmest, most generous friends. They were, after all, genuine 'fighter boys', who lived for the shining hour, who did not take themselves seriously.

Caesar Hull, a lean, husky-voiced South African, lively and always laughing, was a superb and fearless pilot, yet childishly superstitious. He was afraid of 'pheenies' and 'gremlins' and checked every night under his bed, in case there was someone there. Caesar would never fly without his 'pheenie-scarf'. Like all airmen I was superstitious, but not to that degree. I mistrusted talismens.

Fred Rosier was Welsh and musical, a superb pilot too, with a subtle, analytical mind.

Joe Sullivan was different, but a much-loved member of our band. Joe was Canadian, apparently a little bit Red Indian, dry-humoured, always complaining. All of us were obliged to do some daily exercise and one day I asked Joe: 'Have you done your daily dozen?' 'Yeah' he drawled, 'I went for a run – in my car.'

John Simpson, a member of B flight (the one I commanded) was sensitive, immensely likeable and, as a pilot, rather timid – though he later proved his valour.

These were the leading characters in our band of happy, embryonic warriors, among whom I began to find my feet again. John Simpson wrote about me to his friend Hector Bolitho, author of *Combat Report*: 'He used to be rather aloof, going to his room at night and avoiding our games and parties. But we are bringing him out of his shell. He is very shy and has no idea of his own courage. He surrounds himself with armour, but I am slowly breaking through . . .'

I only quote John because of his sensitive portrait of an unfortunate young man who had found that all things were not as bright and beautiful as he had imagined, who had groped through inner and outer darkness, like a lot of young men have to do, and was now reaching the end of the tunnel.

Our training increased in tempo, became more warlike. Battle climbs took us to 30,000 feet, where the Hurricane wallowed, barely afloat in the thin air. We fired our guns at a splash target in the sea, where the bullets kicked up jagged white plumes and churned the water into foam. Nothing, it seemed, could survive in that hail of metal.

Through the clouds we flew, keeping station; and alone into the velvet night, carpeted with the lights of local towns and (with luck) canopied with a starry heaven. Thus suspended between stars and street-lighting, it was easy, despite the torrent of blue flames pouring from the Merlin's exhausts, to keep an even keel. After we had safely landed, the ground-crews pounced on our aircraft to complete the last vital phase of a fighter squadron's functioning: the 'quick re-arm and re-fuel'. Within minutes the aircraft was turned round and ready to go again.

Two things were happening: we were drifting, inexorably towards a conflict and, at the same time, perfecting ourselves as aerial killers. We were on the war-path, and by mid-March 1939, when Hitler, from the Hradchin Palace, Prague, yelled: 'Czechoslovakia has ceased to exist', we felt ready and armed, anxious almost, for the fight – a rather naïve attitude, it is true, for we were David against Goliath, refusing to acknowledge the Luftwaffe's enormous superiority in weight and numbers.

Meanwhile, everyone was being drawn into the vortex of Hitler's dream-war. After Czechoslovakia, we were almost on a war footing. Still, we continued, insouciant, to have fun.

Squadron-Leader Lord Willoughby de Broke led his squadron, No. 605, to Tangmere, their war-time station. Their arrival was the pretext for more parties. Things hummed at Tangmere Cottage, just opposite the guard room, where John and Rachel Willoughby kept open house. There we spent wild evenings, drinking, singing, dancing to romantic tunes:

> A cigarette that leaves the lipstick's traces;
> An airline ticket to romantic places;
> And yet my heart has wings:
> These foolish things remind me of you.

I was beside myself, the self that I had been two years ago, as we danced blithely, relentlessly towards catastrophe. As Hitler himself said at this time: 'The great drama is rapidly approaching its climax.'

The hour struck – for Poland on 1 September, for England and France on the 3rd. That morning, I lay on the grass beside my Hurricane with the rest of my flight. We were at 'readiness' – five minutes notice to take-off, but still there was no word of war. Then we were informed: 'The balloon goes up at 11.45.'

We walked over to the mess, that sprawling building, now covered in autumn-pink creeper, where I had lived on and off for the last four years. Now all was grim and solemn, as we waited in the mess for Chamberlain to speak. While we stood tensely around the radio, Macey and Hoskins, imperturbable as ever, went to and fro through the swing doors, each one carrying his tray of pewter beer mugs.

Suddenly Chamberlain's voice, heavy with disaster, broke the silence: 'It is a sad day for all of us. All the aims I have tried so hard to attain, all the principles in which I believed . . . have come to nought. I hope to live long enough to see the day when, with the end of Hitlerism, a free Europe will be born.'

The tension suddenly broke. The fatal step had been taken; we were at war. Caesar was the first to rejoice. 'Wizard', he kept repeating and, turning to John Simpson, he laughed: 'Don't worry, John, you'll be one of the first to be killed!'

John, like me, would survive, but not Caesar, nor Woods-Scawen, nor Wilkinson in A flight, nor Tiger Folkes, Eddy Edmonds, Pat Christie or Joe Sullivan in B flight. By the time another year was out, they would all be dead. With one chance in five of survival – not counting the burnt and the wounded – only a handful of us would come through.

When the lot of my generation is compared to succeeding ones, I believe that we had it as hard as any. True, we had known a carefree youth and tasted copiously of the joy of living. But six years of war compelled us to live with the horror of dying, day after day; it took from us all we had, our friends included, and left us empty-handed and disillusioned.

We lay down once more in the grass beside our Hurricanes, waiting for the English sky to blacken, as Goering had promised it would, with hordes of his bombers. But only flakey white clouds sailed across England's sky, *our* sky. The larks trilled their energetic songs, and human voices came floating intermittently across the warm air. Never had I known such peace; it was unthinkable that we were at war.

I was twenty-four – quite old for a fighter pilot. Not all that long ago, I had sat on my father's knee, while he told me about Queen Boadicea and King Alfred, Drake and Nelson and all the great company who had fought against the invaders of England. Now it was my turn to be numbered among them, and my brothers too: Michael, a destroyer captain, and Philip, guarding a distant outpost. I believe my father would have felt proud, in his quiet way, that his three sons were in the front line. My mother no doubt felt the same. But now, with my father gone, it was alone that she would have to do the waiting and the praying.

From the beginning, the war in England was a strangely domestic affair. We were all in it; it was everybody's war. We fighter pilots were confined within the base, lived and slept beside our aircraft, in a tense state of alert. But families and friends came to wish their men well, waiting for them by the surrounding barbed-wire fence. My mother came too, with my brother Francis, then fourteen, to talk to me. She was very calm; that was her great quality – she never showed fear nor distress, only joy.

A few alarms and excursions stirred us from our increasing inertia. We waited and waited and became bored and fretful, longing to escape from our barbed-wire enclosure. Then, one day, we were released. We piled into cars and drove hard to the Ship Inn at Bosham. What a party we had; at closing time, we went out into the street and fired our revolvers into the air. Windows were flung open, people rushed from their houses, thinking the invasion had started.

Months were to pass before England was threatened with invasion. Meanwhile, the Phoney War was on.

CHAPTER 10

War: the air battles

The exigencies of war soon changed the pastoral atmosphere of Tangmere. Mechanical diggers came, clawing up the green turf, to clear the way for asphalt runways, and the green itself was camouflaged with soot. Repeated flaps kept us on the alert; but 'bandits' and 'bogies' (code for, respectively, enemy and un-identified aircraft) always turned out to be one of ours. Only once did I shoot – at a stray barrage balloon which flopped down into a field, like a tired elephant, with the local villagers in pursuit.

With ground control still in a rudimentary stage, many fighter pilots, blinded and confused in the unaccustomed obscurity of the blackout, crashed to death. I was only saved by the calm of the controller, David Lloyd. For some minutes, my life hung in the balance, but David kept chatting calmly with me as he brought me down through the murk, finally announcing: 'You'll be over base in five minutes, so we are putting on the kettle to make you some tea.' Our lives were as much in the controllers' hands as in our own.

For thirteen years, Tangmere had been the exclusive home of Nos. 1 and 43 squadrons – the Fighting First and Kate Meyrick's Own (Mrs Meyrick ran the Forty-Three, one of London's most famous night-clubs). Now the time came for both to depart, No. 1 to France and we in 43 northwards to Acklington, a bleak, windswept terrain near Newcastle.

Our Hurricanes were formidable weapons; but we and they were ill-provided. Our dispersal points were concrete slums, poorly heated, sparsely furnished. Mobile starter-batteries were few and often flat. Transport was a rare luxury. At dawn, each day of that bitter winter of 1939–40, the ground crews and we would trudge across the airfield to our dispersed aircraft and, with frozen hands, wind the starting handles. But our lack of equipment was compensated for by our passion for the chase. Though for months the enemy never showed up, we kept our senses sharpened with wild aerial escapades.

Between A Flight, led by Caesar Hull, and B Flight, led by me, was a tense, unsparing rivalry. Caesar, more than any other, had brought me out of my hesitant, timid self and made me feel once more a real airman. He was better than me, but he challenged me to be as good. Though, in the air, we allowed each other no quarter, an inseparable comradeship bound us. We sparred above the clouds; or we would fly together straight at a cliff-face, daring one another to be the last to pull clear. Ignoring the regulations, we looped and rolled in formation at ground level. We borrowed two Spitfires, brand new, from 152 Squadron who, after their slow, square-rigged Gladiator bi-planes, were feeling rather shy of the speedy, sexy 'Spit'. In tight formation we dived those Spitfires low over 152's hangar, pulled them up into a loop, dived again, rolled and gambolled. It looked like terrible exhibitionism, but was really only an expression of *joie de vivre*, which the whole squadron shared. No one, we believed, least of all the Germans, could ever beat us.

Our role being the protection of coastal convoys, we patrolled above them from dawn to dusk, in fair weather and foul. The sea was our one dread. Our single Merlin engine kept us flying; if it stopped we would inevitably fall into the drink where, with nothing but our kapok-filled Mae Wests to keep us afloat, we stood less chance than the mariners below.

Caesar was the first to score: his victim, a Heinkel bomber, crashed into the sea. A few days later, I drew level with him. It was the 3 February 1940. At the head of Blue section, I was skidding low over the sea, Tiger Folkes and Sergeant Hallowes in my wake. Tiger, a mild youth with blue eyes and russet hair, had once protested that I had led him so low past the end of Blyth pier that the flying spray had splashed his windscreen. But only by 'wave-chopping' could we hope to avoid detection by the cloud-hugging Heinkels.

The crew of the Heinkel I spotted that morning never saw us until the bullets began tearing into their bomber. Only then did red tracer come spurting from their rear guns, but, in the first foolish rapture of combat, I believed myself, like Achilles, invulnerable. The Heinkel scraped over the cliffs at Whitby and crash-landed in the snow behind the town – the first German bomber down on English soil since World War I.

I felt elated as I watched the enemy bomber crash. Then the full implication struck me. Someone heard me murmur, as I climbed out of the cockpit: 'Poor devils, I don't think they're all dead'. Two of them were. Remorse, rather than curiosity, impelled me to visit the survivors in hospital. One of them, Karl Missy, the rear gunner, had tried to kill me; he was prevented when the bullets from my guns sawed through his leg and felled him. Despite the harm I had done him, he clasped my hand, but, in his steady brown eyes, was the reproachful look of a wounded animal.

Victory in the air called for champagne in the mess – a horribly uncivilised way of behaving, really, when you have just killed someone. But an enemy bomber down was proof of our prowess, and that was a legitimate pretext for celebration. For the enemy crew, whom we had shot to pieces, we gave no thought. Young, like us, they had existed, but existed no longer. Deep down we knew, but dared not admit, that we had little hope of existing much longer ourselves. So, meanwhile, we made merry.

A few days later, I killed four more men. 'Did you really have to kill them?' asked my 12 year-old Pierre when, many years later, I told him of that morning. I never had the slightest wish to kill anybody, least of all young people like myself, with the same passion for flying. It was not them but their bomber, invading our sky, that filled my sights after I had stalked it, with all my cunning, four miles up in a deserted sky. There I did it to death in cold blood. Only later did I picture the crew, with one more mission accomplished, chatting on the intercom, perhaps munching a sandwich or drinking *ersatz* coffee, as they headed for home and safety, where their comrades and their loved ones waited. How could I escape a feeling of remorse when it was I who put an end to all that, I who struck them down? I, the shy one, ever unsure of myself, afraid of death and darkness, who shunned a fight, of whom it had always been said

'Needs encouragement'. Now I needed none. A terrible change had come over me.

The squadron moved north, to Wick, to defend the naval base of Scapa Flow. There, at the extreme tip of Scotland, we stood guard throughout the long northern days and, during the bitter cold of the night, slept briefly, fitfully, under rough blankets and newspapers. Not that the hard lying was a bad thing – it made it easier to go out, face the weather and the enemy and, if need be, die.

Outside the crude comfort of our wooden huts, the storm raged, dragging our aircraft from their pickets, burying them in snow, lashing the sea, more menacing than ever, and sending it battering against the coast or racing, churned into whirlpools, through the Pentland Firth. One morning, Tiger Folkes, patrolling with me, low above the tumultuous waters, disappeared.

The Luftwaffe men faced the double hazard of our fighters and the sea. We sat, strapped into our cockpits, waiting to sally forth against them. With the approach of the enemy, the radio jamming grew louder and louder, and the tension became so unbearable that it sometimes drove us from our cockpits to vomit. When at last the code word 'SCRAMBLE' unleashed us, we surged forward, throttle wide open, tails up like baying hounds. Only a kill could satisfy our lust for the chase. But the scent, thanks to imperfect radar coverage, was sometimes false.

One night, after searching vainly, high among the A.A. bursts over Scapa, and low, where bombs and unspent shells were plopping into the Pentland Firth, the controller called me in to land. I switched off my radio and continued to search. Then, high up in the glow of the departed day, a speck materialised. With my radio still mute, I began to stalk, silently, stealthily, my eyes glued on the speck in the sky. But when I closed in on my prey, he resisted desperately.

In aerial combat, you usually only hear the enemy's fire if you stop a close one. But there in the darkness, far out to sea, Heinkel and Hurricane were fighting a terrible gun battle at point blank range, so that when I came in for the *coup de grâce* I could actually hear the Heinkel's guns, in their last dying fury, firing just above my head. I was now seized with an irresistible desire to destroy. Down went the bomber into the sea, and with it four more dead men. I all but died with them, as I realised when, next morning, I examined my Hurricane. It was riddled with bullets.

That fight made me think. The killing game was increasing in pace, and this time I had barely escaped death. It was a sobering thought. But a more awful one was that I myself had become an implacable agent of death. Next day, when a small horde of us pounced on another Heinkel, I did not bother to fire – the machine was already foundering. I flew in close beside it. The young pilot and his companions regarded me helplessly as their flying tumbril bore them on, down to the sea. I would have given anything to save them; instead, I found myself escorting them to their grave. A few minutes later they were swallowed up by the sea.

By now, the first care-free rapture of victory had faded. No longer was I an amateur, but a hard-bitten professional. The medal recently pinned on my breast by the King confirmed the fact. But so far the air war had consisted of skirmishes: violent hand-to-hand fighting over the sea. The real air war started, on 10 May 1940, with the German offensive in the west.

A week later, I took command of 85 Squadron at Debden, north of London, where they had repaired after escaping, barely, from the military disaster in France. At our forward airfields, Castle Camps and Martlesham, near the North Sea coast, camping under canvas, in an atmosphere scented with mown hay, heather and wild flowers, and sweetened by the song of birds, I rediscovered the sublime peace of the pastoral life. For a month or so war was not for us an urgent preoccupation. It merely involved us in patrolling from dawn to dusk over the east coast convoys. Occasionally we picked up scraps of talk from the squadrons over Dunkirk; we ourselves were well beyond range of that titanic operation. Then, suddenly, I was ordered to concentrate my entire squadron at Martlesham. The Battle of Britain had begun.

I myself was lucky to survive the first twenty-four hours of the battle. During a sharp fight, miles out to sea, my aircraft was disabled by enemy bullets. One exploded in the cockpit. For some minutes, as I searched vainly for a ship, it looked as if I were going to die, rather slowly, by drowning. But first I had to jump into the sea, three thousand feet below. Faced with the prospect of death, I was astonished to find myself so calm and lucid. I jumped, and my parachute deposited me in the sea, which would have claimed another victim, but for the mine-sweeper *Finisterre*. She seemed to have appeared from nowhere, and was miles off her course.

Back on dry land I telephoned my mother, who feigned indifference and advised me to be more careful in future. That evening I was back again in the air.

The Luftwaffe's increasing offensive against our coastal con-voys kept us patrolling ceaselessly during the day and – those few of us who were qualified – during the night as well. In June, July and August I flew as many hours as in a normal year. I learned not to sleep and, when I did, it was with one eye open and both ears cocked. Gradually, insidiously, fatigue began to weigh down on us, and our nerves tensed more and more to resist it. The south-coast squadrons were having it far worse while we, on the left wing of the battle, waited impatiently to be thrown into the fray.

Our turn came soon after Goering, on 13 August, launched his *Adlerangriff*, Eagles' Attack, which, he promised Hitler, would wipe out the R.A.F.'s fighter defences within a week. 85 Squadron were moved back to Debden where the Luftwaffe were attacking in mass.

My frightening childhood impressions of Germans were as vivid as ever; there still echoed in my ears nanny's terrifying threat. I was still frightened of Germans. The fierce individual combats I had so far fought with them had not made me feel any braver. Quite recently, I had dived slap into a formation of thirty Messerschmitts, hoping to pick one off. The storm of lead which followed my hasty withdrawal into a nearby cloud con-firmed my fears that the Germans, *en masse*, were redoubtable. And now I had to lead my squadron of twelve against hundreds of German bombers and fighters. I dreaded the idea and tossed sleeplessly in my bed thinking about it – luckily for no more than a few nights, for the test came on 18 August, the day after our move to Debden. When I received the order: 'Patrol Canterbury, two hundred plus approaching', I felt not the slightest qualm, even less when I sighted the massed enemy formations, stepped up over thousands of feet like a giant moving staircase, as one fighter-pilot put it.

By the end of the day, the Luftwaffe had suffered a shattering defeat. Goering's boast of victory within a week evaporated in the English air, and it was Churchill, two days later, who had the next word to say, when he paid his immortal tribute to the British fighters: 'Never in the field of human conflict was so much owed . . .'

The enemy's initial onslaught had been repulsed, but the hardest fighting was yet to come. My squadron was now moved up to Croydon, in the fore-front of the battle. Of the twenty pilots I led to Croydon on the 19 August, fourteen, including me, were shot down within the next two weeks, two of them twice. The number in itself looks insignificant; never, in fact, did the R.A.F. lose more than a few dozen fighter-pilots in a day. Yet, during these crucial weeks such losses, especially in experienced pilots, began to spell defeat. As reinforcements, came pilots from other commands, from the Navy, too, and the flying schools – the latter, boys hardly past their 'teens, brave as lions but tenderfeet. Our battle was a small one but on its outcome depended the fate of the western world.

No such thoughts ever bothered us. Obviously, we knew we had to win; but, more than that, we were somehow certain that we could not lose. I think it had something to do with England. Miles up in the sky, we fighter pilots could see more of England than any other of England's defenders had ever seen before. Beneath us stretched our beloved country, with its green hills and valleys, lush pastures and villages clustering round an ancient church. Yes, it was a help to have England there below.

She was behind us, too. When, at the end of the day, we touched down and slipped out for a beer at the local, people were warm and wonderfully encouraging. They were for us, the fighter boys, who had once been the bad boys, who supposedly drank too much and drove too fast. Now people realised that, on the job, we were professionals. They rooted for us as if we were the home team, and we knew we had to win, if only for them.

85 Squadron, like every other, save the homogeneous Czech and Polish units, was a marvellous amalgam of men from Britain and the Commonwealth. Whatever our differences in origin and rank, our view from the cockpit, alone, miles above the earth, was identical. Though we fought wing-tip to wing-tip, each one of us had to fly and fight and, if need be, die alone. It was this sense of isolation and solitude in the air that united us so closely on the ground.

Those days of battle were the most stirring and the most wonderful I have ever lived, all the more so that they were lived in the midst of death. Death was never far away, a few minutes maybe, or a few inches, so it was all the more exalting to be alive. Though our numbers dwindled steadily, no one ever believed that he would be the next to die.

The Luftwaffe's massed formations, laying waste our bases, were smashing their way inland, nearer and nearer to London. Day by day, hour by hour, we took off to battle with them. When possible, I led the squadron in a head-on charge against the enemy bombers. Often, though, we would have to duel single-handed with their escorting fighters.

By the end of August, the Luftwaffe, by sheer weight of numbers – four to one in their favour – was wearing us down; we were weary beyond caring, our nerves taughtened to break-ing-point. On the 31 August the British fighters suffered their heaviest losses. I was among them. The Germans attacked in the middle of our hasty lunch. Their bombs all but hit us as we roared, full-throttle, off the ground. The blast made our engines falter. I never felt any particular hatred for the German airmen, only anger. This time, though, I was so blind with fury that I felt things must end badly for me. But I was too weary and too strung-up to care. For a few thrilling moments, I fenced with a crowd of Messerschmitts. Then, inevitably, one of them got me. My poor Hurricane staggered under the volley, my foot was hit. Down I went, muttering: 'Christ!' then jumped for it. I fetched up in a mass of brambles, feeling rather foolish, as if I had been unhorsed in the midst of a jousting tournament. That evening, at Croydon hospital, the surgeon pulled a heavy-calibre bullet out of my foot.

Two weeks in hospital gave me an idea of the courage of people on the ground. Night after night, the raiders were overhead. Our nurses, charming and serene, pulled our beds away from the windows, which were regularly blown in, occasionally admitting a few bomb splinters. Supposedly a hero of the air battle, I was now terrified, and abjectly ashamed, too, before the resolution of those nurses.

With me wounded, our two flight-commanders killed and more of our pilots dead or wounded, 85 Squadron was, early in September, withdrawn from the front line and sent north. I had to rejoin them within three weeks, or I should be replaced. My wound prevented me from walking, but not from flying, so, when I arrived at our new base, Church Fenton, in Yorkshire, I took the precaution of going straight to the hangars, where I was helped into a Hurricane. Then I took off. When I reported to the doctor, he told me gravely: 'It will be some time before you can fly again.' 'But I've just been flying' I replied, and he said no more.

Early in October, Goering gave orders for what he called 'the complete annihilation' of London. The massive night raids on the capital had started a month earlier and the meagre British night-fighter force, practically powerless to stop them, was now strengthened. My squadron was one of the day squadrons assigned to night-fighting. All through the winter months, we were to grope blindly after the enemy, invisible in the English sky.

Only half a dozen pilots in the squadron were 'night operational'; the others had a month to learn the basic elements. These we imparted to them at Kirton Lindsey, in Lincolnshire. The Luftwaffe took a lively interest: a Dornier machine-gunned the flare-path where I was directing operations – which ended abruptly with my diving under the mobile floodlight. One morning, a few days later, as I talked to Jim Marshall at the dispersal point, he suddenly leapt at me and knocked me flat. 'What the hell . . .' I began, indignantly, then saw tracer whipping past just above us, as a marauding Heinkel slipped low across the airfield.

We moved to Gravesend, at the eastern approaches to London; the very name reflected the dreary atmosphere of the place. A quagmire surrounded our damp dispersal huts, lit by paraffin lamps. There we waited through the night for our turn to patrol, surrounded by the artificial gloom created by our dark glasses, which kept our eyes in a state of night vision. (It takes about twenty minutes for the eyes to become fully adapted from day to night vision.)

Our Hurricanes lacked the proper means for all-weather night-fighting: radar, cockpit heating, de-icing equipment. The ground control, for all their concern for our safety, were seriously handicapped by the rudimentary nature of navigational and landing aids. Fighting by night in these conditions, experience counted more than anything; the weather, not the enemy, proved the greater hazard and killed more pilots. For this reason, it was normal that I, the oldest hand, should do the trickier weather tests. One ended badly for me, when I crashed while landing in a dense fog which had obliterated everything at the airfield, except the red light on the hangar.

Meanwhile London burned, while we, searching blindly in the dark, were impotent, without radar, to find the German bombers. On the airfield at Gravesend, we listened, frustrated to the ceaseless rumble of engines overhead, as they came streaming up the Thames estuary on their way to stoke the fires raging in the city. Ironically, it was the sea of flames below which offered us fighters, stacked up in layers above it, our only chance of discerning the silhouette of an enemy bomber. This crude method occasionally succeeded, but not with us. We continued groping in the dark while below, London was a tumult of explosions and fire. One night at the end of December, a tempest of flame engulfed the city – and in its midst, Saint Paul's Cathedral – and made it seem, at Gravesend, like daylight, in which our weakness was exposed.

We moved back to Debden. To the south, London's fiery

skyline looked like a flamboyant sunset. Yet still, for all our desperate searching, we remained powerless to come to grips with the enemy.

For interception and navigation, we relied solely on radio, directions being transmitted by the controller. One dirty night a generator failure left me erring like a lost sheep. The controller's voice grew dim and disappeared, the cockpit lights faded into obscurity, the signalling lamp was useless. There remained only one way out – to jump.

For some moments I circled, contemplating this hazardous prospect. Then, suddenly, far below in the murk, a light came on, went out and, a little later, came on again, to be extinguished once more. I dived down to investigate. Aircraft, invisible save for their navigation lights, were circling and landing, so I slipped in behind one and landed in its wake. A man climbed up on the wing and I shouted to him: 'I'm the commanding officer of 85 Squadron.' 'We'll see about that' he yelled and pressed a revolver into my back, where it remained until I had taxied in and proved my identity.

Winter, as it deepened, aggravated our problems. In our cramped, dimly-lit cockpits, we sat, numbed by cold, holding the controls, which themselves sometimes became frozen and immovable, while the engine, with ice blocking the air-intake would falter. The Air Ministry's tame scientists were called in. One, having noticed that snowdrops never freeze, made of these pretty white flowers a dirty brown paste which was smeared on our wings and propeller. It was a waste of snowdrops. When, as I approached one night to land, with my windscreen completely iced-up, I found a more effective remedy: I slid my hand round to the front and scraped the ice off with my nails. And when another night, I was caught above a layer of low cloud, I had to invent on the spot a method to get me down. I called up and asked for James Wheeler, a veteran air-line pilot.

James, off duty, was drinking beer in the mess; but a few moments later he called me back from the control tower. 'Keep firing rockets,' I told him, 'and ask for the searchlights to be illuminated horizontally.' The rockets came shooting up through the clouds and, after a few attempts, I managed to break through at the right spot and emerge in the blue glare of the searchlights, with trees and telegraph poles rushing by.

Handicapped as we were by such boy-scout methods, the enemy continued to elude us – even when he landed on our own airfield, as a Heinkel did one night. Realising his error, the pilot took off and escaped in the dark. However, I caught another erring German. His aircraft was held in the searchlights and, incredibly, his navigation lights were burning. Error or ruse? Or was it, after all, one of ours? I got close enough to see the black crosses, then fired. Three parachutes streamed into the dazzling blue searchlight cone and the bomber, a Dornier, its navigation lights still on, dived into the ground. It was the only enemy aircraft to fall to our Hurricanes in six months of futile searching.

Meanwhile, the scientists were foisting on us the strangest lethal devices: aerial mines, trailing hundreds of feet of wire and parachuted across the incoming bomber stream; aerial hand-grenades, to scatter in the enemy's path; and an aerial search-light, the turbinlite, guided by radar and powered by a ton of batteries, which would illuminate the target for thirty seconds, during which a 'satellite' fighter was supposed to make a lightning kill. But we, who had to experiment with these odd contraptions, were convinced that the only solution was airborne radar, electronic eyes to replace our own, and heavy calibre guns. Thus armed, as at last we were, we went forth into the dark and became a scourge to the enemy.

By early 1941, the night-fighter force was inflicting such losses that, after the devastating fire attack on London on 10 May, the Luftwaffe's mass night raids ended.

By now, twenty months of day and night operations had reduced me to a nerve-racked, sleep-starved wreck. I was flying more like a tired chicken than an avenging angel. In my last night combat, a Junkers 88 riddled my aircraft and continued blithely on its way. The fight had gone out of me. I had flown myself to a standstill. The doctors grounded me and put me on barbiturates. In June 1941, I was sent to a staff job with the title 'Wing-commander, night operations' – one that provoked smiles, for it was at this time that I married.

Rosemary lived with her parents hard by our airfield at Hundson, in Hertfordshire. She was twenty, tall and lovely – never more so than that evening we met at a local country house. I could not wait to make her my wife, for life in those dangerous days seemed a brief, precarious thing. So, true to that war-time phenomenon, the urge to reproduce, we rushed hand-in-hand to the altar. In the ancient church at Much Hadham, we vowed – alas, all too hastily – to be one another's for ever. Exactly nine months later, our first child was born.

But, before that, the stresses and strains of the past months had produced in me the inevitable breakdown. Sleep was the gnawing problem. I had learned to do without it, now it evaded me altogether. Unprotesting, I was led before doctors and psychologists, then sent away for three months. Rosemary found herself with an invalid, half-demented husband on her hands, and a baby on the way.

One event which helped, more than any other, to settle my disarray, was the birth, in April 1942, of our son Giles. There was more to it than just becoming a father. Giles's birth had a deeper meaning for me, for while, during all those months of fighting, I had been living in an environment of death and, with my own hands, destroying life, I now found, before my eyes, a life that I had actually created. It was a welcome compensation, if only a symbolic one, for the lives I had taken.

I was sent to command the fighter station at Drem, near Edinburgh. With the Spitfires of 611 Squadron, I began to regain my verve for flying. I flew again, as of old, with daring – fast, hard and low. Regrettably, I once flew, with a Polish officer as passenger, through the local telephone wires. On landing, the Pole, crazy with joy, threw his arms round me: he had never had such a thrill. But, back in my office, a telephone call was waiting, from the regional post office chief. 'One of your blasted pilots has flown through my telephone wires!' he exploded. 'I'm sorry' I replied. 'Please leave it to me. I shall have the pilot severely disciplined.'

Yet for all the new-found thrill of flying, I knew in my bones that I should never again be the pilot I once had been. I had gone too far down the hill ever to get to the top again. The thought haunted me. Hoping to exorcise it, I begged to return to operations. My wish was granted, but my come-back, as commander of 605 night-fighter squadron, was brief and inconspicuous. It was also morbidly reminiscent of the past. Once again, I felt death breathing down my neck. I even got the feeling that I was a harbinger of death. Our new pilots, keen and brave, were babies. Nine were killed within a few weeks. Our aircraft were 'clapped-out' rejects from other units; it was most probably through mechanical failure that our best crew was lost one night over the Channel. When, shortly before taking-off on a night patrol over France, someone stopped me and introduced me to the local curate, that gentle man of God stared at me pityingly, as if I was Isaac being led to the sacrifice. Then he raised his eyes to heaven and murmured: 'May you be spared!' – a prayer that merely strengthened my persistent conviction that I should not be.

For fear had come to dwell within me. It had become, by day, my constant companion, my terrifying bed-fellow by night. In my thoughts and visions I saw myself crashing, over and over again, to a horrible death. I was convinced I was going to die – an abject state of mind, exactly the reverse to what I had felt during the heroic days of 1940, when I was convinced that I was going to live!

The more I flew (and there could be no relenting), the more fear, stark, degrading fear, possessed me. Each time I took off, I felt sure it would be the last. I found myself reacting to the smallest shudder of my aircraft, the slightest engine vibration, gripping the controls tighter and telling myself 'This is it!'

And so my unbearable liaison with fear dragged on. It ended at last when, in October 1942, I entered that seminary for the chosen few, the Staff College. There, I was taught how, at a desk, to destroy on a scale which made my efforts in the cockpit look derisive. But I had no ambition to become a master-mind behind the air war. The course over, I was happy enough to be given command, in January 1943, of the fighter station at West Malling, Kent. It was there, one night, that I was once more 'at home' to the Luftwaffe.

Focke-Wulf 190 'lightning bombers' had been raiding

London. One, which had lost its bearings, followed one of our night-fighters in to land. The special van, operated by two girls of the W.A.A.F. went to guide it in, believing it was one of our returning bombers. The girl driver turned her van and switched on the lighted panel 'FOLLOW ME' – which the German pilot did, until he reached the tarmac, where he switched off. At that moment he felt something sticking into his back: it was a pencil, held by an officer who had left his revolver behind in his room. The German immediately surrendered. During his interrogation, which I attended, he answered every question with '*Ich bin ein Deutsch soldat*'.

This frustrating interview was interrupted when an officer rushed in and shouted: 'Quick, sir, there's another one landing.' The armoured car had already started after it, so I yelled to the crew: 'Don't shoot!' But they did, the idiots, setting fire to the Focke-Wulf, whose pilot, also on fire, jumped down to the ground. We leapt on him, smothering the flames. As the German kept shouting and struggling like a madman, we pinned him down. Meanwhile, his aircraft was blazing some fifty yards away. Suddenly it exploded – at which the German, just as suddenly, stopped his raving. I got off his chest and went to help two of our firemen, badly hit. One had a chestful of splinters (which we, who were kneeling on the German, had escaped), the other a hole in his neck from which blood was spurting.

The German pilot, asked what he was shouting about, replied: 'I was trying to tell that idiot [me] that there was still a bomb in my aircraft.'

Questioned, the German pilots explained their nocturnal escapade: lost in the haze, they had spotted our flarepath, and landed, believing they were in France. The most deeply mortified of them was the one we had sat on. He thought we were Frenchmen.

It was mid-summer 1943 and already the 'second front', the invasion of Nazi-held Europe, was in the air. I was counting on going to France with the 2nd Tactical Air Force. Instead, I was despatched in the opposite direction, to Yorkshire, to command a French training wing.

It was the same, boring reason – another crack-up – that led to this unexpected assignment. I had been rushed from West Malling in an ambulance to hospital, with the first signs of septicaemia – a serious condition when antibiotics were unavailable.

So I found myself once again invalided to a ground job, this time in strange country: Training Command. After a few months I begged to return to flying, but for answer was sent still further north, to Montrose, in Scotland, for a flying instructor's course – the preparatory step to the command of a flying training school. The day I received my instructor's ticket I felt I had reached the nadir of my misfortunes. I had been cut off from the people and the places which were so familiar, exiled, deported to Siberia. Probably I would never be heard of again.

And then, out of the blue, a telegram arrived. It said, curtly: 'You are requested to report to the Chief of the Air Staff . . .' What on earth, I wondered anxiously, had I done to deserve this peremptory summons?

CHAPTER 11

The Palace

On an upper floor in the Air Ministry building in Whitehall, I was led into the presence of Air Chief Marshal Sir Charles Portal, Chief of the Air Staff. His office, with its blue carpet and pleasant furnishings, might have been that of the chairman of a prosperous company, and he himself, the chairman – charming, soft-spoken and with strikingly semitic looks. Dressed in *khaffkir* and *burnous* and mounted on a camel, this remarkable Englishman would have been salaamed as an Arab sheik.

I listened, amazed, as 'Peter' Portal explained to me that the King, whose equerries were traditionally chosen on a personal basis, had decided to widen the net and appoint temporary equerries, who would be picked not for their family or regimental connections, but for their fighting record. The C.A.S., in his soft voice, concluded: 'If you don't find the idea particularly revolting I propose to recommend you for the job of equerry to His Majesty. The appointment will be for three months.'

Rosemary was waiting for me in the street below. In the taxi I told her what had happened and she threw her arms around me and exclaimed, rather indecently I thought, 'We're made.' It was natural, I suppose, for her to be glad – but how tragically mistaken she was. For from now on we were destined, as a married couple, to be un-made.

On the 16 February 1944, after a casual briefing by Sir Piers Legh, Master of the Household, I found myself in the green-carpeted Regency Room at Buckingham Palace, alone with His Majesty King George VI. Outside, there raged a black, violent storm. The King did not try, or even need, to put me at my ease. King though he was, Defender of the Faith and Emperor of India, the humanity of the man and his striking simplicity came across warmly, unmistakably. Despite his easy manner I felt impressed and so kept well within myself. But sometimes he hesitated in his speech, and then I felt drawn towards him, to help keep up the flow of words. I knew myself the agonies of a stammerer.

The King, and everybody else I had seen so far, had been unbelievably nice to me. My interview over, I was thanking Sir Piers Legh when he stiffened slightly. Down the corridor came two adorable-looking girls, all smiles. 'Hullo, Joey,' they chorused, and 'Joey' introduced me to Princess Elizabeth and her sister Margaret. Our meeting might have been a coincidence, but thinking back, I would not have put it beyond the King to have buzzed them on the interphone and told them, 'If you want to see him, he's just left my study'. Elizabeth, then seventeen, and Margaret, fourteen, spent, in those dangerous days, a sequestered life at Windsor Castle; the faintest curiosity, like myself, could brighten it.

A couple of weeks later a taxi deposited me at Buckingham Palace to take up my duties. I went straight to my room, as I had done at Tangmere years ago, and crept into bed.

Seldom have I spent such a night. Towards midnight, the sirens wailed and immediately there came the crash of bombs and the answering blast of anti-aircraft fire. There in my bedroom, somewhere – I was not sure where – in that enormous house, I felt lost and terrified, certain that I should soon be buried under tons of Victorian masonry. Then came a knock at my door. I opened and faced two rather sheepish-looking figures, in pyjamas and dressing-gowns, steel helmets on their heads – Joey Legh and Eric Miéville, the King's assistant secretary. One of them flashed a torch at me, standing there in pyjamas, scared stiff. 'Everything all right?' they asked. Yes, everything from now on was all right. There were, after all, other people in the house.

Buckingham Palace, solid, square-shaped and built around an interior courtyard, is a gray, unlovely edifice. Above the steady hum of London's traffic comes, intermittently, the clatter of sentries' rifle butts on the paving and the thump of their boots as they turn about at the end of their beat – it would be hard to say which suffers most, their feet or the paving.

The use of 'Buck House's' several entrances was determined basically by the rank and station of the user. All normal comers entered by the Privy Purse Door at the right side of the facade; the King's visitors were set down, in war-time, at the equerry's door, within the interior courtyard. When peace came, the Grand Entrance, a little further on, was used for ceremonial visitors who drove up in style, in their own cars or the King's horse-drawn carriages, and stopped under the portico from where, in 1897, Queen Victoria had departed for her Diamond Jubilee drive through London. In the time of her great grandson, King George VI, the Grand Entrance was the starting point for ceremonial drives, like the opening of Parliament. For their personal comings and goings, the King and Queen used the Garden Door, a private entrance on the north facade.

It was vital for the equerry, who had to receive the King's visitors, that the latter be directed to the right door. Once, as I waited for Queen Eugénie of Spain at the Privy Purse Door, her car shot past and disappeared into the interior courtyard, heading for the Grand Entrance – whither I sprinted, down the long corridor, side-stepping startled footmen until, turning into the straight with but a few yards to go, I collided head-on with Her Majesty, who had beaten me to it and was back-tracking in my direction towards the King's study. Grinding to a halt, I lowered my head in the customary bow, like a charging bull (nothing new to a Spanish Queen) and, with my hand outstretched in humble greeting, was just in time to grip that of this spirited royal lady, no light-weight, and prevent her collapsing backward on to the floor.

The Palace Staff were loyal, willing and efficient. They never let you down and expected in return the same of you. In a house as big as Buckingham Palace, internal communications, whether vehicular, pedestrian or telephonic, were vital. The gentlemen who operated the telephone exchange were invariably courteous, patient and painstaking. Very rarely was there a slip-up, but the King himself related a famous one to me: Mr George King, who looked after His Majesty's bank account, called the Palace one morning. The lines got crossed and after some delay

the banker heard a voice: 'Hullo?' 'Hullo,' he replied somewhat testily, 'This is George King.' And the voice, unruffled,
replied, 'Well, this is King George.'

The Palace Staff was headed by the Palace Steward, Ainslie.
Mr Ainslie was a man of high professional capacity, but a man,
too, with a twinkle in his eye, who, in moments of crisis, seemed
to be laughing behind a perfectly straight face. When lightly
admonished one day by the Master of the Household, 'Joey'
Legh, Ainslie's reply was a classic of its kind. 'Let me assure you,
Sir Piers, that my sole object is to obey the orders of the Master
of the Household and give pleasure to the Ladies in Waiting.'

Most Englishmen have the soul of a butler in them – it is
after all only a desire to serve. Butlers, from the admirable
Beech to the sinister Thunder of 'Rookery Nook', are a breed
which has enriched English literature and theatre. They have
provided the grist for many good stories, one of which was told
to me by the Queen, who had a delicious and highly imaginative
sense of the ridiculous.

The butler in question was in the service of a celebrated
London hostess. Unfortunately, he had a weakness for the bottle
and at one glittering dinner party – the Queen was present – he
was tottering so unsteadily round the table that his mistress
decided to act. She wrote out a message on the little pad beside
her: 'Get out, you are drunk', and beckoned to the tipsy butler,
who read it gravely then, unperturbed, placed it on a salver and
delivered it, with a reproachful glance, to one of the distinguished lady guests.

The 'King's Page', an ex-serviceman, who rejoiced in the
official but archaic title of 'Page of the Back Stairs', was in close
and constant attendance on the King. He possessed up-to-the-
minute information on what was going on in the royal presence
and was an indispensable link between the King and the
equerry-in-waiting. The Queen also had a page, 'the Queen's
Page' who, as often as not, was to be seen in the corridor,
dragging, or dragged by, the Queen's three dogs. There were
pages of this and pages of that, of the presence, of the pantry and
so on, conscientious, professional men who worked as a team
and kept the royal machinery running smoothly. I admired

those men; they were the ground troops. I often wondered what they were thinking behind their impassive features.

Communications within Buckingham Palace were, as I said, vital. The vehicular ones ensured the delivery of Their Majesties' meals which were conveyed by trolley from the kitchens, scores, if not hundreds, of yards away. One day, in the course of my duties, I slipped into the kitchen for a word with the chef, a plump, pleasant Englishman who had mastered the best of *la cuisine française* and of English cooking. I asked this dignified paragon, 'Why do chefs always wear that tall, white *toque*?' He thought for a moment, then replied gravely, 'Well, they do say that the brain always works better in a vacuum . . .'

Beyond the circle of the Palace Staff were men who could be, had to be, slightly more demonstrative. They were more like the storm troops, in action in the *mêlée* of an outside royal function. There was Hawes, the King's chauffeur, an ace, who once, with superb coolness, avoided a head-on collision with a car driven by some madman on the wrong side of the road. I was alone beside the King in the venerable, long-nosed, maroon-coloured royal Daimler, which probably, but for Hawes, would have made mince-meat of the other car, though the accident would have caused casualties on both sides.

Alongside Hawes sat Superintendent Cameron, the King's detective, tall, lean and spare of words. Cameron was the King's sole body-guard, bowler-hatted and, as far as I know, unarmed – except with prevision and persuasion, weapons which invariably proved effective. The King had decided views on escorts. He enjoyed, of course, the ceremonial variety (though he had a pitiless eye for irregularities of dress) – escorts like the Royal Company of Archers, the Yeomen of the Guard, the Honourable Artillery Company, with their long pikes and halbards, and, on state drives, the Household Cavalry, glinting and colourful, if precariously balanced (with all that weight of armour), bouncing along beside him on their black chargers. Motor-cycle escorts, on the other hand, were an abomination to him.

Hurle, the Queen's chauffeur, was retained, I suspect, more for his sensitive, human qualities – a factor which always

weighed heavily with the Queen – than for his driving. A middle-
aged man, Hurle was shy and thoughtful of others, and if you
were touched by that sort of thing – I was – you could be more
indulgent of his performance at the wheel. Not that Hurle was
really a bad driver; it was just his style, to which the Queen
seemed innured, but which put the wind up everybody else,
including me. Years later, flying the national airline inside
Communist China, I thought of Hurle. The style and technique
of the Chinese pilots froze me with fear, but their accident
record was low. So it was with Hurle.

That corridor, not much less than a hundred yards of it, along
which I had sometimes to hurry in such unseemly fashion, was
the main business artery of Buckingham Palace. Its walls, once
white, were tarnished by many a London pea-souper and hung
with faded canvases, depicting subjects as diverse as Queen
Victoria's favourite pony, some naval victory against the French,
or a royal ancestor staring vacantly at the passers-by. Book-
cases crammed with weighty tomes; mahogany dressers, sporting on their marble top, an ormolu clock, ticking out the
interminable hours; had been condemned to furnish the sombre
limbo of that corridor. Its red-carpeted floor-boards creaked
under the incessant passage of those on the way to do business
with the King; private secretaries bearing trays of correspondence, pages with red boxes, leather-covered, locked and containing secrets of state from one or another ministry; or ministers
themselves and other persons, the high and the mighty, the
modest also, who had been summoned to an audience with His
Majesty. It was the equerry's job to meet them at the door, and
usher them into the royal presence with a stiff, formal bow of the
head, announcing their name.
    They were of all sorts and conditions, these men – and
women – who were received by the King. The most redoubtable,
of course, was the Prime Minister, Winston Churchill. He came
every Tuesday to discuss business, over lunch, with the King –
who paid him the singular compliment of himself coming to the
door and waiting at the top of a short flight of stairs to receive
him. Sometimes, Churchill was very tired; in the Government

offices in Whitehall he had to be carried upstairs. When, dressed in a black coat, stiff collar and striped trousers, he came to see the King, he shuffled, head bowed, shoulders hunched, crushed by the cares of state and five years of war-time premiership. Mounting those few steps towards the King, he dragged one foot after the other, barely making it to the top.

When, on these occasions, I met Mr Churchill, there was rarely enough time for anything but the briefest and most banal conversation. One day, shortly after the Anglo-American invasion of Europe, I was wondering whether to make the subject Randolph (his son who had courageously parachuted into enemy-held Yugoslavia) or the weather. I happened to tap the glass and it went down. 'Good morning, Sir', I greeted the Prime Minister, 'I'm afraid the glass is going down.' Mr Churchill looked up at me and glowered. 'Why are you afraid?' he growled. I muttered something about our fighters not being able to provide air cover, etc., and as it turned out I was right. But I have never since used that common and meaningless expression, 'I'm afraid'.

One morning, while I waited to take him to the King, he lamented how, because of an electricity cut during the early hours, the water in his aquarium had begun to cool off. The entire Churchill household was routed out of bed to go down to the kitchen and heat up reserves of warm water. The Prime Minister, in dressing-gown and slippers, personally took charge of the operation, pouring kettles full of warm water into the aquarium. Now he waited, at Buckingham Palace, to discuss state business with the King.

Mr Churchill's fish were his pride and part of his life. One evening at a great reception, he looked in the blackest mood, sulking in a corner. Someone said to me, 'For God's sake go and say something to the P.M.' Having nothing in particular to say I asked him why he looked so cross. 'I missed my bath this morning' he snarled. 'One of my goldfish was ill and we had to put it in the bath.' 'Do you like your goldfish that much?' I asked rather stupidly. 'Like them? I'm sweet on 'em' was his emphatic reply.

Burdened as he was with affairs of state, the Prime Minister must have found those formal receptions irksome. Once, however, there came a welcome interruption: Mr Churchill was called urgently to the telephone – to learn from his private secretary the news of some hard-won success. Replacing the receiver, he walked back, singing 'Roll out the barrel . . .', and joined the other guests.

Another time, when Britain's prospects in the Middle East looked far from promising, I listened to Churchill, as he waited for his audience with the King, discussing the situation. Suddenly, he turned towards me, fixing me with his bulldog regard, and growled 'We must hold Suez!' as if assigning that vital task to me.

During my eight years with the King, I led into his presence all sorts of people – British, Commonwealth and foreign. Among them were statesmen and politicians, judges, generals, admirals and air-marshals, ambassadors and governors of His Majesty's territories beyond the seas, heroes and heroines, venerable ecclesiastics and men of letters and of learning. Few of them remained unaffected by their meeting. The explosive Alexander Bustamente, Jamaica's Prime Minister, became as meek as a lamb. General Eisenhower, in uniform, and treating me as if I were his favourite nephew, arrived fifteen minutes too soon and during that time talked pleasantly, if a little nervously, without drawing breath. U.S. Secretary of State Ed. Stettinius seemed in a tearing hurry. On entering the King's study with me, he straightened up his coat lapels, switched on a broad, American smile, and before I could announce him, charged past me, and began warmly to pump-handle the King's hand. On the other hand, Dédé de Jongh, heroine of the Belgian resistance, was so shy that I could only induce her to follow me by commanding her, in my crude French: '*Suivez-moi!*' When, some minutes later, she left, it was obvious that the King had charmed the shyness out of her.

After Labour's sweeping victory in the first post-war election, the socialist ministers – particularly those who had made it the hard way, from mine and meadow, dockland and railway yard – who came for audiences with the King, at first seemed ill at ease in the capitalistic atmosphere of Buckingham Palace. They lacked the assurance, the polished manners and the well-tailored appearance of their Tory rivals. Clement Attlee, the Labour Prime Minister, despite his three years as Deputy Prime Minister in the war-time coalition government, was no exception. Attlee was the very antithesis of his predecessor Churchill – one of the most striking contrasts is his 250-page autobiography which reads like a schoolboy's essay beside Churchill's majestic prose.

Attlee's looks were not impressive. His bald pate and ugly moustache, his flat, unimaginative speech, his timid manner and short, uncertain step, all suggested a rather uninspiring schoolmaster. But his appearance did not do him justice, for there was fire in his soul and when he spoke to you, if only briefly (he never wasted words), you felt immediately the goodness and sincerity of the man. In politics, he possessed the integrity of a judge and on certain problems (like decolonisation) his tenacity and wisdom exceeded Churchill's. What he lacked was the personality and the oratory that made Churchill such an inspiring figure.

Stafford Cripps, Chancellor of the Exchequer, the man who tried (and failed) more than anyone to give back India to the Indians, was a different type. Well-dressed, stiff-mannered, ascetic and looking somewhat dessicated thanks to his diet of nuts and carrots, he sniffed contemptuously the blue, capitalistic air of that corridor.

My cousin, Hugh Gaitskell, with his 13th century face, as someone so exactly described it, and his brilliant intellect, paired off naturally with Cripps. Like him, Hugh later became Chancellor of the Exchequer. Both wore the tie of Winchester, England's oldest public school. Cripps and Gaitskell were the aristocrats, the intellectuals of the Labour party yet managed somehow, with the genuine, earthy 'Labour boys', to paddle along in the same canoe.

The fact that Hugh was a socialist caused me, secretly, I am ashamed to say, some embarrassment, for I was an integral, working part, if only a minute one, in a thorough-going capitalist system, the monarchy; and although the King was, of course, above party, there was not a single socialist – at least above stairs – in Buckingham Palace. The family connection, I felt, might suggest that I was a sympathiser. In truth, I did not care a hoot for Hugh's political views; as far as I was concerned, he was welcome to them.

My own natural leanings were towards the Conservatives. I even, under the aegis of Harold Balfour, conservative Parliamentary Under-Secretary for Air, presented myself as an eventual conservative candidate for a west-country constituency, though with such luke-warm enthusiasm that the chairman, amiably enough, advised me to drop the idea. I was quite certain that I was not cut out for politics. Though I liked a modern definition of conservatism – in substance, to conserve what is worth while and discard what is not – I felt incapable of responding whole-heartedly to Conservative ideology.

There remained the Socialist party. While fully sharing Labour's concern for the under-privileged and a 'fair do' for all, it seemed to me, rightly or wrongly, that they were over-obsessed with egalitarianism and at the same time rather hypocritical about it. I subscribe entirely to the belief that all men are born equal, but not to a policy which would keep them so for the rest of their lives.

Broadly, my political credo springs from the parable of the talents: an equal start for all, a fair chance in life, with the deserving and the undeserving reaping their due reward, and public charity for the sick and needy. Add that the state should be the servant of the people, and exclude war as a means of settling disputes. That would put me about half-way between Left and Right, and, preferably, independent of both – a difficult position to defend. Not that it matters much to me. I accept the thesis that a country gets the government it deserves – as long as I am left a free man. If not, to the barricades!

The equerry, after meeting the ministers at the 'equerry's entrance', would install them, pending the King's summons, in the nearby Chinese Room, amidst whose oriental trappings they looked like a bunch of visiting mandarins. It happened once that I was chatting to one of them when the Home Secretary,

Herbert Morrison, a small man with a cocky air and a quiff of hair above his forehead, arrived to find the equerry's door shut. Wrenching at the handle, he half kicked the door open; once inside, he slammed it behind him so that the glass panes rattled. Then, as if to vent the rest of his spleen against the royal establishment, he pointed to the portrait of King George III, hanging in the corridor, and remarked tritely: 'That's the man who lost us the United States!'

If the style of Ernest Bevin, the Foreign Secretary, was not exactly polished it was more endearing. The massive, misshapen 'Ernie', as he ambled into the King's presence, invariably had his left hand in his pocket. With the other he perfunctorily shook the King's hand. When, before leaving for a conference in Paris, he came for an audience with the King, I asked him, 'Are you taking Mrs Bevin with you?' 'No fear!' he replied, 'Taking your wife to Paris is like taking a sandwich to a banquet.'

The man who most surprised me was Aneurin Bevan, Minister of Housing. He had for years worked at the coal-face and consequently, it was said, had a chip on his shoulder. Reading his vitriolic attacks against the Tories made even my luke-warm conservative blood boil. But when I met him, I took to 'Nye' Bevan, whose rather pudgy, amorphous face was topped by a pair of black, bushy eyebrows and a shock of grey-black hair. Astonishingly enough, the voice which had so loudly and bitterly harangued the Tories was of the softest, with a Welsh accent, and a pronounced stammer. And when Bevan laughed, he did so easily and enjoyably.

The Tories, having been in power for years, knew their way down that corridor, like the back of their hand. In Churchill's steps followed Anthony Eden, debonair, affable and faultlessly groomed – yet, at times, disconcertingly excitable. There were stresses in Eden's life. The loss of his young airman son made me feel a particular sympathy for him; his divorce, in 1950, was to create a relationship, as unexpected as it was impersonal, between us.

Two of the Tory elders, Lords Halifax and Salisbury, could

be paired, like Cripps and Gaitskell, though on a totally different basis: they managed to reconcile a passion both for God and
the chase. Lord Halifax, despite a slight stoop, was immensely
tall. On his thin face he wore a sad, almost saintly expression;
on his left hand, which was artificial, a black glove. At various
times foreign minister, Viceroy and ambassador in Washington,
he was nicknamed for his religious fervour, 'the pope'. In his
spare time, he was a Master of Foxhounds.

'Bobbety' Cranborne, Marquess (from 1947) of Salisbury
and leader of the House of Lords, came almost as often to shoot
with the King as he did to see him on state business. He was one
of the best guns in the country and upheld the Church of
England with equal zeal. 'Bobbety' was a man of unbending
principle, yet his appearance, while far from unattractive, had a
faint suggestion of the slovenly. His speech was slurred, his gait
shuffling and his clothes, though of perfect taste, were worn
somewhat awry.

Another Tory visitor – Tory because he was the Tories'
nominee – was Dr Fisher, Archbishop of Canterbury. Benign
and genial, his face often wrinkled in laughter, Geoffrey
Cantuar cut an impressive figure in his ecclesiastical robes. But
in top hat and gaiters he looked slightly comical, as if he had
walked out of a Ben Travers farce. Like that, of course, he was
more approachable and rather endearing.

I watched this parade of ministers, Labour and Tory, the
most powerful men in the land, of potentates and eminent
personages, with some detachment. Their business was not
mine; and it seemed to me that their passing, individual glory
faded before the mystic, enduring splendour of the throne, so
that they appeared like an actor held in a spotlight – the man
alone was visible, the decor excluded. Thus I regarded each
one, as a man – like myself, who had been fashioned on another
anvil, perhaps, but tempered, all the same, in a fierce fire –
fiercer than some of them had ever known. Some of them made
me wonder how they had ever made it to the heights of fame
and power.

The King and Queen – I would not exclude the princesses,
either – exercised, quite involuntarily, an extraordinary, and

entirely benign, levelling effect on people. They somehow brought them out of their grand, official selves back to what they really, humanly and ordinarily were.

That is how I came to regard the people, so famous and powerful, who presented themselves to the King – as men who had left their arms and armour at the door of Buckingham Palace, and walked on, stripped of their ego and importance, down the corridor and into the royal presence. On leaving, they picked up their arms again, clothed themselves once more in armour, and returned to their well-entrenched positions in the Establishment.

These men were the pillars of the British nation, they supported the Establishment and powered its mills which, like the mills of God, grind slow, but exceeding small.

Lending distinction to the pageant of politicians and important people who crossed the threshold of Buckingham Palace, came Kings, Princes and Princesses, and Presidents. Among them was King Haakon of Norway, a kindly and cadaverous-looking giant who, defying the Nazis, had escaped with Prince Olav, his cheerful, plumpish heir. Another royal Scandinavian giant, King Frederick of Denmark, with his beautiful Queen, Ingrid, paid a state visit. King Frederick had the breezy manner of a sailor, which he was – as well as an accomplished conductor. Towards the end of his stay, I was summoned to his room. The Danish equerry announced me and I entered. There he stood, the King of Denmark, in shirtsleeves. With a casual 'I thought you might like to have this' he handed me a small red leather case. In it was the insignia of a Knight of the Order of Dannebrog.

During the visit of the French President and Madame Auriol, I did nothing in particular, but presumably did it very well, for I was made an *Officier de la Légion d'Honneur*. This time I received the insignia by post, in a brown envelope.

That indomitable lady, Queen Wilhelmina of the Netherlands, had, in 1940, tried, in a cloche hat and a coat-and-skirt, to lead her troops in a counter-attack against the invading Germans. Failing to contact her army, she had escaped, with nothing but what she stood up in, to England. The war over, the brave Wilhelmina returned, still dressed country-style, and, in gratitude for the sanctuary she had received, presented at Buckingham Palace a squadron of big-boned, jet-black chargers to the Household Cavalry.

I was standing quite close to the Queen, watching the ceremony, when something sent me off into a terrible and ill-concealed fit of laughter, in which the Queen immediately joined, skilfully dissimulating her amusement behind a radiant smile. It was the first time (but by no means the last) that I was seized with laughter 'in the presence'. I never mastered the Queen's technique – I had no business to be laughing in public anyway – so my only hope was to bury my face in my handker-chief, and feign a fit of sneezing.

The new Netherlands sovereigns, Queen Juliana, who succeeded on the abdication of her mother, and her husband Prince Bernhard, were refreshingly down to earth. At the banquet in her honour, Queen Juliana made a moving speech – which she herself had written. During a stay at Balmoral, Prince Bernhard would slip off after dinner to his room, there to swot, with his R.A.F. Manual of Air Navigation, for his navigator's ticket. Two young Kings were occasional visitors: first, Peter of Yugoslavia, a fugitive from the Nazis, looking lost and bewildered at being cheated of his throne; and later, Michael of Rumania, whom the Soviets had forced to abandon his.

When the Shah of Iran paid a state visit, I was attached to his imperial person. Cutting quite a different figure then – thin, strained, unsure of himself, with an absent look – he was in the throes of divorcing his first wife, the Egyptian princess, Fawzieh. When, by bus, underground and taxi, I took his Imperial Majesty round London, he relaxed, and apparently, enjoyed it. Back in official circles, however, he once more became taut and uneasy. The Queen, who, as I have mentioned, had a most enjoyable sense of the ridiculous, told me that once when she said to him, 'We are taking you to a show, *Annie get your Gun*', the Shah shot her a nervous glance and enquired 'An' you get your gun? I am so sorry, I left it in my room, I send my A.D.C.'

The next story I can vouch for myself. During dinner one evening, at the Savoy, with the Shah-an-Shah and his A.D.C., who spoke good French but poor English, the latter asked me, 'Were you in the war?' 'Yes', I replied, 'I was a pilot.' 'So you were a big arse!' he exclaimed. I thought the man was insulting me, then realised that, after all, he was complimenting me on being a big ace – *as* in French, which sounds more or less like 'arse'.

Before the Shah departed, I was summoned to his presence at the Iranian Embassy. Charmingly, he thanked me, adding, 'I want to give you a present to remember me – you are standing on it.' Horrified, I looked down, expecting to find the crushed fragments of some priceless Persian antique. Instead, I saw that I was standing on a magnificent rug.

Such was a cross-section of the famous, the high and mighty, whom I met at the entrance to Buckingham Palace and led into the presence of the King, after walking them down that blessed corridor or up a wide staircase which wound up from it to the floor above, where, after the war, the King had his study. Most of the time, I dreaded this ritual. The family stammer got hold of me and, after writing out the names on the King's engagement card for the following day, I spent a sleepless night rehearsing them. My apprehension increased as the moment approached for the visitor's arrival. I knew that the chances were that his name would stick at the back of my throat, at least for a few agonising seconds. I was incapable (as I still am) of reciting a word or a line 'to order'. So with my heart pounding, I tried to keep up a light conversation all the way down the corridor right up to the door of the King's study. It was a stammerer's trick, to help me into a smooth liaison with the dreaded word, Mister, Sir, General or Lord So-and-so.

The King, to whom I had spoken of my problem – which was his – was most sympathetic and helpful. Once I announced the ambassador-designate to Paris, Mr Oliver Harvey, as 'Mr Oliver Hardy'. The King shot me an enquiring glance, as if expecting me to add 'and Mr Stan Laurel, Your Majesty'.

CHAPTER 12

The Courtiers

On to that creaking, red-floored corridor gave the main offices, one after the other: those of the Keeper of the Privy Purse, the King's private secretaries, the Queen's private secretary, the Press secretary and the Equerry, each at a respectful, but easy distance from the King's study. Everyone in that warren was assiduously engaged in the King's or Queen's business. The only one to whom any form of intellectual activity was denied was the Equerry-in-waiting. He was not called that for nothing. His job was to WAIT, which he did uninterruptedly during the King's waking hours. It could happen that the equerry could make the King wait for him, if he was thoughtless enough to drift out of earshot of the King's bell, which occasionally shattered the silence of the equerry's room.

Facing north, as it did, not a ray of sunlight, summer or winter, ever penetrated the french windows of this tenebrous room, with its lofty ceiling and its drab walls lined with shelves of books, massive historical and religious tomes, hardly the kind to provide light reading for whiling away the interminable hours. People dropped in, of course, now and then – members of the Household for a cup of tea or a scotch in the evening. Occasionally the King himself would put his head round the door with a charming 'May I come in?', or during a long summer evening there might come a tap at the window and there would be the King and Queen and perhaps their daughters on their way for a stroll round the garden. They were most welcome visitors.

The dreariest period of waiting was the one that dragged on through the long winter evenings, after the other members of the Household had returned to their home and their family. It was then that I thought most of mine, far away. Then between 11 p.m. and midnight would come a knock at the door: Frederick, the King's page, was there to announce 'His Majesty has retired'.

I came quickly to like Frederick, a quiet-spoken ex-sailor, rather short in stature, not simply because he brought me the good news that my vigil was ended, but because I felt he understood, in his discreet, uncomplicated way, a lot of things that were better left un-said. Meanwhile, being an equerry-in-waiting taught me, more than anything else, to wait. It was to be an invaluable exercise for the future.

After the long awaited release, announced by Frederick, I repaired to the equerry's bedroom, yet a little further along that sombre corridor. Opposite was a bathroom and lavatory. The Buck House loos were solidly built, of seasoned mahogany, with a pull-up flush – old fashioned if you like, but a hundred per cent reliable, which is more than can be said for most other types of flushing devices.

About there, the 'commons' ended with a green-baize, glass-panelled, swing door. Beyond it were the war-time royal apartments (normally on the floor above) and beyond them, in the west wing, the state rooms.

One day, seeing Princess Elizabeth approaching from the other side of the baize door, I bounded forward to open it for her. She did the same and beat me to it, swinging the door open, and with a broad grin, motioning me through. She was then a charming and totally unsophisticated eighteen-year-old, but she already had the heart, if not yet the head, of a queen.

The King and Queen lived in peace-time on the first floor, in the north-west corner of the building. There at least they could enjoy the afternoon sun and a view of the garden and the lake, where ducks nested and raised their young until they were old enough to join higher (duck) society; then the family would waddle off ceremoniously through the gates of the palace to the more animated surroundings of Saint James's Park. As they crossed the Mall, a policeman would hold up the traffic. The whole thing was very civilised.

Facing the garden, too, were the state rooms – the Bow Room and the '44 Room, where the King received ceremonially, where ambassadors presented their credentials and where – an unforgettable sight – the convocations of Canterbury and York, in full ecclesiastical regalia and headed by their respective archbishops, came to do obeisance to the titular head of the Anglican Church. Like a Greek chorus, they advanced in line and bowed to the King – Defender of the Faith. I watched, spellbound in admiration of this formidable bevy of bishops.

Not all occasions went so smoothly. Once, I remember, an aged dignitary came for an audience in the Bow Room. I had been held up on the telephone and had to do a lightning change into morning coat and striped trousers to receive him. Nowhere could I find my braces. In a panic, I turned out drawers and wardrobes. I had to find some means of support for my trousers or else hold them up with my left hand, leaving the right free for handshaking. Suddenly my eye lit on a length of stout string, tied round a parcel of dirty linen. Eagerly I seized it, fastened it about my waist and sprinted for the Grand Entrance.

All went well. I ushered the old gentleman in and bade him take a seat, standing beside him, very close, because he was hard of hearing. Short-sighted, too, I have prayed ever since that day. For looking down, while I talked to him, I perceived six inches of string dangling from beneath my morning coat just in front of his nose.

Opposite the Bow Room the Grand Entrance gave on to the inner courtyard and between the two stretched a long, wide, red-carpeted gallery, practically empty, except on the days when the King held investitures. It was in this gallery that, week after week, he awarded honours to those who had won distinction in the firing line and behind it. For two hours he would stand on a raised daïs with a ramp on each side, along which the recipients would approach and withdraw. While the Lord Chamberlain read out each name, some three hundred of them, 'gentlemen ushers' stood motionless to each side of the King. The equerry stood close behind him, to hand the King a sword when a knight came to kneel for the accolade, and to pass each medal, which reposed on a velvet cushion.

The King's technique was so faultless that he could lay his hand on that medal each time without looking for it. If ever he failed, it was your fault and you had to juggle the cushion, like trying to find the right gear. Very much at ease, he pinned on each medal, spoke briefly to the recipient, and shook hands. At times you could hear him humming the tune being played by the string orchestra, in a gallery opposite. Or he might turn round to you and say, rather too loudly, 'For God's sake tell them not to make such a ghastly noise'.

There was seldom a hitch, though they did occasionally occur. An Indian sepoy, up for the Victoria Cross, marched smartly up the ramp, eyes to the front, straight past the King and down the other side. He made it the second time round.

The King was tolerant of human failings. As he shook hands with a stout elderly lady she dropped her oft-rehearsed curtsey and lost her balance. Luckily, the King still had her by the hand and helped her to rise, if a little unsteadily, to her feet. When Laurence Olivier came to receive his knighthood, his hair was an outrageous blond. He pulled me aside. 'For heaven's sake' he begged, 'tell the King that I haven't gone queer. I'm just playing in Hamlet.'

Tucked away in a corner beyond the state rooms was the Household dining-room, rectangular and red-carpeted – red was the basic colour at Buckingham Palace. There, the Household foregathered for breakfast and lunch. The equerry dined *en tête à tête* with the Lady-in-waiting, his team-mate, one might say, whose official title was Woman of the Bedchamber – on the face of it rather unflattering compared with the Lady of the Bedchamber. They differed only professionally: the 'Woman' did the inside jobs, correspondence, etc. . . ., the 'Lady' the outside ones. I have no idea what they thought of me as my career among them ended. I venture to think that they might have been more saddened than shocked, for I only thought of them as charming, forbearing companions, without spite, rancour or envy.

At first, the table-talk went clean over my head. I had not even a smattering of Debrett and knew not who in the hell was who. So – wisely, I think – I followed the old Chinese proverb: 'It is better to keep your mouth shut and be thought a fool than to open it and show that you are one.' It is wise advice, to be followed when all about you are prattling about things and people of whom you know nothing.

I had, after all, stepped clean out of the cockpit into the Court. Had any of my colleagues found themselves (as occasionally they did) among airmen talking about turbo-compressors and drift-sights, stalling and side slipping, they would have been as perplexed as I.

Joey, Sir Piers Legh, Master of the Household, was, in the Household hierarchy, my immediate chief. A man in his sixties, of average height, frail, myopic, his glasses permanently balanced on the high bridge of his nose, his speech was vague, his walk aimless. But Joey, despite appearances, was far from gaga. His judgement was unerring, his reflexes lightning-fast. He was moreover, a most lovable character.

As equerry to the Prince of Wales he had once attended an official reception in Australia. As the evening wore on Joey, resplendent in Household coat (dark blue tails, brass buttons, and velvet collar) and medals, slipped out to relieve himself. On returning to the room, he had difficulty opening the door, until it suddenly gave and he found himself confronting a giant, liveried Australian who rasped at him, 'How many more times must I say: WAITERS OUTSIDE!'

During race-week at Ascot, I would help Joey to arrange the table-placings for the big dinner parties of some fifty guests. What a comedy! Like old Mr Williams, when he corrected my Latin prose, Joey would remove his glasses and bend low over the red-leather table plans and the confused heap of name-cards so that his nose nearly touched them, trying to place the guests according to their social status and where they had been seated the previous night. After shuffling the name-cards for some time, at least a dozen would have fallen on the floor. 'Where's that ghastly countess,' Joey would mutter, furiously searching among the name-cards. 'You are standing on her, Joey,' and I would pick the card up, only to hear another outburst: 'Blast! we can't have her next to Lord So-and-so. He had her last night.' 'Steady there Joey, that remark might be taken literally,' I would tease him and he would give a funny, staccato little laugh.

One day, Joey, who prefaced every remark with 'I say', asked me 'I say, do you think I can tell this one to the King?' And he proceeded to tell the story of a young cavalry officer who was reporting for the first time to his new unit. 'Your name?' asked the colonel. 'Ponsonby, Sir', snapped the subaltern. 'Really? No relation of old Poker Ponsonby of the Blues, I suppose?' enquired the colonel. 'Yessir, my father' replied the other. 'Delighted to hear it, young man. Old Poker was a great friend. By the way, are you married?' 'Yes, Sir' answered the subaltern. 'Great! Who was she?' 'A Miss Warburton, Sir.' 'Not true! No relation to old Wobbles Warburton of the 11th?' 'Yes, Sir, as a matter of fact he's my father-in-law'. 'Splendid! Used to go pig-sticking with old Wobbles when we were together in Poona. You two must come and dine with me tonight.' 'I'm sorry, Sir,' apologised the young officer, 'My wife's in bed with cramp.' 'Good God'! exploded the colonel, 'Not old Crumpy Cramp of the "Tins"'!'

I told Joey I thought it would be safe to go ahead.

As time went on, I found Joey more and more endearing in his sincere, unhurried way. He was a very sure friend. Once the King told me that, when it came to purely personal advice, he would turn to Joey before any other of his staff. I can understand why. Joey remained a staunch friend throughout my problems. He died as they neared their climax.

While on the subject of pale blue stories, I should like to tell the rather charming one of *The Little Hut*, a somewhat *risqué* (for the time) comedy by André Roussin. One morning the house telephone rang. It was the Queen. 'Good morning, Peter. I was wondering whether you might know if *The Little Hut* would be a suitable play for us to see, or do you think it is a little too, you know . . .' I did not know the play nor, at that time, its author, so I called the Lord Chamberlain's Department, which then had the absolute right of censorship on all plays. The Assistant Comptroller, red-faced, moustachioed Norman Gwatkin, ex-Guards, with a permanent, mischievous glint in his eye, answered, 'Of course it's O.K.' and uttered one of his diabolical chuckles. 'It will do Their Majesties good to see it.' I saw it with them. Years later, when André Roussin became a good and a gentle friend, I told him this little tale, which brought one of those marvellous, wrinkled smiles to his rather oriental face.

Another of my colleagues of whom I was particularly fond was Sir Arthur Penn, the Queen's Comptroller. Sixty-odd years old, he might have stepped clean out of the 19th century, wearing modern, impeccably tailored clothes. His white, wavy hair and drooping moustache gave Arthur a solemn, distinguished look but from beneath the cover of his moustache there would often break an uproarious laugh, which made me feel that Arthur was as young as I was.

One day, a friend accompanied him to a stiff tea-party. Arthur found himself seated next to an aged dowager, stone deaf, but armed with an ear-trumpet. After attempting vainly to get through to the old lady, he whispered desperately to his friend, 'What on earth can I say to the old girl?' 'It doesn't matter, say anything!' Arthur turned back towards the dowager, who once again proffered her ear-trumpet. Into it Arthur bawled 'Get me Whitehall 1212, please.' Like Churchill, Arthur had a gift for the burlesque and the serio-comic. It is the kind of humour that pleases me, most.

The Queen's Chamberlain was Lord Airlie – Joe – who looked best in a tweed jacket and kilt, even in the highlands of Mayfair or Belgravia. His mother, the dowager Countess of Airlie, was Lady-in-waiting to Queen Mary. Well into her seventies, Lady Airlie was essentially Edwardian – a gay, spectacular figure and a wonderful *raconteuse*. She also had a capacity for getting involved in droll situations.

One day, it was related, she left London in the Flying Scotsman, bound for Aberdeen. An hour later she found herself locked into the first-class lavatory with still another hour to go before reaching Grantham. Arrived there, she beat on the window and called for help. The guard arrived and unlocked the door. Foolishly, though, he was determined to prove to Lady Airlie that there was nothing wrong with the door-lock. Joining her in the lavatory, he closed the door and locked it. 'Now', he said triumphantly, 'I'm going to show your Ladyship how to open that door.' He turned the lock, but in vain; the door refused to budge. At that moment the train puffed out of Grantham station. Lady Airlie spent another two hours in the lavatory, this time with the guard. They were finally released at York.

Sir Harold Campbell, the senior equerry, was a sailor. His nose resembled the prow of a battleship and he walked in a curious manner, hardly right for the quarter-deck, bouncing off his toes. This, I think, was merely a symptom of his astonishing fitness. He possessed a tall, lean figure, straight as a mizzen mast. However, he did not possess – any longer – his own teeth. Once, after I had taken over from him, he wrote to me, 'Dear Peter, I have left my maulers in the right-hand top drawer of the equerry's writing table. Please send them.' I did, post-haste.

The man with the most difficult and delicate job was the King's private secretary, Sir Alan Lascelles. In his own words, 'Life in that office is not by any means beer and skittles.' Professor Laski amplified this earthy phrase: 'The private secretary', he wrote, 'is the confidant of all ministers . . . Receiving a thousand secrets, he must discriminate between what may emerge and what may remain obscure . . . It is a life passed amid circumstances in which the most trifling incident may lead to major disaster . . . He must move serenely amid all the events which move other men to passionate statements.' This Tommy Lascelles did admirably, except, I was one day to feel, when men began to be moved to passionate statements about me.

There was a mutual affection between us. I admired his dry, pungent wit, though less when it turned to pitiless sarcasm. Tommy's character was written all over him: spare of frame, his steel-rimmed spectacles and World War I moustache were the main features of his thin, pallid face. He still dressed in the fashion of the 'twenties, in dreary, out-moded grey or brown suits, with waistcoat and watch-chain and narrow trousers. The points of his stiff collars were rounded, his ties were sombre and colourless. There was great kindness in him, but in purely human affairs, affairs of the heart to be more precise, he had an archaic, uncomfortable outlook which irked me. Perhaps it was just as well, when the monarchy was like an island in a world evolving at a frightening speed around it. Tommy did not adapt himself to the changing times nearly as well as the monarch himself. Profoundly perspicacious in political and constitutional matters, he was, I felt, on the human side, cold, rigid and inhibited.

His assistant, Michael Adeane (who, in 1953, succeeded him), was a warm character. The grandson of Lord Stamford-ham, the sagacious and trusted secretary of King George V, Michael had the same qualities in his blood. He was close enough to the 'lower echelons' to understand them. He possessed an earthy wit, brief and pithy. Like many of the King's men, he was an Old Etonian. When Pandit Nehru, a one-time pupil at Harrow, Churchill's school, came to see the King, I asked Michael what he thought of the Indian leader, the idol of three hundred million Hindus. Michael summed him up in four words: 'A typical Old Harrovian', he said, with some disdain.

Table-talk in the Household dining-room taught me much – it helped me to avoid many pitfalls and it sharpened my wits. Quick repartee was appreciated. Once everyone was discussing Princess Margaret, who was suffering from a torticolis, a stiff neck. What kind of specialist should be called in? they wondered. A masseur, a chiropractor, an osteopath? Who could cure the stiff neck? I suggested a necromancer.

This, then, was the new milieu, social and sophisticated, into which I had fallen. Let it not be thought from what I have said that the business of monarchy is frivolously conducted in England. On the contrary, I believe the English have no equal in democratic government or in constitutional monarchy. They invented both, and by keeping a subtle blance between the two, practise them with unrivalled success. But behind the mystique and the majesty of the British monarchy there are lots of laughs.

CHAPTER 13

The royal homes

Before I had time to adjust myself to the fusty, august atmosphere of Buckingham Palace, Easter brought a dramatic change of scene. I found myself alone, except for the lady-in-waiting, with the King and Queen and their daughters, in a small house, Appleton Lodge, on the King's estate at Sandringham. It was my first opportunity to see them out of their royal context, thinking and acting for themselves, behaving and looking more or less like anybody else. It was then that they were at their best and most enjoyable.

The King was a man of medium build, lean and athletic. His head, rather small, was statuesque, so finely chiselled were his features; his hair and his skin had the look and the luminosity of bronze. The steady regard in his blue eyes only changed – and then, to an alarming glare – when he was irked, or rattled. Then, he would start to rant, noisily, and the Queen would mollify him with a soothing word or gesture; once she held his pulse and, with a wistful smile, began to count – tick, tick, tick – which made him laugh, and the storm subsided. In those moments he was like a small boy, very lovable. 'The most marvellous person in the world', the King called his wife. Although, as yet, I hardly knew her, I came, within my limits, to think so, too.

At your first (and every subsequent) meeting with Queen Elizabeth, you did not notice her small stature, her *embonpoint*. You were simply swept off your feet by her warm and totally captivating charm. It radiated from her smile; you felt it as you took, but never shook, her small, soft hand – which members of her household were privileged to kiss. In her quiet, enquiring voice, she would invariably, first, ask a stranger about *himself*. That was the secret of her charm; she gave people the feeling that she was interested, primarily, in them; that she knew them,

THE ROYAL HOMES

almost. And when she laughed, her very blue eyes laughed, too. The Queen enjoyed laughing. Only rarely did she betray anger – and then it was in her eyes, which blazed, bluer than ever.

The two princesses had the same coloured eyes as their parents. Those of Elizabeth were the porcelain blue of her father, of her German ancestors; Margaret's were of a darker blue, like that of a deep tropical sea. Both had inherited their parents' flawless, luminous complexion, their shortish stature, too. Elizabeth, the sturdier built, had not yet attained the full allure of an adult. She was shy, occasionally to the point of gaucheness, and this tended to hide her charm. When it showed through, it was with a touching, spontaneous sincerity. Her younger sister was as unremarkable as one would expect of a 14-year old girl – except when she came out with some shattering wise-crack; then, to her unconcealed delight, all eyes were upon her.

So charming and thoughtful was this family, whom I hardly knew, that they they made me feel more of a guest than an aide, showing me over the 'Big House' at Sandringham (closed for the duration of the war), where daffodils bloomed, a mass of gold, on the lawns; driving me – the King at the wheel – to the Royal Stud, where the stallions were paraded, and to the museum, guarded by the vigorous bronze statue of the Derby-winning Persimmon.

The Princesses led me in a hair-raising bicycle race, pedalling headlong down the switch-back slopes of the lawn, round the pond and down the narrow paths between the flower beds. Then through the woods, now coming alive with spring-time, we walked – and talked

> 'of shoes and ships and sealing wax,
> of cabbages and Kings . . .'

Talking of Kings, Princess Elizabeth told me of her grandfather King George V: 'His manner was very abrupt; some people thought he was being rude.' 'I rather like people like that,' said I, unwittingly putting my foot into it, 'because if they are rude to you, you can be rude back at them.' 'Yes, but you can't very well be rude to the King of England,' retorted the heir to England's throne. I took note to be more wary in future of what I said.

Easter, I think, is the most soul-shattering of all church feasts; after humiliation and disaster – triumph, to which the Easter hymns give full vent. The Royal Family attended matins as usual. The King was deeply religious; he knew the Bible well. Some of his favourite quotations were the ones with a double meaning that crop up here and there in the Bible and the hymns. He laughed when I told him that Mr Williams, at Wychwood, had found two mentions of cricket in the Bible: when Peter stood up with the eleven and was bold, and when Rachel came out with a full pitcher. That Easter morning we sang the traditional Easter hymn, No. 140: 'Jesus lives!' We came to the lines

> 'This shall calm our trembling breath
> When we pass its gloomy portal'

Portal. I glanced across at the King, wondering whether the same thing had struck him. It had. Our eyes met and he grinned broadly at this unexpected and quite undeserved allusion to the Chief of the Air Staff, Sir Charles Portal.

What struck me during those few days *en famille* with the King and Queen and their daughters was the astonishing affection generated by that small family. Perpetual currents of it flowed between them, between father and mother, sister and sister, between the parents and their daughters and back again. Then it radiated outwards to the ends of the world, touching thousands of millions of hearts who sent, rolling back, a massive wave of loyalty and love to the Royal Family.

The King and Queen were good and upright people who had inherited a gigantic burden to which they were selflessly devoted. Everybody knew that. But now I saw them not as King and Queen, but as the father and mother of two rather adorable and quite unsophisticated girls, as affectionate, understanding parents who had succeeded in creating a family atmosphere which every other family could admire, even envy.

The disputes, the sulking, the voices raised in protest or dis-approval, that were to be found in the households of his subjects, never – at least, so that you could notice it – occurred in the King's home. People talk about royal training; well, this was a part, a very basic part, of it. 'Our family, us four,' the King once wrote, 'the "Royal Family" must remain together . . .' Everything was subordinated to that warm, heart-felt sentiment.

In that small house, Appleton Lodge, as in all the King's private residences, we, 'the Household in Waiting', shared the recreational hours of the day with 'the Family', lunching and dining with them and remaining with them until the evening was spent.

Outdoors, this could involve one in walking, riding or shooting, and possibly, even, fishing. The Queen was an enthusiastic angler – though these activities were, of course, curtailed in war-time. Indoors, the basic attractions were games, like consequences or charades – in which the Queen, particularly, joined with incredible gusto – or cards, and a great jigsaw puzzle, whose hundreds of pieces were gradually assembled, during the stay, on a green, baize-topped table in the drawing-room. Anyone could have a go, but the most zealous contributors were the King and Princess Elizabeth.

Never one for indoor games, I became, when Canasta was the rage, quite an adept. Because it was never played for money, but to the accompaniment of a 'snifter', I enjoyed it – particularly when I partnered the Queen or Princess Margaret, both of whom played well, but with so little respect for the seriousness of the game, that each *coup* was accompanied either by loud groans or gales of laughter.

There were people who took the view, and sometimes openly expressed it: 'It's all very well for them. They are spared the hurts and banalities and chores of everyday life which the rest of us have to endure.' But it was not as simple as that. Britain and the Commonwealth were now in their fifth year of war. The King Emperor, as titular leader of this vast Empire and its 500,000,000 subjects, had lived, very personally, the anxieties, disasters and dangers of the war, as well as being constantly separated from the family he adored. The war had made him a very tired man, if not yet a mortally sick one.

Yet during those few days of springtime in the country, he seemed to shed the cares and the burdens of kingship and became once again *pater familias* and squire of Sandringham. Echoing the feelings of his father, George V, he said of it, 'I have always been so happy here and love the place'. It was the place where he was born and where he was to die.

The Easter holidays over, the King returned to London, there to pick up his burden once more, to live again the anxious days – now more anxious than ever, with the preparations for *Overlord*, the invasion of Europe, nearing completion, and D-Day at hand.

On the 15 May the King drove to the Headquarters of General Montgomery's 21st Army Group at St Paul's School, near Hammersmith, for the historic conference of the invasion commanders. Tommy Lascelles, his private secretary, accompanied him. I also went, seated on the strapontin in the back of the royal Daimler and feeling very much a 'spare part'. I was bidden to remain outside – very naturally, for, within, the whole plan of the Anglo-American invasion was being exposed to an audience which, apart from the King, included Winston Churchill, the War Cabinet, Generals Smuts and Eisenhower. One bomb on that schoolroom and the invasion would have been off. Each commander having said his bit, the King, to everyone's surprise, rose to his feet and, in a short address, put Operation Overlord, the liberation of Europe, in a nutshell. 'This is the biggest combined operation ever thought out in the world . . . a combined operation of two countries: the United States and the British Empire . . . With God's help you will succeed.'

Exactly three weeks later, on Monday, 5 June, the great invasion armada was due to sail from British south-coast ports. That week-end, the King and his family were at Windsor Castle. Sunday was sunny, but a stiff wind was blowing, so they had tea, sheltered beneath the wall of the east terrace of the castle, whose first grey stones William the Conqueror had shipped from Caen in his native Normandy.

The King's thoughts seemed far away; he hardly spoke at all, and I wondered why. He gave the reason in his diary for that day: with the wind at gale-force on the south coast and a high sea running, General Eisenhower had postponed D-Day to 6 June. 'This added to my anxieties,' the King noted that evening, 'as I knew the men were going aboard the ships at that time and their quarters were very cramped.'

The King's thoughts were always with his fighting men. He would dearly have loved to be with them himself and even mooted the idea to Churchill – who happened, already, to have made his own plan to be there. At which the King remarked that Churchill could not very well say no to him. The King then told the Queen about his idea. 'She was wonderful,' he wrote in his diary, 'and encouraged me to do it.'

What a superb example of leadership the King and his Prime Minister envisaged – not for the first time. They had both – with their wives – lived through the German air-raids on London. Now, they wanted to be with their men in the firing line and not, like the common run of Kings, presidents and politicians, well behind it. Unfortunately the King's plans were frustrated by cautious men of lesser calibre. He was put off by questions, like that of his private secretary: 'Was His Majesty prepared to advise Princess Elizabeth on the choice of her first Prime Minister if her father and Mr Churchill were killed simultaneously?' In the map-room at No. 10 Downing Street he was given a scary picture of bombs and mines and torpedoes, of shells fired from the shore batteries.

So what? Did not the Kings of old, their ministers and even bishops, accompany the fighting men into battle? That is the least that the old men who make wars owe to the young ones who go out and fight them. The King's brother, the Duke of Kent, (killed on active service) and his cousin, Lord Louis Mountbatten, who went down with his destroyer (but fortunately bobbed up to the surface again) had in this war given a splendid example. But the King's advisers succeeded in forcing him to see the 'sense' of staying behind and in convincing him equally, that it would be disastrous to give way before Churchill's obstinate determination to emulate his celebrated ancestor:

Malborough s'en va-t-en guerre.

The King's private secretary told him gloomily: 'It is not going to make things easier for you if you have to find a new Prime Minister in the middle of Overlord.' Churchill, when he heard of this argument, dismissed it jauntily: 'Oh that's all arranged for and, anyhow, I don't think the risk is 100 to 1.' But by now the King, whose own chivalrous spirit had been dampened by the dark counsels of his advisers, was himself begging Churchill not to go, and Churchill, who had already left London for Eisenhower's H.Q. at Portsmouth, deferred only at the last minute to his sovereign's wishes, 'since Your Majesty does me the honour to be so much concerned about my personal safety'.

Thus perished the noble intentions of the King and his Prime Minister.

I was, at this time, living with Rosemary and Giles among the Kentish orchards and hop gardens. Rosemary's unhappy lot, like all courtiers' wives, was to become a 'court-widow' during my spell of waiting – two weeks. Then for four weeks she had me more or less on her hands, an unbalancing routine. But who were we to grumble? Many men in the forces, including my two brothers, had it much worse. Yet, in our case, the imbalance proved more upsetting than the absence.

Exactly one week after D-Day, at 5 a.m. on 13 June, we were awoken by a shattering explosion. Believing it must have been a stray bomb dropped by a German raider, we thought no more of it. Two nights later, the sky was overcast, the 'ceiling' low. Some time before midnight, approaching from the south-east, there came an unaccustomed droning which rapidly crescendoed into an ear-splitting thunder until we could see, against the clouds, the silhouette of a small and villainous-looking winged projectile darting overhead, trailing a jet of red, roaring flame.

Hitler's V1's (vengeance weapons) had arrived. One of the first of them had shattered our sleep two days earlier. But that night they kept coming in a continuous stream. Totally indiscriminate weapons, they were aimed at London, but hundreds fell all along 'bomb alley', between the Kentish coast and the capital.

That night, as they thundered overhead, the thought occurred to me that these remotely controlled weapons took the glory out of war. The German who pressed a release-button at some distant launching-site would win no medal or title of valour, whatever the toll of death and destruction his act might cause. A new age of warfare had begun. There would be no more battle-fields where men won glory and honour, but just the mutual destruction of anonymous masses of the population of rival powers. As such, there seemed some possibility that war might lose its attraction for man.

When the postman knocked next morning, he was trembling, partly with fear, partly with anger. 'The bastards,' he said between his teeth. 'Takes a bloody Hun to think up something like that.' I still feel the same about Werner von Braun, father of the V-bombs, which caused such widespread, indiscriminate slaughter among British and Belgian civilians.

At Buckingham Palace, waiting in the equerry's room, I would listen to the V1's as they came roaring in to London. As long as that pulsating noise continued, all was well for those below; but as soon as the ram-jet engine spluttered to a stop it was time to get your head down, thrust your fingers in your ears, open your mouth and wait for the shattering blast.

The King showed remarkable phlegm under fire, as he had done when, as a nineteen year-old midshipman, he had manned A-turret in the *Collingwood* at the Battle of Jutland. He was inclined to fuss when 'ordered' below to the underground shelter; the royal quarters were tiny and the rest of us had to make do. My first night in the shelter, I slept on the floor in a narrow passage, swept by a piercing draught. My spinal column, already shaken by various falls, including a couple of parachute jumps, was next morning paralysed from the cervical vertebrae down to the lumbar, and I winced painfully as I bowed to the King.

Once, an investiture was held in the shelter – for the comfort and reassurance of a number of elderly and distinguished gentlemen who had come to be knighted. Other investitures, for the young and the brave, were held in a room on the ground floor. While the 'doodle-bugs' buzzed incessantly overhead, the

King continued to pin on medal after medal. Only when one of those sinister missiles was actually visible through the window might he turn and remark 'that was a close one'.

In July I accompanied the King and Queen when they visited an A.A. battery in Sussex. On the way, they called at East Grinstead, where a V1 had just fallen. This deviation was for me a god-send. An experienced courtier had once said 'Never miss an opportunity to relieve yourself'. At that moment, it was, for me, less a question of opportunity than of dire necessity. As Their Majesties talked to people in a débris-strewn street, I dropped to the rear of the cortège of municipal officials until I was level with a junior police officer. To him I made known my problem. 'Follow me,' he said, 'the public convenience is round the corner.' Alas, it had received the full blast of the bomb, so that I had to stand there in a surrealist *décor* of chains and cisterns and shattered urinals.

That afternoon, at the A.A. site, six flying-bombs streaked over in quick succession while shot and shell filled the air around them. The King – the Queen too – looked on with as much detachment as if it had been a duck shoot, while I prayed fervently that the guns would miss and so spare Their Majesties the possibility of a V1 crashing at their feet.

The V1's died away in September, but not before one had blown a gaping hole in the garden wall at Buckingham Palace – its ninth hit. The V2's then took up the bombardment of London. Being supersonic, they hit before they were heard, so the possibility of running for cover did not arise. Bomb for bomb, they killed three times more people than the V1's.

During those empty, endless hours in the equerry's room I was all too conscious that my next breath might be my last. One evening, the lady in waiting and I were invited to dine with the King and Queen; perhaps it was a gesture of solidarity under the V2 bombardment. During dinner a terrific explosion rocked the palace. The King asked me to find out where the V2 had fallen; it had hit a pub off Oxford Street, killing over a hundred people. In ten months, they killed, in Britain, over 10,000 civilians.

In autumn, 1944, Rosemary and I moved from 'Bomb Alley', in Kent, to a house in Windsor, which we shared with two young and attractive newly-weds, Lord and Lady Rupert Nevill. (Rupert belonged to a secret élite unit called the Coates Mission, whose job it was, if ever the King and Queen should be threatened by a German commando, to remove them to safety.) Nothing puts a bigger strain on a friendship than sharing a house. Micky and Rupert Nevill withstood the test and remained always my most loyal and helpful friends.

In the spring of 1945, with our second child on the way, the King proposed that we should move our abode to a small 'grace and favour' house, Adelaide Cottage, in the Home Park of Windsor Castle. It was a generous gesture for which I felt deeply grateful, despite the limited amenities of the house.

Adelaide Cottage was built in the early nineteenth century as a tea-house for Queen Adelaide. The site, a stone's throw from the Thames, was one of the dampest in England; the house possessed two radiators; they and the meagre coal ration were insufficient to warm it. In the drawing-room, surrounded by french windows, it was sometimes necessary to wrap up in an overcoat and scarf. The house was an ice-box in winter; in summer it was delightful.

By early spring 1945, the allied armies were across the Rhine. But the Germans, holding out in the Hague, were able to bombard Antwerp, now an allied port, with many thousand V1's and V2's. They killed over 3,000 Belgians.

One little Belgian girl, not yet six, had a narrow escape from death when she was riding on the back of her nine-year-old brother's bicycle through Antwerp's *Nouveau Parc*. Suddenly the bicycle and the children on it were knocked flat by the completely unheralded explosion of a V2; it fell just the other side of a grassy bank which deflected some of the blast. The little boy led his sister home; she was badly cut and shaken. Her name was Marie-Luce; today she is the mother of three of my children. Marie-Luce's parents moved with their children to Brussels. The following day a flying bomb demolished their house.

The last V2 I heard rocked Adelaide Cottage early one spring morning. About a month later, on 8 May, deliverance came, at last, from the European war. VE- day was, as Churchill said, the signal for the greatest outburst of joy in the history of mankind. It brought welcome release, too, for the young princesses imprisoned, more or less, in a tower in Windsor Castle. The King's thought for them was, 'Poor darlings. They have never had any fun yet.' That day they did. They broke out into the crazy, rejoicing world which was London and I stood near them in the dense crowds in front of Buckingham Palace as they cheered, with everybody else, each time their parents, the King and Queen, came out on to the balcony.

Six weeks later, Hugo, our second son, was born. He was christened in Saint George's Chapel where his godfather, the late King, now sleeps. For reasons doubtless valid, but best known to himself, Hugo would later abandon the church of his fathers – and godfather. Today he is a brother in the Roman order of Carmel.

Slowly, England began to come alive again, though rationing and restrictions, which lasted another few years, kept the pace slow. The King holidayed, for the first time in six years, at Balmoral, his Dee-side residence in Scotland, built by Queen Victoria in the mid-nineteenth century. 'This dear Paradise' she called it and her feelings found an echo in my own heart. Of all the King's estates, I loved Balmoral best. I liked it less for the house itself, a solid pile of dour grey granite, with its interior of tartan-clad walls and emotional Landseer engravings; I loved Balmoral first and foremost for 'the hill'.

Beyond the Dee valley, wooded with fir and birch, the 'low ground' was all rounded, heather-covered hills. Further, beyond the Gelder Burn, the 'high ground' rose up and culminated in the rugged peak of Lochnagar. You could go to the hill and be very close to yourself and to the earth. I loved the hill, open to heaven and horizons, unlike the forest, closed and mysterious, dark and menacing in its silence.

As an Englishman, I suppose that my first love should be for the sea. I was brought up by the sea and there is salt in my veins. The sea's chief attraction for me is that it leads to the

unknown, to far away lands and people. It answers an irresistible
yearning in me for change, for the exotic. The hill brings me
down to earth; it is more symbolic of life, with its ups and
downs, its steep gradients, its summits and skylines and its warm,
sheltered valleys. In the hills you can feel the strength of your
legs and lungs and heart. The hills lead you up, like an aeroplane, towards the sky; seen from above, the petty things of the
world and its anxieties fade out of sight. And when the wind
sighs on the hill it brings the smell of pines and heather. When
it roars on the high tops it does not trouble the hill, as it does the
sea. The hill remains immovable.

Once, at Balmoral, I drove out in the station wagon with
General Smuts, that great sage and world statesman, yet such a
simple man at heart. As we rounded a bend and the hills came
in sight, Smuts, suddenly moved, gave voice: 'I will lift up mine
eyes unto the hills from whence cometh my help.'

At Balmoral, more than anywhere, the King and Queen were
on holiday, the house full of guests. The equerry's duties were
not onerous, but generally enjoyable. He acted, unobtrusively,
as a kind of general handy-man, with eyes and ears alert, wary
even, to the wishes of the royal hosts and the needs and foibles
of their guests – a shy girl arriving, late and blushing, for dinner;
a young blood with a drop too much inside him; a cabinet
minister, still wearing the pallor of Whitehall, and often ill-at-
ease in this highland lair; a reverend minister, distractedly
contemplating the sermon he was to preach on the morrow and
finally, their Majesties' old and intimate friends who knew the
form better than the equerry himself – and consequently needed
the most delicate attention.

The royal holidays were really the ultimate test for members
of the Household, for, while they might perform impeccably in
the formal decor of Buckingham Palace, (where protocol was
well-defined) the relaxed, familiar atmosphere of Balmoral
demanded of them more natural, human qualities – in two
words, that they should 'fit in'. The Royal Family were perpetually surrounded by the members of their household, so the least
they could ask of the latter was that they should be bearable to
live with.

Those who attained to this ultimate standard did so each in
their own, individual style. Among the ladies-in-waiting Katie
(Lady Katherine) Seymour did it by almost total self-efface-
ment, though she did, occasionally, and most enjoyably, break
out in a burst of unbridled, if somewhat nervous, laughter.
Marion (Lady Hyde), was tall, straight, brown-eyed and un-
demonstrative. I believe she often longed to laugh outright, but
rarely did so. Delia (Lady Delia Peel), on the other hand, a
tireless – and trenchant – commentator of the passing scene,
could become helpless with laughter and take everyone else with
her.

For Tommy Lascelles, there was no problem: as private
secretary his day was already full. He was not expected, nor did
he try, to be sociable, but retired, a saturnine expression on his
face, into a corner. Harold Campbell, old salt as he was,
participated loyally, in his quarter-deck manner, up to a point
– beyond which he, too, retired, not to a corner, but to the
equerry's room, there to restore himself from the whisky
decanter, while sadly contemplating its diminishing contents.

Of my immediate contemporaries, Peter Ashmore, another
sailor, but young, always pleased by his pure and charming
simplicity. Patrick (Lord Plunket), highly sophisticated, yet
shy, conquered with his cool, ineffable charm – that of the
classic, faithful courtier – and as such was to die, sadly, long
before his time.

As for me, I felt rather as if I were on a stage, playing a part,
a minor one, in a wonderful comedy, human, colourful, animated
and at times intensely moving, with an extraordinarily varied
dramatis personae. Yet, more than the play itself, it was the
players, each one of them, the 'royals' and the members of their
household, down to the pages of the presence, of the pantry and
of the back stairs, the stalkers, keepers and ghillies, whom I
found both friendly and fascinating. Though I had no particular
qualifications for my part, it seemed to suit me, for I hit it off,
apparently, with the other players, and not least the leading
ones – the King, the Queen and the princesses.

The days at Balmoral passed pleasantly, energetically. The
King and the rest of the guns, dressed if the King had favoured

them, in the green-grey tweed of the royal estate, left for the hill, at 9.30, to shoot grouse. After seeing them off, I would discuss with that dear man, Ainslie (the palace steward), or his deputy, the immediate commitments on the domestic front.

One day I told Ainslie, 'Please note: Tomorrow King Faisal of Iraq and the Regent will be staying. They are Moslems, forbidden to eat pork. So for heaven's sake, no bacon or sausages for breakfast.' Ainslie raised his eyebrows: no bacon and sausages. This was a serious break with tradition.

Next morning, at breakfast, I led the King's Moslem guests to the sideboard and raising the lid of a silver dish, invited them: 'Please help yourselves; you have a choice of haddock, kippers or scrambled eggs.' But there was nothing of the kind; the dish was full of bacon and sausages, upon which those royal sons of the Prophet fell with unconcealed relish. Ainslie, in the background, smiled approvingly.

While the guns were at the morning drive, there would gather, back at the ranch, a small posse of riders, headed by the princesses. Elizabeth, on a horse, was competent and classic, Margaret pretty and dashing. I often rode with them on the hill.

With the King's permission – and encouragement – I took enthusiastically to deer-stalking. The instinct was strong in me; I believe that, of all forms of hunting in our island, deer-stalking is the purest. With the stalker, a dour, straight-spoken high-lander, you are alone between the hill and the heavens, pitting your skill and your patience against the defensive instincts of the quarry. It is a hard sport, demanding keen eyes, strong legs and lungs, and a stubborn resistance to the elements, which in the Highlands can be savage. Sometimes it rains all day and a macintosh cannot be used – it can be seen and heard. A solid tweed keeps out some of the wet, and when the rest soaks into your bones, it can be warmed out by a wee drop . . . never does whisky taste so good as on the hill, with water from the burn.

I liked the stalkers, hard men who wasted neither words nor feelings, who spoke a language among themselves which was barely understandable and invented pretty diminutives like 'staggie' and 'pathie'. As with all true hunters, there was that strange complicity between them and their prey. MacGregor, scrutinising a measly old stag through his telescope, whispered to me 'Yon staggie *badly* needs a slug in him' as if he were asking me to do the poor brute a favour. MacHardy, the dourest of them all, was one day gutting the stag I had just shot. He slit open the belly, pulled out the entrails, then as he severed the penis with his knife, remarked: 'Ye'll nae be needin' that no more.'

Another time, with MacHardy, I fired and missed. 'Damn bad shot' was his only comment. Yet I became quite a crack at this sport, which I loved, not least because it took me away for a whole day to be alone on the hill.

One day, the King invited me to go stalking with him. The cold numbed our fingers and His Majesty, as he fumbled painfully with the bolt of his rifle, muttered a volley of oaths. But his aim was unerring. He was one of the best shots in the land, though he had a decided preference for driven birds. Occasionally, he invited me to join the guns. One of the first grouse I ever shot came plummeting down and exploded in a flurry of feathers at the King's feet. Not only did the bird nearly hit His Majesty, but worse – it was his bird.

Shooting from a line of butts never greatly attracted me, no doubt because, instinctively, I always preferred to follow a lone trail (as I did with the deer) than to take part in a general free-for-all.

I was more than content, when not stalking, to accompany the ladies, at midday, to the butts and, after a picnic lunch, to sit out the afternoon, admiring the grouse, swift and determined flyers, as they came on and on, braving the deadly barrage put up by the shooting men. While appreciating the latters' style and skill, my sympathies as a flyer, having been shot at so often myself, were for those daring but foolhardy birds.

The King's daughters held differing views on shooting, and more particularly, on stalking, which Princess Elizabeth loved. She was a tireless walker and an excellent shot. Princess Margaret detested stalking. Oddly enough, I found this rather endearing. As time went on and I became something of an expert, she helped me not to take myself too seriously.

The sporting day ended, sportsmen and spectators foregathered in the drawing-room. Its bay-windows gave on the distant hill; its pictures, furniture and bibelots exuded so strongly the intensely romantic, if somewhat vetust, personality of Queen Victoria that you almost felt that you were in her august presence. Which did not dispel the pleasure of downing a well-earned drink, chatting animatedly about the day's sport, or getting drawn into the wiles of canasta.

Then, invariably too late, everyone would hurry to their room, hurriedly change, and hurry back, just in time for dinner – to learn that the Queen had returned only a few moments earlier from fishing and would not be down for half an hour.

Dinner at Balmoral was a joyous feast which capped the day's sport. The Scottish gentleman, resplendent in kilt, jacket and jabot, far outshone the sassenachs like me, in our dowdy black dinner-jackets. Grouse, slightly high, but delicious, was on the menu each night during the six-weeks' stay. For one half of the meal, conversation was directed to one neighbour, then switched (following the Queen's cue) to the other.

Towards the end of the dinner, the King's pipers, numbering up to a dozen, entered and blew their way round the table, to the stirring, moving but deafening wail of airs like *Scotland the brave*, *My home* or *Flowers of the Forest*. Those inimitable, nostalgic airs, better heard from the other side of the hill, penetrated, at point blank range, to the depths of my heart. I often asked the pipe-major for a repeat on the following evening.

Dinner over, the ladies retired and the King passed the port to the gentlemen. It could happen (and often did) that the Queen, half an hour later, had a message passed to the King, telling him that the ladies were getting impatient. So the gentlemen then joined the ladies and the reunion led to crazy games, or canasta, or, most enchanting of all, Princess Margaret singing and playing at the piano. Her repertoire was varied; she was brilliant as she swung, in her rich, supple voice, into the American musical hits, like 'Buttons and bows', 'I'm as corny as Kansas in August . . .'; droll when, in a very false falsetto, she bounced between the stool and the keyboard in 'I'm looking over a four-leaf clover, which I'd overlooked before . . .'; and lovable when she lisped some lilting old ballad: 'I gave my love a cherry, it had no stone . . .'. No one remained unmoved.

Quite another kind of evening was the Ghillies' Ball, held in the castle ballroom and attended by all the braw lads and the bonnie lasses of the Balmoral estate, and even by those dour, weather-beaten stalkers, MacGregor and MacHardy, looking, in kilt and buckle shoes, slightly sheepish.

Time was given for pipers and dancers to warm up; then, when the air was vibrating with the wail of pipes and the measured beat of feet, the King, the Queen and the princesses, followed by their guests, joined the reels – the sassenachs, including myself, rather reluctantly. I much preferred to remain a wall-flower and simply watch the handsome, kilted, screeching Scots pirouetting on tip-toe about their ravishing, tartan-sashed ladies, rather than cut a ridiculous figure, in black dinner-jacket, trying vainly to emulate them. I thought then, as I still do, that native dances are best performed by the natives.

The Royal Family celebrated the Scottish sabbath in the Kirk of Crathie, hard by, whose incumbent was the Reverend John Lamb. A man of small stature, the Minister had about him an astonishing radiance: snow white hair, a lean face, shiny pink, and a pair of pure and piercing blue eyes which gleamed like light. From early spring to late autumn, Johnny Lamb dived into the River Dee, no doubt convinced that its icy waters were every bit as cleansing as those of the Jordan. If not a man of great intellect, he was one of purity and simplicity. He preached, as did every Presbyterian minister who was privileged to address the Royal Family from the pulpit of the Kirk, like an Old Testament prophet, dispensing, in the name of the *Lorrd*, both fire and brimstone and the blandishments of divine love and mercy. As with the men of the hill, what I liked about these Scottish men of God was that they spoke a direct, clean-hewn language. The truth for them was as hard and straight-cut as the red granite of the Kirk, yet they were readier than many of their clerical brethren of other Christian cults to forgive the weakness in men. I always found Minister Lamb's support and friendship a great stay.

About mid-September the King would go south, via London, to

Sandringham, for the partridge and pheasant shooting. The Queen and the Princesses stayed on at Balmoral till early October, when the hill echoed with the melancholy roar of rutting stags. I often stayed on, too, and day after day went, with MacHardy, to the hill to shoot out the 'rubbish'.

Though I loved the hill, I disliked this kind of shooting. The stags, exhausted with rounding up their ladies (as MacHardy called them), defending them against challengers and of course serving them turn by turn, were in wretched condition and had about them a rank and revolting odour. Sometimes a young stag would attach itself to this wandering harem and it seemed to me unjust to shoot the old stag and leave all his hard-won concubines to the young hanger-on – not that he was likely to keep them to himself for long.

At this time skeins of wild geese, silhouetted against a cold blue sky, began flighting south. Then the Queen and the princesses departed in the same direction and the family was reunited in London for the winter season.

In London I was making a number of enjoyable, interesting and occasionally distinguished friends, though, unfortunately for Rosemary, I was never able to match her enthusiasm for the social life. I enjoyed dining out: a dinner party, particularly a small one, is a pleasant and civilised pretext for intelligent – and audible – conversation. For precisely the opposite reason balls, to my mind, are a bore, cocktail parties an unspeakable curse and night-clubs the nadir as a form of social intercourse.

Week-end parties in the country are another enjoyable feature of English life. It is there that major business or political matters are often discussed and decisions made. Though this aspect did not – yet – interest me, I enjoyed them for the opportunity they gave to meet people and their possibilities for fun and civilised conversation in pleasant surroundings.

A memorable exception was a week-end, otherwise quite delightful, when conversation was made difficult owing to an unusual idiosyncrasy of our hostess, a dowager duchess. You would have thought that this wonderful lady was several thousand years old; her *maquillage* made her look like an

Egyptian mummy who had just climbed out of a pyramid. Yet the duchess was still incredibly energetic, voluble and witty. Unfortunately, she had the disconcerting habit of breaking wind without the slightest regard for the company and the circumstances. I first became aware of it as I strolled with her round the garden. There came a series of reports. Not daring to believe my ears I tried to convince myself that they were just some miscellaneous garden noises. In vain. More reports followed, while her grace continued, quite unconcernedly, to extol the glories of her beautiful garden. There was no let-up at dinner, during which the startled guests either looked fixedly at the ceiling and bit their lips, or conversed, shouting at each other, hoping to drown the cannonade.

For the first time since the war started, the King spent Christmas in the 'Big House' at Sandringham. The interior of Sandringham House, for all its labyrinthine passages and staircases which seemed to lead nowhere, exuded warmth and a genial sort of comfort. It had the feel of an ancestral, a family home; it smelt of winter and log fires and still gave off a strong aroma of its first royal owner King Edward VII and the *aisance* and elegance of his times.

From without, the house presented a hideous, nondescript silhouette, a bizarre mixture of British, baroque and byzantine. That worried no-one, least of all the King. Sandringham was the place that he loved most on earth. It was essentially his Christmas abode, associated with rain and fog and snow and crisp, bright mornings. The east wind brought cold, strong, salty air off the North Sea and the surrounding pinewoods added their savour. The furrowed fields smelt good, of earth and dung, and the standing green pastures gave off their subtle, delicious smell. Sandringham air was revivifying; it was what the King needed. After six long years of war, he was, as he put it himself, burnt out.

Not surprisingly, considering the Royal Family's continental affiliations, the royal Christmas smacked somewhat of a continental *réveillon*. The Christmas parade began the evening before. In the tinsel-hung ballroom the King's family and his closest relations gathered about the Christmas tree to open their

presents. Within a few minutes they were standing amidst a
débris of paper wrappings and coloured string, embracing one
another with thanks and kisses – a simple, heart-warming scene
which, on the morrow, would be repeated throughout the land.
For once, in the whole year, the Royal Family and their nearest
kith and kin could be together in private.

The principal guest was Queen Mary, a grand and most
gracious lady; if there was a certain stiffness about her manner
it was because she was (like her son, the King) shy. When first
placed next to her at dinner I said to myself 'Speak before you
are spoken to' (exactly the opposite to what nanny used to say)
'otherwise you may never speak at all'. Queen Mary's first
responses were monosyllabic, but I talked on and was soon
enjoying the warmth of her conversation. At the end of dinner
she took a cigarette and puffed away at it gently, but contentedly.

Queen Mary was the most admirable of all the old ladies I
have met. I was moved by her dignity, the straightness of her
carriage, her flawless porcelain complexion, her majesty and her
touching simplicity. One evening, after dinner, the party
warmed up and people began to dance. Queen Mary, now in
her 80's, did not hesitate. I found my arm linked with hers as we
danced round, singing the Hokey Cokey:

> You put your left foot in,
> Your left foot out,
> In out, in out,
> Shake it all about,
> You do the hokey cokey and you turn around
> And that's what it's all about

The King's younger brother, the Duke of Gloucester and the
Duchess – Uncle Harry and Aunt Alice – were always there
with their boys, the Princes William and Richard. The Duke
was of a different stamp to his brother. *Gourmand* and more
carefree about what he ate and drank, he cut a substantial
figure compared with the King's lean silhouette. 'Uncle Harry'
was a jovial type, reacting instantly to the most faintly funny
remark with a gusty, high-pitched giggle. He always made you

feel good, if not particularly clever. 'Aunt Alice' possessed classic, serene good looks and sincerity shone from her mild face. But she was painfully shy, so that conversation with her was sometimes halting and unrewarding, for you felt that she had so much more to say, but could not bring herself to say it. Her two sons had the refreshing look of prep. school boys, with no hint that they were princes of the blood.

Another Christmas guest was the Princess Royal, a sister of the King. As a girl she had been the despair of her brothers' tutor who, as long as she was around, found it impossible to keep order. Princess Mary was still full of fun, a very dear lady, so dear that you could tease her and she loved it.

The Duchess of Kent, 'Aunt Marina', completed, with her three children, the inner family circle. Princess Marina's face was of an exquisite, almost tragic, beauty, with a permanently wistful expression. She was sensitive, artistic and *sympathique*, going straight to the depths of a subject. Her husband, an airman, had been killed in an air crash only a few years earlier; perhaps it was because I was an airman, too, that I found areas of common ground with the beautiful, bereaved duchess. I longed to know this gifted woman better, but felt too shy to insist in face of the sophisticated company with which she often surrounded herself. I believe that wit and brilliance were more effective at buoying up her spirits than the searching, nostalgic conversations I had with her.

For all her sophistication, the Duchess of Kent was a devoted mother, presiding at her children's tea-parties at her house, to which my children were sometimes invited. Prince Eddie, her eldest son, was diffident and hypersensitive; Princess Alexandra easy and enchanting, with unmistakable signs of becoming a great beauty; Prince Michael a plump little boy with the charm, already, of his father.

The Christmas tree ritual over, the family trooped off to the carol service in Saint Margaret's Church, Sandringham, where the Reverend Hector Anderson, 'Hector the Rector', with his rich, unctuous voice, officiated. As the heretic father of my present catholic family, I must say in all truth and humility, that no catholic *Messe de Minuit* that I have ever attended has surpassed the beauty and joy of the simple Christmas carol service in the little church at Sandringham, repeated in thousands of other churches up and down the land that holy night.

Sandringham afforded the King a sporting holiday; the partridge and pheasant season was in full swing. He loved duck-shooting, too, and shot with his neighbours. One of them was the Earl of Leicester, whose seat was Holkham Hall. I believe it was the father of Tommy Leicester, the then earl, of whom a nice story was told. Old Lord Leicester had invited a French general to shoot duck at Holkham. On the eve of the shoot he drove the general round the estate. As they stopped before a piece of water where mallard were known to flight in large numbers, Lord Leicester announced: '*Ici, mon général, nous tuons toujours beaucoup de malades.*'

Shooting was the King's passion; he dealt directly with the game-keepers and took charge, personally, of each day's operations. Nothing escaped his keen, observant eye, especially when the action was fast, as when the cry went up 'Woodcock!' and the guns blazed away wildly at this somewhat rare and elusive bird.

From which there hangs this little tale: a neighbouring game-keeper, having attained the age of ninety, was asked: 'How have you managed to survive to this ripe old age?' 'Well', replied the veteran, 'every time they shouts "Woodcock!" I always throws meself flat on me face.'

CHAPTER 14

South African trek

I had now been with the King not, as originally intended, for three months, but for two years. As I came more and more to know the King and his family, my affection for them grew. I desired to serve them to my utmost, yet I felt restless and frustrated. The simple if rather special duties I performed were difficult to reconcile with the responsibilities, the stress and the danger I had known when commanding a squadron and a station, or the functions I was trained for at the Staff College. My job, to some extent exacting, if only because of the empty, interminable hours of waiting, was far from taxing my energies, either mental or physical, to the full. I longed to be more actively, more usefully employed.

The chance came with the Royal Tour of South Africa and Rhodesia. The King and Queen and the Princesses were to leave England on 1 February 1947; they would be away for three months. Peter Ashmore and I were to go along as equerries. I had also to act as master of His Majesty's reduced Household, a kind of chief of personnel-cum-purser-cum-social secretary.

Britain's six-year war – longer than any of her allies or indeed of her enemies – had left her bankrupt and half-starving. Now she was hit by the cruellest winter in living memory. The country was still living on a basic ration of 1/2d worth of meat a week, one egg and a 2-lb loaf. Shortages of clothes, equipment and houses made life a drab and difficult affair. And now the fury of the elements descended on Britain: gales and floods, frost and snow paralysed communications. Power cuts left Britons shivering in their homes; factories were shut down and $2\frac{1}{2}$ millions were thrown out of work. British agriculture was devastated in its worst crisis in three centuries. And, on top of all these calamities at home, the King faced immense and pressing problems in his Empire: India, Burma and Palestine – two-thirds of its population – were in turmoil, demanding independence from the British crown.

Such was the situation as the King prepared to leave, in the battleship *Vanguard*, his forlorn and frost-bound United Kingdom for the midsummer of South Africa. He was loth to leave and would rather have stuck it out at home with his people. But the King of England was also King of South Africa, and South Africa claimed him.

I had never before made any serious attempt to keep a diary, but during the next three months I recorded, day by day, simply and spontaneously, my thoughts and impressions. My main object, since I would be away so long, was to keep my wife informed. I was deeply attached to her and my two small sons and it was hard to leave them to the rigours of life in Britain and sail away to a land of sun and plenty. Periodically, I sent my notes home to Rosemary. I have not read them for nearly thirty years but am lucky to be able to draw on them now instead of on faded memories.

For the next three months were to be a key-period in my life, with thoughts, frustrations and desires erupting in my mind and horizons widening before my eyes. Not since I went to Singapore, eleven years earlier, had I travelled so far from England. The effect on me was similar. It liberated me and altered my outlook.

I had reached a crossroads. My generation had gone to war inspired by the ideal of freedom. We had fought successfully to save our country – and a good many others – from Nazi tyranny. What was the gain? To judge by Britain's present plight, there was no gain, only loss – at least for her. I had survived the fighting; now I wanted nothing better than to help in the reconstruction of a new Britain. I believed in the future of my country and above all of the British race – who could not after going through six years of war with them? In my present position I had perhaps a unique opportunity to help, but was I going to be able to give of my best?

I was far from sure. But I instinctively felt that the South Africa tour would open up new horizons. It did, but sadly enough, some were darker than I imagined.

Snow lay thick on the ground as the royal procession left Buckingham Palace. At Waterloo there was time for a few words with Rosemary and Giles, a fond farewell, yet it marked the first stage of a parting which would eventually separate us for ever. The *Vanguard* sailed from Portsmouth early next morning. Three colleagues waved us away – Joey Legh, Tim Nugent and Edward Ford – black silhouettes beneath umbrellas, standing ankle-deep in the snow, a sad little spectacle which seemed to symbolise the cold, confined England we were leaving behind us. I felt remorse for them, remorse mingled, all the same, with the excitement of heading away towards the sunny spaces of a new world.

The Navy and the R.A.F. escorted the *Vanguard* down-channel; then, after some delay the splendid French battleship *Richelieu*, which the Royal Navy had tried to sink at Mers-el-Kebir in 1940, took up station alongside. The King, on the *Vanguard*'s bridge, fretted at the delay, even more so when the *Richelieu*, instead of firing a royal salute, emitted a silent puff of white smoke. Could it be a gesture of contempt for Mers-el-Kebir? No, a technical hitch. Despite the heavy seas, the *Richelieu*'s decks were manned and her brave sailors were getting a soaking.

For several days the *Vanguard* pitched and rolled through stormy, violent seas. The King, a seasoned sailor if, at present, a weary one, stayed in his cabin and slept, though he became impatient as the days passed and the storm showed no signs of abating.

I love a storm at sea, the wind howling in the rigging and the grey wastes of angry, tormented water. In life it is a rare experience to feel totally unimportant. A good storm at sea can do the trick.

At last we sailed into calm waters; a warm wind blew and the Queen remarked 'It's like being stroked.' At night, sitting on deck, as the *Vanguard* rolled gently through the swell under a full moon, I felt great peace of soul and at close quarters with the Infinite.

If only I could have felt closer to my family. Released from the worries, the cold and shortages of life in England, I began to

Two visits to the theatre. *above*: at the Strand Theatre in August 1946, seated between Queen Elizabeth and the then Princess Elizabeth. *below*: Escorting the two Princesses to the Palace Theatre in July 1947

With the royal family in South Africa, 1947. *above:* Watching as Queen Elizabeth is presented with a model zebra and *below:* driving with Princess Elizabeth and Princess Margaret through the streets of Cape Town

In attendance at Badminton, 1953

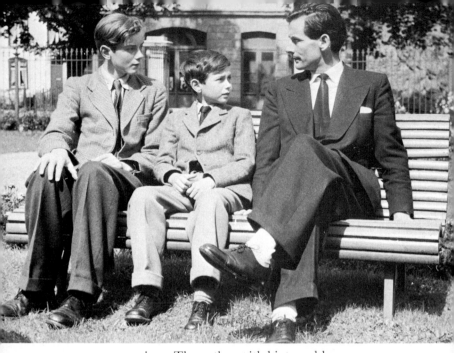

above : The author with his two elder sons,
Giles and Hugo, in 1955
below : Taken by surprise by an intrusive reporter

dream up schemes for my wife and sons, schemes which were, alas, but dreams. From mid-Atlantic I called Rosemary. 'We've just crossed the line,' I told her and she replied, 'I know. I heard you got a ducking.' She had followed King Neptune's ceremony, of which I was one of the principal victims, on the radio from 4,000 miles away. It was snowing hard, she told me; we were sweltering in the heat.

As we sailed on into the limpid blue waters of the southern hemisphere, the sun began to warm out the discontent that had eaten into my soul. I poured out my feelings in my diary. I felt frustrated and unsettled in England. Though I felt for her and desired no better than to stay with her during her post-war struggle, I began, as the voyage continued and my thoughts grew clearer, to doubt whether the England that I had been brought up to love and to serve would ever turn out to be the promised land that I had so passionately believed in. It irked me to be restrained, imprisoned, driven in on myself within her shores – a feeling which made me desperate, but which was not new. I had felt exactly the same at the end of my 'teens and my longings were only satisfied by my departure to Singapore, at the other end of the world.

As I sailed on towards South Africa, I looked back at England's horizons, and thought how narrow they were. Yet how could my English soul ever find an outlet from my English body, chilled, neurotic and overwrought as it was, after six years of war and privations? My soul was bursting for an outlet and if I could not find it in England, I would remove it elsewhere. I thought a lot about myself, it is true. But, quite truthfully, I thought as much about my beloved wife and family, intending that they, above all, should benefit from my adventurous projects.

I saw little of the Princesses during the voyage, save at meals. A couple of days out from Cape Town I sat next to Princess Elizabeth at dinner. We talked at length about sleep, of which she said she had had far too little during the voyage – so indeed had we all and we were to have even less during the tour. We talked on, about the tour; the Royal Family were feeling rather apprehensive about the strong republican feeling in South

Africa. But General Smuts, the South African Prime Minister, would soon be there to reassure them.

On 17 February the Royal Family landed at Cape Town, 'the fairest cape I ever did see' wrote Admiral Drake when he sighted it nearly four centuries earlier from the bridge of the *Golden Hind*. The Royal Family stayed at Government House and for four days Cape Town feted them.

Apartheid was not yet a policy of government, though there was a distinct feeling of apartness between the different communities, the Coloured (a mixture of races), the Africans ('natives') and even between the white races, Afrikaners and English. Due recognition was, of course, given by Their Majesties to each and all, but the most demonstrative response came from the Coloureds. At the Coloured Ball, a dense throng, gaudily dressed, swung it with frenzied enjoyment in the presence of their royal guests, greeting them with cries of 'Hullo you darlings!', 'Oh you're pretty!' and so on.

By comparison, the opening of Parliament was a solemn occasion. The ceremony inside Parliament House over, the royal cortège proceeded outside. But the King and Queen were not at its head; I was. Before the crowd and the flashing cameras, I had to lead down a long flight of steps. Suddenly there came a shout from the King: 'Stop!' Presumably the Queen thought the message was for her, for I then heard 'No, not you!' Halfway down the steps, the King shouted another command, 'Tell the guard of honour to present arms!' In as dignified a manner as possible, I hurried on down the stairs to find the guard commander, relaying to him the royal command, 'For Christ's sake present arms!'

Meanwhile, behind my back, the King had signalled the waiting royal car out of the way. The car reversed and hit the kerb, carrying the red carpet with it. By a miracle, the King and Queen were not swept off their feet. Laurel and Hardy could not have thought out a better act nor – once we were safely back at Government House – could they have given us a bigger laugh.

From Cape Town, the King and Queen and their daughters

set off on a two-month's marathon around South Africa and Rhodesia. Most of the way, they travelled in the splendid air-conditioned White Train. In it, they slept thirty-five nights. They also motored and flew hundreds of miles. It was a rudely exhausting, but fabulous journey. From my own point of view, while I was lucky to average four or five hours sleep a night, I had the good fortune to get to know and to love that beautiful, romantic, colourful – in one word, beloved – country.

Everywhere, even in the toughest Nationalist republican strongholds, South Africans gave their King and Queen a warm and heartfelt welcome. It obviously sprang, not from any political feeling, but straight from the hearts of that multi-racial, multi-national people.

There was another reason. The simplicity and sincerity of the King and Queen appealed to the South African people. They immediately became a great hit. At Paarl, known for its wine and its republicanism, the population turned out in force to greet them. Laughing boys and girls, cool and clean and sun-burnt, their fair hair blown by the wind, cheered them through the streets.

The King, his profile as fine as if etched on a postage stamp, stopped before the Town Hall to receive a loyal address. In the middle of it, a sudden gust of wind stirred the oak trees over-hanging the royal dais and sent a shower of acorns bouncing off the King's head and the Queen's hat. Everyone, republicans and royalists, led by the Royal Family, dissolved into fits of laughter.

As they trekked across South Africa, the Royal Family were welcomed by all races. People shouted from the crowd 'Stay with us!' or 'Leave the Princesses behind!' Black and white, they had trekked in from farms, miles away, by car, on horse-back, or by foot, to places where the train halted.

The horsemen – boys and girls too – often galloped alongside the train. A gnarled old giant, mounted on a clean-legged Basuto pony, caught up with the train when it reached Power, in the Outeniqua range. Breathless, he told me, 'I'm a Dutch-man and a nationalist, but the King's visit is doing us a lot of good', and added, 'Yes, I'm a Boer. I fought the British in the

Boer War and joined the rebellion in 1914. Now I've seen the King, I'm through with being a republican.' Then he whipped off the handsome belt from around his waist and handed it to me. 'I've had it thirty years' he said, 'Here, give it to the King'.

We often stopped at wayside halts on the *veldt* where Africans, bearing banners of welcome, had been waiting all day. When at last the train steamed in, they would break into haunting, melodious airs, drifting on the limpid night air, under a starry sky. As they sang, they swayed, dreamy-eyed, carried away by the harmony of their own voices. Never had I heard such moving songs.

At Alice, thousands of students chanted the African anthem *N'Kosi Sikeleli Africa* (God bless Africa). The lisping treble of the children, answered by the refrain of the male voices, a low murmuring hum, sounded like the wind murmuring in the trees. And again, at Sanaspos, in the middle of the *veldt*, school children lifted up their voices and sang the Hallelujah Chorus with the verve of a cathedral choir.

When the King and Queen and their daughters alighted from the train at wayside halts, the crowd often had difficulty in distinguishing them from the rest of us, dressed as we were like them, in relaxed clothes. A police officer was once heard explaining to a group of piccaninies: 'That is Mr King and next to him Mrs King; then just behind, Princess Elizabeth King and Princess Margaret King.'

Government ministers took it in turn to travel in the royal train. General Jan Smuts, the prime minister, took over as minister in attendance as the King and Queen reached Ladysmith. During the Boer War, Smuts and his men (Queen Victoria's 'presumptuous little foes' as *The Times* called them), had tried to shoot their way into the town, where the British were besieged. Now the old Boer leader drove side-by-side with Victoria's great-grandson into Ladysmith, to be greeted by British ex-servicemen (including Boer War veterans) with cries of 'Hullo Janny!' To which he answered: 'You see, it was worth fighting it out!'

Smuts possessed, like all great men, simplicity and humility.

His vision was clear and far-sighted and he spoke to you as if he
had know you all your life.

With Smuts, we all stood at the foot of a grassy hill, Spion
Kop, where the Boers had defeated Victoria's men (and where,
incidentally, a wiry little Indian had served bravely as stretcher-
bearer – his name was Mohandas Gandhi). It was sad to think
that so many men from far-away England had been killed
there, yet a soldier could hardly wish for a more lovely place to
die than on the fair slopes of Spion Kop.

It was when we came to the Natal National Park hostel, high
in the forbidding Drakensberg range, that, one night before
dinner, I had a long talk with Smuts – alone, under the stars,
while lightning cleft the darkness, momentarily revealing the
massive peaks towering up behind us. Smuts loved the mountains. He talked of the Basutos and their mountainous land that
we had recently visited; of the wisdom of their chief, Moshesh,
who outwitted the Boers and the Zulus, too, and created the
Basuto nation. He told me of Chaka, the tyrant who welded the
Zulus into a nation; if a man so much as sneezed in Chaka's
presence he was put to death and when Chaka's mother died, he
ordered the massacre of seven thousand Zulu mothers. Chaka, in
his time, murdered over a million Africans; his fugitive lieutenant, Mzilikatzi, 'Pathway of Blood', murdered half a million
more.

The British had, in 1879, subdued the Zulu's, who now
hailed the King as 'the lion whose roaring silences the rest of
creation'. The Swazis, too, and the Matabeles, Barotses, and
Bechuanas all showed reverence and affection for the Great
White Queen's descendant, who, on the side, gained quite a
reputation as a rain-maker and was often greeted with the cry
'Pula!' Rain!

The 'native problem', Smuts went on, was of course South
Africa's greatest problem, but he did not see in it all those many
difficulties and dangers. It was, after all, the world's problem:
there were more blacks than whites in the world and if only the
whites – in South Africa and the world at large – would stop
their futile fighting between themselves, they would come to an
understanding with the blacks. That would not happen in his

life-time, but Smuts did not think in terms of the present moment or place; he saw hundreds of years ahead, thousands of miles away.

I could understand why, to each of its many races and colours, it was such a beloved country. I, too, had fallen in love with it. It had happened somewhere between Kingwilliamstown and Kei Road, a district of green hills and broad pastures, full of horsemen, leather-faced old farmers and boys and girls, hair blowing, shirts billowing, sitting their horses with ease as they rode to school or market. I had even begun to weigh the possibilities of settling there, in the hopes of starting a new, fuller and more creative life.

Talking to Smuts warmed my enthusiasm. He himself, he told me in his clipped accent, was inspired by South Africa: 'Its hills and mountains, rivers and far horizons make me think beyond the immediate cares of life to greater things. They give me a feeling of permanence.'

Permanence. It had been so lacking in my own life since 1940 when, with my aircraft hit, I had stepped out into space, all but stepped out of this life into the next. All of us who had been through the worst of the war felt more or less the same. We were living, now, in a world of changing ideas and values, of dying or discredited traditions, of possessions destroyed, lost or decayed. Life seemed transitory and uncertain as never before. The feeling of permanence, the anchor and the rock-like security that I had known in my youth had vanished.

A feeling of permanence: that is what I sought. Not that I saw security as an excuse for inactivity; on the contrary, it meant a base, indispensable to further action and adventure. How could I, I kept wondering, employ myself more usefully, more creatively? In South Africa, perhaps. Sitting there, in the stillness of the night, high up in the Drakensberg, I felt captivated by this land.

Torn between South Africa and England, I poured out to Rosemary, by way of my diary, my tormented thoughts which, I believed, might lead to a new and more constructive life for us. Back came her reply – by cable, followed by a letter to drive home her feelings. They shook me rudely out of my dreams and set me back on the straight, monotonous and narrow road which leads on through a settled, conventional existence. That had been Rosemary's background; mine savoured more of adventure. I could not blame her; she could not help, any more than I, the conflicting attitudes.

Meanwhile, from the Drakensbergs, the King and his family trekked on, only partly restored, for the tour was being very strenuous – 'doubly hard for Bertie', wrote the Queen, because of his constant anxiety about the hardships of his people back in Britain. Although, in appearance, the King was the most phlegmatic of men, he drew heavily on his reserves of nervous energy.

The Queen and Princess Elizabeth seemed tireless. Princess Margaret played a relatively thankless rôle for, beside her sister, heir to the throne, she cut a less prominent figure in the eyes of the public. She was not yet seventeen. Yet, throughout the daily round of civic ceremonies, that pretty and highly personable young princess held her own.

Distractions were rare during the tour, but there was one which the Princesses seldom missed. At most stops, horses were waiting for those who felt like a gallop before breakfast. With the Princesses, we sped in the cool air, along the sands or across the *veldt*. Those were the most glorious moments of the day.

But neither they nor their parents could often relax and be themselves. Occasionally the King had the chance of a few sets of tennis. He still showed the class of the top player he had once been, though he was impatient with his faults. Once, when I was playing a singles with him, he had a bad run; finally he picked up that damned, evasive ball and hit it miles out of court. I thought to myself, 'I'm not going to get that one – you are', and he did. He wandered off into the garden, beat about the flower beds and bushes and returned, rather shamefacedly, with the offending ball.

On a Sunday near Ebb and Flow, Cape Province, the King and his family had another of their rare 'whole holidays'. Matins were held, with all of us sitting round a long table, in a shaded grove, (which had been previously cleared of a dozen deadly puff-adders). Afterwards, the King and his family embarked in a small boat; they were accompanied by the Minister of Transport and his wife, whose combined weight – no mean one – gave the royal boat a decided list as it navigated towards the place where a *braaivleis* (barbecue) had been arranged. The *braaivleis* over, the Royal Family and everyone else stretched out on the grass and dozed off.

Not long afterwards, a loud snoring woke me; it was the King, who lay on his back, dead to the world, affectionately watched by his elder daughter. He slept on another ten minutes, while, one by one, people around him stirred and sat up. Then he himself awoke, with that shy, boyish look he always had when slightly embarrassed. In a moment he was on his feet and striding off on a walk through the bush, leaving his youngest daughter, Margaret, still fast asleep.

One evening I had a long talk with the King, 'something of a heart-to-heart' I wrote in my diary without further details, except that I asked him if he could suggest to the Princesses, in a fatherly way, that they might talk more to people in the crowd, for it had been remarked that they were shy and hung back.

The King owed so much to the gracious – and tenacious – support of the Queen; she was indefatigable and even the hardest republican hearts melted before her radiance. The King moved people more by his simplicity and goodness, which were so obviously genuine. When a huge black crowd of Africans roared their greeting *A Sozizwe!* Father of Nations! it was with real feeling; and at Pretoria, veteran *Outstryders*, Boers who had fought against Queen Victoria, knelt and kissed the hand of her great-grandson.

And so the King of South Africa journeyed on among his people, Boer, Bantu and British; through Natal, with its British connection, and the rich pastures of African Swaziland, and on into the one-time Boer republic of the Transvaal. There, the King and his family came to Johannesburg, the city of gold, the greatest city in all Africa – which but a generation ago had been a collection of shacks huddled about the gold diggings.

They drove all day in torrid heat for some 120 miles, through the mining towns of the Rand, and received their most massive welcome of the whole tour. Hundreds of thousands of sweating, screaming, frenzied blacks lined the route, pressed about the car, waved frantically and hollered their ecstatic joy at the sight of this little family of four, so fresh and white and – apparently – demure, seated in the back of the open royal Daimler. I was up front, next to the chauffeur.

Despite appearances, however, everyone in that car was uncomfortably tense; we were all in for a rough ride. The King, as I have said, looked as if he were the most phlegmatic of men. In reality, he possessed a very highly-strung temperament which at times got the better of his self-control. He was by now exhausted by his travels and the cares of state and, that day, his nerves were badly on edge.

He immediately took over the driving from the back seat and soon had the chauffeur rattled. Hemmed in by the teeming, hysterical crowds, the car edged its way through the Reef towns: Waterkloof, Zesfontein, Putfontein, Geduld Mine and on through Springs and Brakpan. While the incessant tirade from the back seat continued, I kept up a patter with the chauffeur, trying to calm and encourage him. Behind, the Queen was doing her best to sooth the King and the Princesses were trying to make light of things, which became so bad that I felt there was only one thing for it. I turned round – and shouted angrily – and with a disrespect of which I was ashamed: 'For Heaven's sake, shut up, or there's going to be an accident.'

Then it happened, not an accident, but something which looked far worse. It was as we entered Benoni. First, I saw a blue-uniformed policeman, ahead of the car, come racing towards us, with a terrible, determined look in his eyes, which were fixed on something behind us. I turned, to see another man, black and wiry, sprinting, with terrifying speed and purpose, after the car. In one hand he clutched something, with the other he grabbed hold of the car, so tightly that the knuckles of his black hands showed white. The Queen, with her parasol, landed several deft blows on the assailant before he was knocked senseless by policemen. As they dragged away his limp body, I saw the Queen's parasol, broken in two, disappear over the side of the car. Within a second, Her Majesty was waving and smiling, as captivatingly as ever, to the crowds.

At Benoni town hall, where we stopped, I discovered that the African, who had looked like an assassin, was in fact one of His Majesty's most loyal subjects. As he rushed towards the car he was crying 'My King! My King!' and in his hand he clutched a ten-shilling note, a birthday present for Princess Elizabeth, soon to be twenty-one. The King was upset about this mis-guided gesture of loyalty and asked me to find out if the man was all right. 'I hope he was not too badly hurt,' he said.

It was typically thoughtful of him, but did nothing to allay my own feelings of remorse and disgust – at the King's disarray and my own angry and ill-mannered reaction. That evening, at Government House, I talked to Tommy Lascelles, telling him that I felt like throwing in my hand. Never again did I want to get involved in such a lamentable scene.

Tommy was soothing; he convinced me that I was doing a useful job. But he added, 'When I first saw you three years ago, I remarked to Joey that it was a pity to let you in for the job, little knowing, as you did, what was in store for you!'

It was nearly midnight when the King sent for me. All he said, very simply and with complete sincerity, was: 'I am sorry about today. I was very tired.' More than ever before, I realised how lovable the man was.

The Royal Family now made a side-trip to Rhodesia. At Salisbury, the King of Rhodesia opened parliament, which paid homage to His Majesty. A few days later, he himself stood in awe before the splendid, puissant majesty of the Victoria Falls, where the Zambesi, a mile wide, plunges over a 400 foot precipice, while a column of spray, *Mosi-oa-tun-ya*, the Smoke that thunders, rises to twice that height into the air above.

From the Victoria Falls, the southward trek began, by way of the arid spaces of Bechuanaland (Botswana), Mafeking and Kimberly, where £3 million worth of uncut diamonds – a month's output – were displayed. While Their Majesties were admiring them, I slipped off to the Bank to cash a cheque for £50, to pay for a few small gifts they had bought.

By 20 April we were back where we started, at Government House, Cape Town. When I woke up next morning it was as if I had dreamed the whole of that fabulous two-months' odyssey, the thousands of miles we had travelled, the hundreds of thousands of people we had seen.

Thirty miles from Cape Town is a beautiful seventeenth century Dutch farmhouse, Vergelegen, and it was there that all my impressions of the beloved country were consummated. Three mornings running, I rose at 5 a.m., drove out to Vergelegen for a gallop over the hills, and returned in time for the day's work.

When I spoke to the Queen of this enchanted place, she asked me to take the King and herself out there. They were overcome by its loveliness; never did I hear them express such pleasure. The Princesses resisted my attempts to persuade them to come and ride over the hills into the dawn. They were too tired. I thought of Rosemary and wrote, 'You must come with me one day to this lovely place.'

CHAPTER 15

Pressures on a marriage

Rosemary, however, was in no mood, either, to be persuaded, as I discovered when I returned to England two weeks later, in May 1947. I hurried back to Adelaide Cottage, eager to see my wife and family. Within a few moments I gathered that something had come between Rosemary and me.

Ours had been a typical wartime marriage. After nearly two years of non-stop operations I had stepped out of my cockpit, succumbed to the charms of the first pretty girl I met and, within a few weeks, married her. We might have loved each other and left it at that, but that was not a solution to my craving for a rock and an anchor. I was determined to have and to hold her – till death did us part, and that we knew, like every other young couple who married in war-time, might be all too soon. The consciousness, in wartime, of impending death, spurs people on to urgent, reckless marriage.

I cannot help feeling that the sex-urge is a rather unfair device employed by God. He needs children and counts on us to beget them. But while He has incorporated in our make-up an insatiable capacity for the pleasures which flow from love, He seems to have forgotten to build in a monitoring device, to warn us of the unseen snags which may be lurking further on. Unless it be intelligence. But sex is an enemy of the head, an ally of the heart. Boys and girls, madly in love, generally do not act intelligently. The sex-trap is baited and set and the boys and girls go rushing headlong into it. They live on love and kisses, until there are no more left. Then they look desperately for a way of escape.

In 1945, the year the war ended, there were some 15,600 divorces in England and Wales, over 33,000 the following year and, in 1947, 52,000. That was when our marriage began to founder.

On the surface, we had everything going for us. I had a
steady job and, thanks to the King's kindness, my family were
installed in a most charming, if chilly, house. Yet it was at
Adelaide Cottage that our marriage finally broke up. But not
before we had held on for another five years, while our in-
compatibility weighed more and more heavily and our paths
separated. We did our best to avoid hurting one another, but
hurt one another we did, inevitably, for a dying marriage is a
very hurtful process.

Our problems were intrinsic and personal. One of them was
that Rosemary's fierce opposition to my ravings about South
Africa and my longing for horizons beyond the narrow life at
home, had brought to the surface a fundamental difference both
in our outlook on life and our approach to it. This discovery
triggered off in me a reaction, latent since the air battles and
congenital, I dare say, to some airmen – Lindbergh and Saint
Exupéry were famous examples – against the conventional
existence, the 'system', the establishment, with its taboos, its
shibboleths and its obsession with class status. Rosemary
preferred to remain ensconsed in her world of the 'system' and
its social ramifications – and why not, if that was her pleasure?
But in me there were stirrings of a revolt against it; a state of
mind that had been affected by the passion, the danger and –
inevitably – the horror which belonged to flying, with the
resultant contempt it created for the earthly order.

The occupational hazards of a member of the King's household occasionally, it is true, put a strain on family life but they
were no greater than in a number of other situations. My own
duties kept me away from my family a certain amount and
sometimes sent me off far from home.

In the autumn of 1947 I was attached to Princess Margaret's
small entourage when she went to Belfast to launch the liner
Edinburgh Castle. Watching the liner as it glided down the slipway, I thought back to that early morning long ago at Bideford
when I had run with my brothers to the little shipyard to watch
my first launching. Even more, I thought of my family at
Adelaide Cottage and longed to be back with them.

With the *Edinburgh Castle* launching, the Princess launched herself, also, on her career of public service. Though only seventeen, she stepped up to fulfil some of the tasks previously left to her elder sister, who, in the immediate future, had more pressing and personal things on her mind. Princess Elizabeth was shortly to be married to the Duke of Edinburgh.

Before I ever met Prince Philip, I was prepared to like him. He had served in the destroyer *Chequers*, whose captain was my brother Michael. Michael had often extolled to me the Prince's virtues as a sailor. My admiration for him increased when he became a pilot. I never, however, got to know Prince Philip well, though we quite often fought each other nearly to a standstill in the squash court at Buckingham Palace and on the badminton court at Windsor Castle. These sporting affrays left me with the impression, which remains indelible, of the Prince as a genial, intelligent and hard-hitting extrovert.

Princess Margaret, meanwhile, was getting into her stride as a public figure. In the autumn of 1948, she attended Queen Juliana's inauguration at Amsterdam. Once again, I was attached to the Princess's entourage, a larger and more distinguished one this time. Without realising it, I was being carried a little further from home, a little nearer to the Princess.

That summer I had accompanied the King on his customary visit to the Palace of Holyroodhouse, Edinburgh, that somewhat sinister landmark in Scottish history, where, from a small upper room, David Rizzio, the private and rather too personal secretary of Mary Queen of Scots, was dragged, shrieking, from the Queen's presence, to be stabbed to death. Taking a few of the uninitiated, including me, under her wing, Princess Margaret led us up a narrow staircase and, not without a touch of ghoulish pleasure, showed us the fatal spot.

Once, I climbed with the King towards the summit of the hill behind the palace, Arthur's Seat. Normally, he walked with a remarkably long, steady stride, but that evening he laboured and kept muttering, 'What's the matter with my blasted legs? They won't work properly!'

He had first noticed the cramp in his legs earlier in the year but, instead of complaining or doing anything about it, he insisted, typically, on going through with his heavy programme of engagements. Only at the end of October, some weeks after Princess Margaret's return from Holland, did he send for his doctor, Sir Morton Smart.

On further examination, the King's medical advisers discovered that he was suffering from arteriosclerosis; they even feared that the right leg might have to be amputated. However, the risk of amputation was removed by rest and treatment, and the King got better. But in March 1949 his doctors decided that, to maintain the improved condition of the right leg and enable him to get about normally, a right lumbar sympathectomy operation was necessary. It was successfully performed on 12 March.

About this time, the King's junior private secretary, Edward Ford, was due to leave for Rome in an aircraft of the King's Flight. His mission, no concern of mine, was to discuss arrangements for a forthcoming visit to Italy by Princess Margaret. I thought it would be fun to go along, just for the ride; so I asked the King and he agreed.

It was my first visit to Rome, and Edward rivalled Karl Baedeker himself, showing me every museum and monument worth seeing. One evening, he announced: 'Tomorrow morning we have a private audience with Pope Pius XII' – we two heretics, Edward dressed in rather loud brown checks and I, in a grey flannel suit and brown crêpe-soled suede shoes! 'But Edward, we can't, not in these clothes,' I protested. 'You're supposed at least to wear a dark suit, if not morning dress!' 'Don't worry' Edward replied, 'I have a pair of evening shoes – they'll tone down my check suit.' 'No they won't,' I groaned. 'They'll make you look exactly like an Italian waiter.'

Edward refused to be put off and next morning, with his black patent leather shoes gleaming and the soles of my brown ones squeaking on the polished floor, we bowed our way into the presence of His Holiness.

What struck me most about the Pope were his hands, with their long, sensitive fingers, delicately, suavely expressive, smooth as satin. Pius XII, who had once been a diplomat, chatted away in good English; he made most of the running, answering our own remarks with a single, oft-repeated word: 'Fine, fine . . .' Then he gave us each a little medallion and blessed us.

On my return home, I passed the medallion on to Giles. He was then seven and at a kindergarten in Windsor, run on non-denominational lines by catholic sisters. Apparently unable to impress his teachers, Giles lingered near the bottom of his class, so I told him to show the medallion to the sister-in-charge and tell her where it had come from. It produced a small oecumenical victory. Things went better for Giles in future.

The cruellest problem posed by an unsuccessful marriage concerns, nearly always, the children. We were both devoted to ours, yet the differences between us, evidently irreconcilable, were bound sooner or later to affect our small sons.

Meanwhile they were growing up happily. Giles went on to the local school, St George's, in Windsor, where he cultivated his little circle of friends. One of them was blue-eyed, fresh-faced and fair-haired, like him. Together they careered along the narrow paths of the Home Park on their bicycles, trying to excel one another in speed and daring. Years after, I met Giles's friend again at Monaco; he was driving in the Grand Prix. His name was Piers Courage. Sadly, the day came when Piers died for his love of speed.

CHAPTER 16

Death of a King

When, in June 1949, Princess Margaret returned, via Paris, from her Italian holiday, her lady-in-waiting, Jennifer Bevan, asked me to go with her to London airport to meet the Princess. The latter's comings and goings were of no particular concern to me; airports, on the other hand, were and since I enjoyed Jennifer's company, I readily agreed. I was glad of this small break from the monotonous routine, all the more so because it answered, in a very small way, a complaint, recently expressed by an Air Ministry pundit, that 'the R.A.F. was not sufficiently represented at court', no doubt a hint that he expected me to push to the front.

But there came to my mind an original idea which would represent the R.A.F. at court not in a social but in a thoroughly airman-like way. I put the idea to Princess Margaret. She was the youngest of the Royal Family, the Royal Air Force the youngest of the services. Would she, I asked, consent to enter an aircraft for the annual King's Cup air race – which I had so passionately watched as a school-boy, when Ashcroft took me to Heston for the finish, and in which I now proposed to compete, piloting the Princess's aircraft. Sportingly, but with no wild show of enthusiasm, the Princess agreed.

The aircraft in question was a Miles Whitney Straight and the race was held over a closed circuit near Birmingham at the end of July. Thinking that it might make a pleasant change for Rosemary, I took her along with me. She, of course, stayed on the ground during the race, in which I finished nowhere, though I sweated a lot and frightened myself even more. Two aircraft collided, killing the pilots.

As if this was not enough to put Rosemary off flying for ever. my engine, after the flogging it had received during the race. began to grumble unpleasantly on the way home. As I flew on, my ear tuned finely to the engine note, my anxiety was not relieved by Rosemary's repeatedly expressed conviction that we should finish up like those other two unfortunate pilots. Instead of providing the pleasant distraction that I had planned to help us forget our marital problems, the day ended with our nerves more on edge than ever.

And so we drifted on, month after month. When, next year, 1950, I flew a Hurricane – again entered by Princess Margaret – in the King's Cup, Rosemary was not there. This time I decided to make a determined effort to win the race – again a handicap one over a closed circuit, held at Wolverhampton. I practised over the course until, flying on the 'deck' at nearly 300 m.p.h. in my hotted-up Hurricane, I knew by heart every vital tree and steeple, contour and cabbage patch along the course. My most dangerous rival looked likely to be a Spitfire, piloted by a lady, Miss Sharpe. It had a slightly greater handicap than my Hurricane, but neither of us started until many of the lighter aircraft had already completed their first circuit.

Down went the starter's flag and for the next forty-five minutes I streaked across the fields at full bore in the brave old Hurricane, nicknamed 'The Last of the Few', feeling, as I flashed past the smaller aircraft, as if I, too, was back in my hey-day. Five miles from the finish I had only one more aircraft to catch. I failed, but by such a narrow margin that I had overtaken it before it reached the far side of the airfield – where there happened to be a cricket match in progress. I enjoyed some malicious pleasure at seeing players, umpires and all fling themselves flat as my Hurricane skimmed over their heads.

The Spitfire, meanwhile, had got itself lost, otherwise its pilot might have done what I did – create a world's speed record over a closed circuit. Not until years later, when reading a newspaper clipping, did I hear about my remarkable feat!

A couple of months later, in August 1950, there came a pleasant surprise, in the form of my appointment as assistant Master of the Household – a position which, while it tended to confirm me as a permanent fixture in the King's household, tended also to dislodge me further from the insecure place I occupied in my own.

My office, cosy and green-carpeted, was on the south side of Buckingham Palace and the sun, when it shone, came clean through my window; it was a little paradise compared with the gloomy equerry's room, and well off the beaten track of busy secretaries and distinguished visitors who trudged up and down the red-carpeted corridor in the north wing. Green was the basic colour on our side of the house. It felt fresher, almost rural and, above all, less regal and ceremonial.

Now that I had a full-time job, Rosemary and I drifted even further apart, each of us going more and more our own way. It was a difficult and sometimes heart-rending time, with the conviction growing on us that a break-up was inevitable. Ours was the classical divorce story; there still remained between us vestiges of real affection, yet conjugal life, practically, emotionally and sentimentally, had come to a standstill. Both of us, in our own way, continued our sterile, uneasy existence.

As usefully and as energetically as I could, I went about my new duties. The King, since his lumbar sympathectomy operation some eighteen months earlier, had been faithfully observing a go-slow régime, though there was no escape for him from the burden of state affairs. By May 1951, people noticed that he was looking very tired. In mid-May he and the Queen managed to get away to Balmoral, taking Princess Margaret with them. A lady-in-waiting and I accompanied them.

His elder daughter, Princess Elizabeth, was the King's pride; she was his heir, his understudy, his affectionate admirer, and played her role, as he did his, dutifully, punctiliously, charmingly.

Princess Margaret was the King's joy. She amused and delighted him and appealed to the lighter side of his nature – he had after all, as a boy, been something of a devil himself. The young Princess gave him a lot of fun. She enchanted him.

The King was not the only one to fall beneath the spell of Princess Margaret. If her extravagant vivacity sometimes outraged the elder members of the household and of London society, it was contagious to those who still felt young – whether they were or not. She was a girl of unusual, intense beauty, confined as it was in her short, slender figure and centred about large purple-blue eyes, generous, sensitive lips and a complexion as smooth as a peach. She was capable, in her face and in her whole being, of an astonishing power of expression. It could change in an instant from saintly, almost melancholic, composure to hilarious, uncontrollable joy. She was, by nature, generous, volatile. She was a *comédienne* at heart, playing the piano with ease and verve, singing in her rich, supple voice the latest hits, imitating the favourite stars. She was coquettish, sophisticated.

But what ultimately made Princess Margaret so attractive and lovable was that behind the dazzling façade, the apparent self-assurance, you could find, if you looked for it, a rare softness and sincerity. She could make you bend double with laughing; she could also touch you deeply.

I was but one among many to be so moved. There were dozens of others; their names were in the papers, which vied with each other, frantically but futilely, in their forecasts of the one whom she would marry.

Yet I dare say that there was not one among them more touched by the Princess's *joie de vivre* than I, for, in my present marital predicament, it gave me what I most lacked – joy. More, it created a sympathy between us and I began to sense that, in her life too, there was something lacking.

That spring of 1951, Balmoral was never more lovely. The sun warmed the scent from the pines and the crisp nights were full of stars. His short holiday in the Highlands gave the King a much-needed rest. But it was not long enough. He needed not a week, but months, to get him over his weariness. Instead, he returned to his endless day of work. Before May was out he was down with 'flu. His doctors found that his left lung was inflamed; they gave him penicillin, but his recovery was slow. He spent June and July convalescing.

In June 1951 I had hoped to compete once again in the King's Cup. The Hawker Hurricane was not available, but Hawkers kindly offered a pre-war Hart biplane which, despite its age (and mine), Princess Margaret once more agreed to enter under her name. This was our third King's Cup, but our chances, slender though they were, with the veteran Hart, were not put to the test. Bad weather prevented the race.

As I flew the Hart back at a leisurely pace from Hatfield to the Hawker airfield at Langley, there was suddenly a loud and alarming bang as one of the interplane bracing wires came adrift. Another of Fate's curious jokes; had the wire broken during the race, in a tight turn at full throttle, the Hart's wings might well have folded.

The King's two months' convalescence had done him good. Early in August he went north to Balmoral, hopeful that the bracing air of the Highlands would restore him completely. At first he enjoyed the shooting and seemed to be in good form.

One day, after a picnic lunch with the guns, I stretched out in the heather to doze. Then, vaguely, I was aware that some-one was covering me with a coat. I opened one eye – to see Princess Margaret's lovely face, very close, looking into mine. Then I opened the other eye, and saw, behind her, the King, leaning on his stick, with a certain look, typical of him: kind, half-amused. I whispered, 'You know your father is watching us?' At which she laughed, straightened up and went to his side. Then she took his arm and walked him away, leaving me to my dreams.

On 21 August, Princess Margaret celebrated her 21st birth-day, at Balmoral, among a small circle of friends, including the Earl of Dalkieth and Mr Billy Wallace. Johnny Dalkieth, war-time sailor, red-haired, tweedy, droll, and Billy, tall, gangling and half-brother of one of my best Cranwell friends, killed in the war, were the two who were most strongly tipped as a husband for the Princess.

Tommy Lascelles favoured Johnny – with some feeling, per-haps, for Johnny's mother, the Duchess of Buccleuch, was a Lascelles. Drily, Tommy remarked to me: 'Dalkieth and the Princess were making sheep's eyes at each other last night, at dinner.' That, as far as Tommy was concerned, apparently clinched matters.

The weather at Balmoral turned wet and cold. The King caught a chill, yet insisted on going out to shoot. But now he no longer strode on the hill as of old, with his light, long gait, but laboured, coughing and leaning on his crummock. After dinner, while the house-party continued, singing and dancing and gaily laughing in the drawing-room, the King would retire to his room on the floor above.

One evening he rang for me. I entered his room and found him standing there, a lonely, forlorn figure. In his eyes was that glaring, distressed look which he always had when it seemed that the tribulations of the world had overcome him. Above the rhythm of the music and the dancing coming up from below, he almost shouted at me: 'Won't those bloody people ever go to bed?'

It was the Queen who, suspecting that the King was suffering from something worse than a catarrhal inflammation, made him send to London for his doctors. They examined him at Balmoral on 1 September, only some ten days after the rejoicings of Princess Margaret's twenty-first birthday. Their suspicions concerning the King's health were confirmed by a bronchoscopy made on him in London on the 15th, when they identified a malign growth in his left lung. The King made light of his infection, but on 18 September the doctors informed him that his left lung would have to be removed.

The operation was performed on 23 September by Mr Clement Price Thomas in the Buhl Room at Buckingham Palace. During it, the doctors saw that the other lung was also affected. The King could not be expected to live for more than two years.

Despite which, those who hung about the throne expected him to employ to the maximum his remaining time on earth. Only three days after this ghastly operation, along came the King's private secretary to lay before him state papers for signature. He signed, though still very weak, in his long sloping hand.

In this condition I met him, one day, in the corridor outside his room. Clad in a blue dressing gown, he looked frail and thin; he had lost 21 lbs since the operation. But he smiled warmly, almost apologetically, for when he spoke it was not in his firm, deep voice, but in a thin whisper.

The King now knew that the two operations for his arterial and lung complaints placed him under a double sentence of death. He was condemned and the execution might not for long be stayed. This supreme test he faced with the courage that he had always shown in the past. When still in his 'teens, it had been said of him that he showed 'grit and a never-say-die spirit'. Someone else had said 'He has tremendous guts'. This sort of courage, the quiet kind, had seen him through the humiliation of his stammer, the torment of his elder brother's abdication, the blackest moments of the war and the post-war gloom in which his empire broke up and his kingdom retrogressed into economic ruin.

The King surprised everybody by his rapid recovery. Less than a month after his operation he was writing to his mother, 'I must now start to get up and do more to get stronger'. From Dr Malan, now Prime Minister of South Africa, the anti-monarchist who had snubbed the King during his visit to that country, there came a warm invitation to His Majesty to spend his convalescence in the prime minister's official residence in Natal. The King sent me to look at the house.

In mid-January 1952 I landed at Johannesburg where reporters questioned me about the King's health. I had seen him a few days ago, I told them, and he looked fine. One reporter, a toad-like gentleman called Eric Kennedy, asked me if I could confirm a report that Princess Margaret was going to marry Lord Dalkieth. I told him I could not. It was, unfortunately, not the last time that I should hear from Eric Kennedy.

I reported to the King at Sandringham at the end of January. He seemed well and cheerful and was looking forward to his holiday in South Africa. On the 30 January, on the eve of Princess Elizabeth's and Prince Philip's departure on their tour of Africa, Australia and New Zealand, he came to London for a family reunion. That evening he took his family to Drury Lane Theatre to see South Pacific and I had the good fortune to accompany them.

Next day, at London Airport, he stood, hatless, in a bitingly cold wind and waved his daughter farewell. His face, haggard and drawn, bore the signs of all that he had been through. Both the King and his daughter knew that they might be parted for ever. If that were to be, Princess Elizabeth would always remember that last sight of her father, upright, fearless, his face turned towards the future which, sooner than either imagined, would pass from his hands to hers.

The King returned to Sandringham, there to throw himself into his work and his favourite sport. On Tuesday, 5 February, he enjoyed a great day's shooting. He spent the evening quietly with the Queen and Princess Margaret. At 10.30 he kissed them good-night and retired to bed. A few hours later he died, very peacefully, in his sleep.

CHAPTER 17

Princess Margaret

During 1952, Princess Margaret and I found increasing solace in one another's company. The year began with the Princess's grief, caused by the sudden death of her father; it continued with the change in her own family situation – living alone with her mother (whom she adored) – and the steady deterioration in mine; it ended in the break-up of my family. Not that there would normally have been the slightest connection between her private affairs and mine but for the sympathy which had grown up between us in our particular and purely fortuitous circumstances: the King's death had left a greater void than ever in Princess Margaret's life, while my own was clouded by the failure of my marriage.

If on the material plane, as well as temperamentally, the Princess and I were worlds apart, we responded, in our feelings and emotions, as one.

The King was buried at Windsor on 15 February. His body had lain in state at Westminster Hall, that ancient place of kings and courts of justice, and it was from there that the cortège left that crisp winter's morning. To the measured and mournful beat of the funeral airs of Handel and Chopin, the coffin, borne on a gun-carriage and closely escorted by the King's equerries, proceeded up Whitehall, along the Mall and Piccadilly and through Hyde Park to Paddington station. Never had I known a walk so long, so slow, so sad. From London the train took the coffin to Windsor where, to the lament of bagpipes, it was borne on to Saint George's Chapel. There the great company of mourners stood with bowed heads, as we watched King George VI laid to rest among his ancestors.

In the reshuffle of the late King's and the new Queen's households, I left my post as deputy Master of the Household to become, at the request of Queen Elizabeth, now the Queen Mother, the Comptroller of her household – which meant supervising its internal organisation.

My admiration and affection for Queen Elizabeth was, like everybody's, boundless – all the more so because beneath her graciousness, her gaiety and her unfailing thoughtfulness for others she possessed a steely will. For some months, Queen Elizabeth and Princess Margaret lived on at Buckingham Palace, while Clarence House, in the Mall, was being re-decorated. White, square and solid, Clarence House had only acquired central heating when it was renovated, in 1947, for Princess Elizabeth and Prince Philip. They, on the Princess's accession to the throne, moved, of course, to Buckingham Palace.

This was a busy time for me; my preoccupation with the work going on at Clarence House helped me to keep my mind off my own troubled home, which was now in the last stages of disintegration. Yet we kept up the pretence of conjugal unity. In June, the Queen, the Duke of Edinburgh and Princess Margaret were our guests at Adelaide Cottage. Six months later, to the day, I was awarded a decree *nisi* against Rosemary with the legal custody of our two boys, who were left in the care of their mother. Two months later, she married John de Lazslo. His father, Philip de Lazslo, the celebrated painter, had done portraits, long ago, of both the King and Queen Elizabeth.

For Rosemary, as for me, the calvary was over. I was now on my own and my first taste of solitude in my newly-found state of bachelorhood came a few days later with Christmas, which I spent alone. The break-up of my family had been a traumatic process. When, during the hearing of my case, a photograph, a particularly lovely one, of Rosemary was shown to me for identification, I felt a huge wave of sorrow crash against me and go rolling back across the eleven years of our marriage. Divorce may be the only solution to an unsuccessful marriage, as I believe it was in our case, but those who have never tried it should not imagine that it is a painless process. It is a sad and tormenting one and amputates a part of yourself which belongs both to you and your former partner.

Momentarily, I felt as if I were orbiting in outer darkness. Masochistically, I even wanted to continue that way, to get the full effect of what had happened, to get lost in my loneliness and to see where it would lead me. My reaction was unmistakable: I gravitated back into the atmosphere of that person who all along had shown me such generous sympathy and affection.

A spell of duty took me to Sandringham, where I found Princess Margaret. It was there, one winter's evening, that she had kissed her father good-night, only to receive the cruel news next morning that he was dead. A year had passed since then and now, too, my own ordeal was over. We rediscovered one another, and in a new frame of mind.

We had known each other for nine years, during which time she had grown up from a school girl into a young woman whose beauty, charm and talent had attracted scores of admiring and faithful personal friends. Yet among none of them had she found the man of her choice. That – incredibly – was the lot that destiny had reserved for me. Completely in love with life as she was and surrounded by friends who were both eligible and available – which could not be said of me – I saw little of her as she grew to womanhood, nor was I in the least concerned with her private life. Yet, as the daughter of her father, I had come to know her so well that we could confide in one another.

One afternoon, at Windsor Castle, when everyone had gone to London for some ceremony, we talked, in the red drawing-room, for hours – about ourselves. It was then that we made the mutual discovery of how much we meant to one another. She listened, without uttering a word, as I told her, very quietly, of my feelings. Then she simply said: 'That is exactly how I feel, too.' It was, to us both, an immensely gladdening disclosure, but one which sorely troubled us.

The times that we could share each other's company were infrequent. When they did occur, it was at no social function, nor dinner, nor dance, nor night-club, but on a terrain which was to me, the stranger who had walked into her life, as dear and familiar after all these years, as it was to her, who had always belonged there. It was in her own home that we met, among her own people, surrounded by her memories, which she loved to recount. For Princess Margaret, if she was sophisticated and enjoyed the high-life, loved, more passionately than anything else, her home and her family.

So, with due allowances, did I. Ever since that first visit, in 1944, to Appleton Lodge, I had felt most happy and at ease with them in the atmosphere of their own homes: Royal Lodge, their private house near Windsor, Sandringham and, dearest of all, Balmoral. It was in these places, more than anywhere, that I had come to know and to love this family, and appreciate their kindness, their affection and the feeling of permanence – which, for years, had been so lacking in my own life.

My relationship with them was a simple one, with none of the gloss that some people have put on it: that I was the 'King's adviser', 'closest confidant', etc. That is rubbish. The King's closest confidant was, obviously, his wife, Queen Elizabeth, and, on political matters, his private secretary, Tommy Lascelles. Nor was there any question of my 'advising' the King. He was just about old enough to be my father and had no reason, on important matters, to ask my advice, nor had I any to give him. The relationship, I repeat, was a simple one, motivated as it was by sympathy.

So it was in the midst of her family, in those familiar, well-loved surroundings, that I came to discover Princess Margaret – the person she really was. At Balmoral, dressed in tartan skirt and green tweed jacket, she would sometimes walk with me between drives, a discreet but adequate distance from the rest of the party, so that we could talk en tête-à-tête.

People usually do that in a quiet corner of a bar or bistrot, over coffee or a bottle of wine. We talked while walking on the hill, among the heather, with the breeze in our faces; or riding, in the Great Park at Windsor, along drives flanked with rhododendron and venerable oaks and beeches; or through the pinewoods and across the stubble at Sandringham.

We talked. Her understanding, far beyond her years, touched me and helped me; with her wit she, more than anyone else, knew how to make me laugh – and laughter, between boy and girl, often lands them in each other's arms.

Her individual world and mine may have been widely separated, but we had discovered another world which belonged, jointly and exclusively, to us. In it there grew up between us a warm, profound affection. Absence, distance and our difference of station only tended to deepen it. Now that, at Sandringham, we were together again, we longed, as never before, to remain so – God alone knew how – and never be parted.

Our love, for such it was, took no heed of wealth and rank and all the other worldly, conventional barriers which separated us. We really hardly noticed them; all we saw was one another, man and woman, and what we saw pleased us. How to consummate this mutual pleasure was the problem. Marriage, at this moment, seemed the least likely solution; and anyway, at the prospect of my becoming a member of the Royal Family the imagination boggled, most of all my own. Neither the Princess nor I had the faintest idea how it might be possible for us to share our lives. That depended finally on the British constitution and the Church. But we were not there yet; all we could hope was that, with time and patience, some solution might evolve.

At all events, we wished the Queen to know of our feelings, and these Princess Margaret confided privately to her sister. A few days later, at Buckingham Palace, Her Majesty invited us both to spend the evening with her and Prince Philip. Both were in good spirits and the evening passed off most agreeably. From it there stands out in my memory one unforgettable impression: the Queen's movingly simple and sympathetic acceptance of the disturbing fact of her sister's love for me. Prince Philip, as was his way, may have tended to look for a funny side to this poignant situation. I did not blame him. A laugh here and there did not come amiss. That evening we had several. But, as I sat there with them, the thought occurred to me that the Queen, behind all her warm goodwill, must have harboured not a little anxiety.

Princess Margaret also told her mother, who listened with characteristic understanding. I imagine that Queen Elizabeth's immediate – and natural – reaction was 'this simply cannot be'. But thoughtful as ever for the feelings of others, for her daughter's above all and for mine as well, she did not hurt us by saying so. Without a sign that she felt angered or outraged – or, on the other hand, that she acquiesced – the Queen Mother was never anything but considerate in her attitude to me. Indeed she never once hurt either of us throughout the whole difficult affair, behaving always with a regard for us both, for which I felt all the more grateful because of my own responsibility in the crisis.

Princess Margaret had broken the news to her family: if disconcerted, as they had every reason to be, they did not flinch, but faced it and us with perfect calm and, it must be said, considerable charity.

This was hardly the attitude of the Establishment to which, in the person of Tommy Lascelles (now the Queen's private secretary), I undertook to broach the news. I entered his sombre but spacious office. When, first, Air Chief Marshal 'Peter' Portal, then the King, had initiated me to my job of equerry, both had received me, at my own level, standing. Now that I was on the point of leaving it, Tommy remained seated, regarding me darkly while I stood before him and told him, very quietly, the facts: Princess Margaret and I were in love. Visibly shaken, all that Tommy could say was: 'You must be either mad or bad'. I confess that I had hoped for a more helpful reaction.

Though not entitled, perhaps, to any sympathy from him, it would all the same, have helped. He was a friend and I was asking for his help. I was describing to him a state of affairs which, if thoroughly undesirable, reprehensible even, in his eyes (and, eventually, in a good many others'), was, equally, impossible to ignore. The situation in which the Princess and I found ourselves might be criticised, ridiculed, it might not last. But at the present moment it existed; it was a reality – and a pretty dramatic one, considering all the other factors involved. I was, I told Tommy, quite ready to face the immediate consequences and leave the Queen Mother's household.

Tommy consulted the Queen, of course, doubtless reminding her that under the Royal Marriages Act of 1772, Princess Margaret would have to obtain Her Majesty's consent to her marriage – at least before her 25th birthday. Thereafter she would be exempt from the Queen's veto, but would still need the consent of Parliament, and of the Dominions' parliaments as well.

The crucial point, when it came to the Queen's consent for her sister to marry me, was that I was divorced. The Queen, as titular head of the Church of England, whose canon No. 107 of 1603 forbids divorce, could not, constitutionally, give her consent, unless her prime minister saw fit to advise her otherwise. When the Queen put the matter to Sir Winston Churchill, the prime minister replied, with good reason, that it would be disastrous for the Queen were she to consent, during coronation year of all times, to the marriage of her sister with a divorced man. There was an ironic twist to the premier's counsel, for Churchill's own son, Randolph, was divorced and remarried.

That, then, was that. Princess Margaret would have to wait another two years, until she was twenty-five, before she could hope to contract a legal marriage with me.

Tommy Lascelles (not that I was aware of it) also consulted the Prime Minister. Both agreed that I should leave the Queen Mother's household. Lascelles wanted more – to banish me, forthwith, abroad. However, the Queen, characteristically, would not hear of such drastic measures to separate me from her sister. She insisted, and the Queen Mother agreed, that I be allowed to stay on at Clarence House.

I was not admitted to, or even kept informed of the consultations between Lascelles and the press secretary, Commander Richard Colville, concerning the Princess and myself. I was unaware, therefore, of how events were developing, both locally and in the foreign press. So I can only surmise that the sympathetic gesture of the Queen and her mother was made without full knowledge of all the available facts.

For, incredibly, neither the Queen's nor the Prime Minister's advisers seemed to be paying sufficient attention to reports already circulating in the U.S. and the continental press, not to speak of the rumours flying round London (but not yet in the British papers) about Princess Margaret and myself, and of which we ourselves were ignorant. We two had innocently confided our secret to the inner circles of the Royal Family and, by extension, to the competent authorities – notably the Queen's private secretary, press secretary and prime minister, who were secretly discussing it while the press of America and Europe were openly informing their readers about it. Yet neither of us knew, nobody told us: our secret was out.

The Queen's press secretary, Commander Richard Colville R.N., a thin man with a thin face, straight black hair, black-rimmed spectacles and dressed (invariably, it seemed) in formal black clothes, was a naval paymaster who had distinguished himself gallantly during the war. Richard came to his post, a delicate one and the object of constant, world-wide attention, without any professional experience. After six years of it, he was still being criticised for his handling of press problems, of which, from now on, he was to have more than his fair share.

Whether Colville or Lascelles, his immediate chief, knew anything about the rumours in the foreign press, I do not know. It seems incredible that they did not; in which case, they might have whispered a word in my ear. We were, after all, colleagues. Had they only taken me into their confidence and alerted me to the danger, I would have got out of the way fast, on my own initiative – dutifully, for the sake of the Royal Family, and selfishly, for my own sake. I should have got well clear of the target area, Clarence House and Buckingham Palace – withdrawn, resigned, done anything reasonable to avoid the attention of the press, which at this moment was con-centrated on the Queen's approaching coronation. Now was the time. But the Queen and the Queen Mother, apparently, were not fully aware, while the Princess and I were not aware at all, of a situation which was bound, very shortly, to explode.

Explode it did, on Coronation Day. That morning of Tuesday 2 June, after the splendid and moving service in Westminster Abbey, a great crowd of crowned heads, of nobles and com-mons – and newspapermen, British and foreign – were gathered in the Great Hall. Princess Margaret came up to me; she looked superb, sparkling, ravishing. As we chatted she brushed a bit of fluff off my uniform. We laughed and thought no more of it.

But American reporters, not to say British, had apparently been observing us almost as closely as the coronation itself. Next day, that charming little gesture made the headlines in the New York press.

Even now, Colville did not react, at least towards me, to the reports circulating abroad. I never read the foreign press, and neither he nor anyone else breathed a word to me about the sensation that the Princess and I were providing in the U.S. Had they done so, there would still have been just time for me to fade out before the storm burst, for twelve more days passed before it did so.

Then, on 14 June the news hit the British public. The Sunday newspaper, *The People*, spoke out the first. '*It is high time*' it said, under a banner headline, '*for the British public to be made aware of the fact that newspapers in Europe and America are openly asserting that the Princess is in love with a divorced man and that she wishes to marry him . . . Every newspaper names the man as Group Captain Townsend.*'

Several more paragraphs followed, *The People* remarking that newspapers outside Britain had for weeks printed reports of their forthcoming marriage '*without meeting any official denial*'. Unbelievably, nobody, including Commander Colville, R.N., had taken what sailors call avoiding action. This was only the beginning of a series of incomprehensible blunders.

Next day, Monday 15 June, Lascelles and Colville could only tell the Queen what was very obvious, that it was now too late to stop the British press from discussing the case of Princess Margaret and myself. Things had been left too late for a denial; what they now proposed was instead virtually a confirmation. They advised the Queen that I should quit my post forthwith and leave the country. The Prime Minister concurred and insisted on a period of one year's separation.

Mr Churchill told the Air Minister, Lord De L'Isle, to find me a job abroad without delay. A choice of three air attaché posts were communicated to Lascelles who summoned me to decide my place of exile: Brussels, Johannesburg or Singapore.

At first I thought he was joking. A few months earlier, as he well knew, I had been awarded the legal custody of my two sons, eleven and eight years old. How did Tommy expect me to exercise legal custody, let alone keep in touch with my young sons, from Johannesburg or Singapore? I chose Brussels – it was Hobson's choice.

Princess Margaret and I were prepared for this sentence of exile, harsh as it was. The Queen, however, was not to be rushed. She was due to visit Northern Ireland on 30 June and, in a most gracious and touching gesture, asked me to accompany her as equerry-in-waiting. The Royal Family, despite the embarrassing circumstances, showed me every possible consideration, for which I now repeat my warm and humble thanks.

The Queen Mother and Princess Margaret were to leave on 29 June for a long-awaited tour of Rhodesia. As the Queen Mother's comptroller, I was to have accompanied them but now, of course, this was out of the question. Lord Plunket, the Queen's equerry, went instead; Patrick was a dear friend, so I was consoled.

Sunshine warmed the Queen Mother's sitting-room at Clarence House when, towards midday on 29 June, I took leave of Her Majesty and Princess Margaret. The Princess was very calm, for we felt certain of each other and, though it was hard to part, we were reassured by the promise, emanating from I know not where, but official, that my departure would be held over until her return on 17 July. We talked less, I think, of her forthcoming journey than of our next meeting, in about three weeks' time. Her mother – I blessed her for her exquisite tact – left us alone for a few precious moments. Then the Princess was gone. We were next to meet, not in three weeks, but in over a year.

Next day, I accompanied the Queen and Prince Philip to Belfast. It was my last duty for the Queen and a most agreeable one – until, in the middle of the civic luncheon, attended by the Queen, in the Ulster capital, Colville's press office announced my appointment as air attaché to the British Embassy at Brussels.

That put the cat among the pigeons. For the rest of the Belfast visit, the public were treated to the embarrassing spectacle of photographers concentrating almost as much on me as on the Queen. It was when she alighted from the aircraft at London airport that they got their final scoop. There on the tarmac, for all to see, the Queen, smiling and charming as always, chatted with me for a few moments. I never admired her more, above all for publicly defying the cries of scandal which were resounding about her sister and me. She was truly Elizabethan. She and Prince Philip shook my hand and wished me good luck, as I bowed and took my final leave.

The sensation caused by the announcement of my transfer to Brussels caused the wheels of Whitehall, closely geared as they were to the secretariat at Buckingham Palace, to accelerate to full speed. Summoned by Tommy Lascelles, I was informed that the final date for my departure was now 15 July – two days before Princess Margaret's return. Instead of our expected farewell, we were to be torn apart. The decision, conveyed to the Princess in Umtali, Rhodesia, came as an unpleasant shock.

Hurriedly, I began packing and saying my goodbyes. The most touching of all was to Joey Legh, my one-time chief, now in retirement. It was he who, over nine years ago, had conducted me to my first meeting with the King. Joey was entirely non-political, essentially human – the surest and most understanding of friends. I never saw him again; he died two years later.

The parting with my sons was particularly harrowing. Those two little boys were boarders at a prep. school in Kent, far from their mother, to whose good care they had been entrusted. Giles was brave, but Hugo, then only eight, cried a lot. He had seen a newspaper headline saying that I, his father, was to be banished and taken it in its literal, medieval sense. I hugged him and promised to come back. But Hugo, I believe, has never quite recovered from that brutal separation.

There was indeed a medieval atmosphere about my impending departure. I was being despatched, willy-nilly, to a virtually, sinecure post in a foreign capital – a hefty come-down after the commands I had previously held in the R.A.F. and my nine years in the Royal Household. I felt rather like a political deportee. I was never consulted, only informed, on occasions, by Tommy.

To add to my discomfort, false statements were being made publicly and in high quarters, about me. To a press enquiry about my post as Comptroller to Queen Elizabeth, Colville's office replied, 'The Queen Mother has never had a Comptroller.' Yet it was she who had personally invited me to accept the post, a new one it is true. An Air Ministry spokesman, replying to a question about my new post in Brussels said, 'This is a natural move if he wishes to pursue his career'. It was, in truth, an unnatural move to an obsolescent post, in which my R.A.F. career was to end.

At this point a wave – it was fortunately only a passing one – of disgust and disillusionment hit me. The R.A.F. had thought well enough of me to recommend me for my post with the King. I had been with the Royal Family for nine years. Now I was being booted out of England. But I quickly got over these feelings; self-pity was no remedy in the present crisis. I had no right to complain. I had offended the Establishment by falling in love with the Queen's sister, for whose heart, let alone hand, I was, by Establishment rules, quite ineligible. Now I was getting my deserts.

I put away rancour and bitterness as a waste of effort. My time at school and my flying years had hardened me to all manner of hazards, hardships and deceptions; they had been an education for survival, and survive this present situation I would. But I never imagined how hard it was going to be.

So I reconciled myself to my exile. It was obviously my duty to accept – anyway, there was no alternative. But by precipitately deporting me the Establishment chiefs were, as it turned out, making a serious error. They counted on my exile to break up our relationship. It did not. It led, on the other hand, to a lamentable crisis in which Crown, Government and Church were all embarrassed.

CHAPTER 18

Exile in Brussels

At daybreak on 15 July 1953, I drove out of London. I felt no regrets at leaving – what had to be, had to be. What sickened me was the manner of my leaving – hustled out of the country so swiftly that my future Ambassador, Sir Christopher Warner, had no warning of my arrival. He was away, touring the Belgian Congo; when he returned he was naturally embarrassed to find that his quiet embassy in the Rue de Spa, Brussels, had become a hot-bed of world speculation.

Though I longed for nothing more than to fade out, pick up the threads of a normal life and go about my business like anybody else, it was at first not possible. I was still hot news and as I drove into Brussels, in shirt-sleeves and looking like anything but a diplomat, let alone a pretender for the Princess's hand, I was surrounded, every time I stopped to ask the way, by an animated little crowd. At last I found the embassy. Even there a crowd had collected.

Once inside the courtyard I mopped my brow; it was going to need tact and patience to settle down in my new surroundings. The counsellor, Joe Parrott, came to the rescue, taking me off to his home where he and his wife protected me, aided by a police guard outside, and helped me to make my first steps into the diplomatic milieu of Brussels.

In the quiet of Joe Parrott's house I was at last able to think over recent events. The inescapable fact was that Princess Margaret and I, much as we loved each other, could not, if ever we married, do so for another two years, because of the Royal Marriages Act. It was an insurmountable bar, unless or until Parliament abolished it. The act did indeed, at this moment, come in for much indignant criticism and there was a clamour for its abolition. But in a country like Britain, where the monarchy owes much of its stability to the hereditary principle, the act was a safeguard, if an unjust one on legal and humane grounds, to this principle, a safeguard not lightly to be set aside.

The Royal Marriages Act was conceived by the Queen's ancestor George III who believed that royalty should marry royalty. George's brothers, the Dukes of Cumberland and Gloucester had thought otherwise – they married commoners. So did George's son (later George IV) who – heinous crime – wed a catholic lady, Mrs Fitzherbert. The Royal Marriages Act was intended to clear up the mess and, above all, protect the succession from undesirable pretenders.

Broadly, the Act stated that no descendant of George III could marry, before the age of twenty-five, without the sovereign's consent. Beyond that age, if the sovereign still disapproved, the consent of the British (and Dominions') Parliament would be required. The wretched royal lover was caught either way. The Act was presented to Parliament in 1772. Walpole, presaging Winston Churchill in another context, said of it 'Never was an act passed against which so much, and for which so little was said'. Nevertheless, in 1953 the Act was still law. Not all the conjugal extravagances of the Princess's forbears provided a pretext for contravening it – the contrary, rather. Princess Margaret was bound by it until her twenty-fifth birthday, two years hence, on 21 August 1955.

Could Princess Margaret and I have been left in peace, privately to live with our problem, time would have worked its soothing, helpful influence. We should have been able to discuss the immense and possibly insurmountable problems that marriage would involve. But now that our story had hit the world's headlines it was no longer our private affair, one that we could reason out among family and intimate friends. It had been tossed into the forum of world-wide debate, bandied about from continent to continent.

The immediate reactions were diverse and sometimes piquant. The Queen was Head of the State, which permitted divorce; she was also Head of the State Church, which did not. The Queen then, constitutionally, was contradicting herself. The Church formally opposed an eventual marriage, yet its right to do so was not incontestable. Its Canon 107 (unchanged since 1603) forbade divorce, but the Church had always been divided on the question, as well as on the re-marriage of divorced persons whose former spouses were living. At that moment there were hundreds of such people, many of them well known, whom the Church had remarried. One of the most recent was a first cousin of the Queen.

The Cabinet, for political reasons, was against a marriage; morally, however, they were on shaky ground. Mr Eden (later, the Earl of Avon), soon to become prime minister in place of the aging Mr Churchill, had recently divorced and remarried. Four members of the government had been through the divorce courts; three had remarried. Many people objected that it was pure hypocrisy for ministers to uphold the law of the state church in public and to ignore it in their private lives.

A pertinent answer to this objection was that the private life of Mr Eden and the other ministers' – indeed of every citizen – was his own affair; Princess Margaret's private life was the concern of the nation and of the Commonwealth. Against which, it was argued that it would be unjust to deny to the Princess, if the sister still a subject of the Queen, the right to marry a divorced man when every other of the Queen's subjects was allowed by the law of the land to do so. A cry went up, 'If they want to marry, why shouldn't they?'

All this highly embarrassing speculation was in any case premature. There was no thought in the mind either of the Princess or myself of immediate marriage. We had two years to think about it – but that, with me exiled in Brussels and the public proclaiming their different opinions, was not made any easier.

A fortnight or so after my arrival, Sir Christopher Warner returned from his Congo trip. I was beginning to integrate myself into his embassy. He quickly got over his umbrage at my unheralded arrival and became, with his sister, Miss Warner (who ran his bachelor household), the warmest and surest of friends.

Briskly, amiably and most effectively, Miss Warner organised Her Britannic Majesty's ambassador in Brussels and, when she got the chance, the rest of us on his staff, as well. He himself was always imperturbable; his speech, however serious the subject, was flavoured with humour. He was the classical diplomat.

The ambassador held a weekly meeting on Tuesdays to which I looked forward as the brightest hour in my decidedly boring week of office work, for I was then able to get a glimpse of the work of my diplomatic colleagues. One Tuesday the ambassador raised a grave problem. He had recently visited the battlefield of Waterloo, some fifteen miles south of Brussels; having studied all the exhibits, films and so on, 'I came away,' he told us sadly, 'with the unmistakable impression that the French had won. We *must* do something, gentlemen, to put the record straight.'

I settled into a modern ground-floor flat, pleasantly furnished, with dark blue curtains and grey carpeting, in the Square Louise, next to the Bois de la Cambre. It suited me perfectly, as did my immediate neighbours, Mademoiselle Orban, a dear person, physically handicapped, and her one-time English nanny, Miss Frances Williams. Living, as I was, cheek by jowl with them, they were good neighbours – kindly and not inquisitive.

Madame Wagner, from the English north country and married to a Belgian, came in daily to keep house. She treated me so severely that I felt like a small boy, but she invariably collapsed into hilarious laughter when I outraged her conventional outlook. Madame Wagner, or Mrs as she liked me to call her, was one of those rare, faithful servants who are, indisputably, the bosses.

I warmed quickly to the Belgians, '*les petits belges*', whose small country is full of generous-hearted giants who welcome the foreigner with open arms. There is a Bruegelian side to every Belgian; they are earthy and fun-loving and, like the English, have an instinct for maintenance and order which they apply to their gardens, their artistic treasures, their folklore and their friendship. '*La joyeuse Belgique*': I soon felt at home there.

Since I was recognised everywhere, I avoided going anywhere. My social life was limited to two main outlets. First the official, with its endless luncheons, dinners and cocktail parties. To some of them I was invited less, I suspect, because of my gifts as a diplomat than to provide the other guests with a close-up of me. I always responded to other people's curiosity in me with an equal curiosity in them. It is a rewarding and invariably successful defensive technique.

The other outlet was provided by my growing circle of friends. There was the diplomatic circle: Colonel James Curry, the U.S. Air-Attaché – with quiet Jim and his vivacious wife, Donna, I could relax and laugh. Colonel René de Wattre, the French Military Attaché, always gave me the pleasing senation that I was breaking his conventional military French ice. Considering that I was supposed to be a suitor for the Princess's hand, he was faintly scandalised by my disrespect for diplomatic usage. 'Peter, you are a naughty boy' he would reprove me, with his delicious French accent.

Colonel Drummond-Wolff, the British Military Attaché, a formidable giant in his Black Watch regalia and bristling moustache, was my closest colleague. At first, he sniffed contemptuously at this upstart from the junior service who had caused such an unseemly flutter. Robin Drummond-Wolff was one of those bulwarks of the Establishment who put the regiment first and the griefs of the soldiery afterwards. But behind his terrible, tartaned façade I discovered a mellow heart. He melted towards me, no doubt encouraged by his redoubtable but kind-hearted wife, Anne, and I came to enjoy them as human beings.

In the *Force Aérienne*, the Belgian air force, I rediscovered friends who, during the war, had escaped to join the R.A.F. in England. The old ties were still strong: Leon de Soomer, 'Mr D.' who commanded No. 3 Fighter Squadron at West Malling, where I was station-commander, was now a top-ranking general. In order to furnish information to London on air matters in Belgium, I did not have to be a James Bond. I just asked Mr D, or one of his colleagues, and got the answer.

My own diplomatic colleagues showed much kindness to this odd creature in their midst. Another good friend was Henri Claudel, of the French Embassay, son of (and incidentally with a remarkable resemblance to) the great Paul Claudel. In the

little square where I lived were affluent neighbours who nonetheless took me, an impecunious and somewhat renegade airman, into their midst. One, Prince 'Bertie' de Ligne, had been
a corporal in the war-time R.A.F.

And there was Renée Lippens, a kind of Boadicea, as big of
heart as she was of frame. She, too, had escaped to England in
the war. Lingering, pending identification, in a British prison,
she had been delighted by an official letter from the War Office
which ended 'I am, Madam, your obedient servant.' Her
identity established, she was parachuted back into Belgium.

Renée was a woman of courage, and a great morale-builder.
A fervent catholic, she invited me to her home, where I met
priests and savants with whom, *en têtê-à-tête*, over the dinner
table and late into the night, I discussed the Christian doctrine –
and many others, too – on matters of life and death, and notably
on the indissolubility of marriage.

I found these holy and erudite men very straightforward,
understanding and easy to approach, and I was struck by their
tolerance for the frailty of men and their mercy towards me, a
sinner in their eyes. It would not be betraying them, I think, to
say that they saw my point. But as servants of the Roman
Church they were unable to identify themselves with it.

By the end of 1953 I was settling down quietly in Brussels. A
British newspaper, looking back over the events of that year,
recalled the 'rumours which had linked' me with Princess
Margaret 'handsome and reassured at the Coronation, harassed
and distraught' during my precipitate departure in July. It now
depicted me as 'faded from the limelight – lapsing into slow
oblivion'. This was fine. I desired nothing more than to retire
into the shadows and find peace in which to think clearly.

How much more profitable could it have been, had I been
able, to discuss these pressing problems face to face with
Princess Margaret. We wrote almost every day, but that was
not the same. Audibly, visually and tangibly we were separated.
Our own world was a vacuum which had to be endured day in,
day out, and during the yearning hours of the night.

If I was 'the loneliest man in Brussels', I had found a

welcome port of call in Antwerp. Pure chance took me there. One autumn afternoon shortly after my arrival, friends took me to a horse-show in Brussels. I was watching spell-bound, like everyone else, a young girl, Marie-Luce Jamagne, as she flew over the jumps with astonishing grace and dash. Suddenly, with a timber-shivering crash, her horse fell. Its young rider lay senseless, practically at my feet. I immediately left my seat and went to where she lay. My friend Didi van Derton, one of the judges, was already there. 'She'll be all right,' he said. Later he introduced me to her parents.

Early in 1954 they invited me to their home in Antwerp. They had not forgotten the days when the Canadians had liberated Antwerp and they had welcomed them to their home. I was no liberator; rather, I needed liberating from myself, and this 'la famille Jamagne' did. They showered me with kindness; their home, far from the guessing and the gossip which surrounded me in Brussels, was a safe and a blessed haven. It was always open to me and in time I became one of the family. That is what I still am today. Marie-Luce, the girl who fell at my feet, has been my wife for the last eighteen years.

It was no doubt because Mr Sydney Rodin was convinced that I was the loneliest man in Brussels, that he flew there 'to seek the truth' as he said. The 'news exclusive' that Sydney wrote about me, 'the man with the royal romance rumours', was nauseating.

Under the heading 'Townsend and the beautiful countess', Sydney Rodin now had me hooked up with a charming but completely disinterested acquaintance. According to Rodin, the 'former Buckingham Palace aide', whose air of sadness was so marked, now seemed deliriously happy in the presence of the countess, whom he was free to marry. The simple truth was that the lady, a close friend of a friend of mine and not, therefore, a likely bride for me, owned a horse called Tourbillon. I bought it. That was all.

I had had some encouraging success in hunter trials in England; I wanted, now, to try my hand at show-jumping. Unfortunately, Tourbillon was nearing the end of his brilliant show-jumping career; I was only starting mine, which was to prove far less brilliant.

Slowly, I was coming out of my shell. Encouraged by Jacques du Roy de Blicquy, Belgium's leading amateur rider, I rode my first gentleman-rider race in April, at Groenendal, a gem of a race-course in the woods near Brussels. It was the start of a new and exciting sporting career whose only drawback, I was soon to find, was that, among gentlemen-riders, the gentlemen are fewer than the riders.

Every morning I would rise at dawn and drive through the Forêt de Soignes to the gallops at Groenendal. Spring had begun to brush a timid green on to the gaunt, leafless trees, and day by day the foliage grew until the forest was swathed in green.

Then, in the midst of this idyllic prospect of spring and peace and pleasantness, the press began sniping again. Nothing serious, but they were the last people I wanted to hear from. Mr Kennedy hopped, like a toad, from out of some dark corner. I once more appeared in print, this time as 'the man who once made the headline news'.

In July I flew to England. Unknown to me, the official in the B.E.A. office in Brussels booked my ticket in his name. So, quite innocently, I travelled as 'Mr Carter'. When the *Sunday Pictorial* found out, it asked, the following sabbath, with grinding irony, '*Are we to understand that this comparatively junior diplomat has a private life to justify a device normally used by people high in the affairs of state?*'

What the *Sunday Pictorial* had not, fortunately, discovered is that when I reached London I went straight to Harrods, to the bookshop, where, as arranged with Princess Margaret (who had of course told the Queen), I met Brigadier Norman Gwatkin of the Lord Chamberlain's office. His rubicund face shone like a friendly beacon among all those books. Norman led me to a waiting car and we drove to Clarence House, straight in through the main gates. The press had no idea that I was in England.

Princess Margaret and I had not met for a year. Our joy at

being together again was indescribable. The long year of waiting, of penance and solitude, seemed to have passed in a twinkl-
ing. We were together for a couple of hours and talked as if we
had left off only yesterday. We did not discuss the future; all we
knew was that for the present our feelings for one another had
not changed. Another year's wait remained, until the Princess's
twenty-fifth birthday, when she would be free of the Queen's
official veto on her marriage. Until then, there was nothing for
it but to hold on and wait. Until then . . . But events were not to
turn out so simply as that.

It was a joy, too, to be reunited with Giles and Hugo. I had
been forcibly separated from my sons for a year; now they were
reassured that their father had not been banished for life.

Then I returned to Brussels. There, every morning, I rode a
gallop at Groenendal, under the benevolent but eagle eye of
Alfred Hart, one of Belgium's leading trainers. Dear Alfred, he
was one of my truest friends. Thanks largely to him, I had
become passionately keen on amateur racing.

Though, as a spectacle, racing bores me, I found race-riding
was, of all sports, the most exhilarating and required the greatest
exertion. I kept my weight at a constant 10 stone 3 lbs and often
went below to make the weight. I began to understand what
drove Fred Archer, the greatest of English jockeys before Gordon
Richards and Lester Piggott, to suicide. He was over 6 ft tall.
Physically and mentally, race-riding kept me in hard condition.
I felt I should need to be, in order to survive the future.

An odd mixture of language streamed forth from Alfred's
racing stables; basically it was the *Bruxellois* dialect – French,
heavily accented and flavoured with Flemish. But the lads invariably (and frequently) swore in English. Evidently, they
found the vocabulary richer and more satisfying.

I rode my first winner for Alfred soon after my return from
England. We celebrated a win when we could, by dining together. Alfred was a lover of *la bonne chère* and would always say,
as he filled my glass with a sturdy Burgundy *'Allez, buvez, c'est du
sang!'* Alfred, incidentally, was English and proud of it. But he
could hardly speak the language.

I kept on riding in horse-shows, too, but I enjoyed it less and less until it became torture. It was partly a question of nerves – performing alone in the presence of a crowd was never my line. Then, Tourbillon was not in form. He was still a great jumper, but there was invariably one jump which he refused – I, almost invariably, arrived in a heap on the other side.

The press enjoyed these performances much more than I. Photos were captioned 'Flying feet and empty saddle' or 'The airman who didn't take off'. Fun for them; for me it proved that they were still on the watch. A man called Harry Proctor wrote a silly piece for the *Sunday Pictorial*: 'Silent Peter is so choosy . . . I wanted to see him on official business. I report my failure . . . All this because someone in London court circles put around a rumour that Princess Margaret was in love with him. That rumour made Peter Townsend. He is adopting the rôle of a male Garbo.' Harry knew nothing, and I continued to keep my peace.

CHAPTER 19

Marking time

Early in March 1955, I took ten days leave. For the first two I enjoyed perfect peace, walking alone in the Forêt de Soignes, listening to the urgent chatter of migrating birds, feeling the 'day-spring from on high' as it woke the forest into new life. Nature was stirring to the call of spring. So, unfortunately, was the press.

Princess Margaret returned from her Caribbean tour – and suddenly I was pitched out of my placid retreat back into world headlines. A New York paper, hearing that the chapel in Saint James's Palace was to be restored, immediately deduced that the Princess and I were to be married in it. Some London newspapers (which I did not read) were loudly proclaiming that now the 'Dolly Princess', as they called her, was back from the West Indies, she must make up her mind – about me, of course.

On Monday 2 March I walked out of my apartment and was immediately surrounded by a posse of newspapermen. They took me completely by surprise. Howard Johnson of the *Daily Mirror* thrust a copy of the *Sunday Pictorial* under my nose. 'Please read it,' he said. I could have done so from a mile away. A huge headline screamed 'PRINCESS MARGARET MARRIAGE SENSATION'.

Then the questions began. I could have replied curtly (but for how long?) 'no comment'. But I decided there and then to answer the reporters. It was a question of honesty, logic and courtesy. It was illogical to run away from the press. I had my life to live, my job to do. It was not possible to remain locked up in my apartment and withstand a siege of dozens of international reporters camped, 24 hours a day, on my doorstep. Besides, their presence caused considerable annoyance to my neighbours. It was obviously not possible to placate that host with denials and 'no comment'. The least that courtesy demanded, both to my neighbours and the reporters themselves, was to come out and make terms with the latter – who proved to be extremely accommodating.

Unfortunately, I found myself alone, in that little Square Louise, facing the world's press. I badly needed professional advice. I should have welcomed a word from Richard Colville. He was the one person who might have helped. I have not the impudence to claim that I had any right to Colville's advice; only that, since I was so closely bound up with Princess Margaret's future, it might have been better if Richard Colville, instead of leaving me to cope alone, had co-operated with me. But not once, during the whole affair, right up to its bitter end, did he contact me or attempt to evolve a joint front with me towards the press.

Colville and the Queen's advisers, including, of course Lascelles' successor Michael Adeane (for whom my warm regard remains, nonetheless, undiminished) apparently believed that the feverish speculation about Princess Margaret and myself which, after two years, had suddenly flared up more intensely than ever, could be quietened by their own silence. I agree, silence is a most powerful weapon, but it was not, in this case, effective. The clamour, over the next six months increased to a deafening crescendo while the 'Margaret-Townsend' affair sank deeper and deeper into a morass of frantic, popular sensationalism. Today, twenty-two years later, that is really the only bitter memory that still lingers with me.

For one whole week, as I went about my daily round, I was questioned and pursued by the press. The weather was bitterly cold and snow lay on the ground. I rose betimes every morning to drive to Alfred Hart's stables at Hoeillart. The reporters were there, shivering. 'The Dawn Patrol', they called it.

I am not clever at beguiling people, nor do I believe in it. The reporter's questions were based on a premise which I knew, and they suspected, to be true: that the Princess and I were in love. All I could do was to parry them as best I could. I stood, like Lars Porsena, trying to defend the bridge which led across the turbid waters of speculation to the factual truth. In the clash of question and answer one reporter said: 'The simple way to stop rumours, would be a denial.'

Exactly. But there was nothing to deny. The truth was there. All I could do was to try to shield it.

Day after day the combat continued, while the flood of speculation mounted. In down-town Brussels the names of the Princess and myself were being flashed in neon signs – as they were in capitals the world over. In Kingston, Jamaica (where the Princess had just been) there were headlines, 'Engagement. Royal wedding'. Traditionally, Buckingham Palace never makes denials. Tradition was respected, as the flood of rumour continued. In Australia the public were told, 'Romance moving to its climax' and the *New York Post* confidently predicted, 'Meg, flier will wed'. Though the Paris *L'Aurore*'s comment was decidedly acid, the implication was the same. 'Modern princes and princesses hardly hesitate between their right to the crown and their sentimental comfort.'

By mid-week I was so exhausted by the press offensive that I asked the reporters for a truce. They had me, back to the wall, and were not going to let me go, but they sportingly allowed me a respite. I also called Serge Nabokov, Reuter's correspondent and a reliable, discreet friend. 'Please come and give me a hand,' I begged Serge, although this meant giving him an exclusivity, too. He did not abuse it. His help was timely, for things were getting into a mess – the climax came when the correspondent of the *Sydney Sun Herald* quoted me as saying, 'If the situation should demand my exile and that of a certain lady, we should accept it'. With Serge's advice I put out a categorical denial. 'It was pure invention . . .' I stated, and the newspaper must have agreed, for the reporter was sacked.

Unpleasant as this incident was, it gave me the initiative. I told the reporters that, while grateful for their fairness and consideration, as one of them had let me down I should no longer be available. Henceforth they left me alone, but, anyway, salvation was at hand. Mercifully, my leave was ending. On Monday 14 March I was back in my office, safely within the solid precincts of the embassy, among my own friends.

That week had left me shaken and above all disgusted. The British nation and the Commonwealth, the whole world indeed, were clamouring for a word on the Princess's future. It was perhaps reasonable to claim that her private life was the concern of the nation. But that was no reason to leave me as a solitary target for the world's press.

Even worse was the cynicism of those who reproached me for not keeping mum (though I had revealed strictly nothing). They knew quite well that the Margaret-Townsend affair was a live – if embarrassing – reality, but pretended that it was all moonshine. The *Daily Mail* spoke smugly for them: 'We hope the Group Captain has said the last word and that if there is any more to say, the Royal Family will be allowed to say it.'

That had always been my hope, too. But the unbroken silence continued; in it, a more terrible storm was brewing.

The recent fracas with the press had shattered my precious, hard-won independence and landed me back where I was before, an object of curiosity and comment (not always favourable), tracked, questioned and publicised in headlines the world over. I did not at all like the look of things. I asked myself – and the Princess (we wrote, as usual, almost every day) – was it wise to go on? Our feelings for one another had not in the least changed; they were as sure and as strong as ever. Yet they seemed to be sapping us, rather than inspiring us to greater things, creating about us, too, an uncomfortable atmosphere of sensation and controversy. Emotively, I was ready to go through anything for her. But logically . . . where would it lead us?

In any case, now that the press was in a state of ferment, I did not feel that I could endure to wait much longer for a decision on our future. What we needed to know – urgently – was whether marriage was feasible – and this, only the Princess could ascertain. In five months' time, on her twenty-fifth birthday, the Princess would be free of the Queen's veto under the Royal Marriages Act – but not of her formal disapproval, as Head of the Church.

For the Church still had its word to say.

I had met Dr Fisher, Archbishop of Canterbury, several times. He seemed a genial, jolly type and I liked him. If there was anything against him it was his appearance; he looked more like a stage character than the Primate of All-England.

At all events, he now gave a remarkable performance on arriving at Cape Town aboard the *Edinburgh Castle*, the ship that Princess Margaret had launched at Belfast when I accompanied her. A reporter of the *Cape Town Argus* bearded the Archbishop in his cabin and, reminding him of the enormous publicity given to the fact that Princess Margaret and Peter Townsend wanted to marry, asked, 'Was the fuss justified?' To which His Grace replied, 'The whole thing – and you can quote me – was purely a stunt.' 'So there was no truth in the rumour?' pursued the reporter. 'None whatsoever' replied Geoffrey Cantuar.

Was the Archbishop telling lies, if only white ones? Perish the thought. Yet there it was: he was denying a fact to which the Queen, Head of the Church, was privy and upon which she had sought his advice. It was a sorry thing to see this good man joining the ranks of those who knew the facts, but manipulated them in public as they saw fit.

Despite his critics, and they were many and fierce, Dr Fisher's attitude towards divorce was, in my view, movingly Christ-like. He held that the Church must witness to Christ's teaching that marriage was indissoluble, and though he admitted that divorce could relieve the suffering of parents and children, he insisted that divorced people (whose former spouses were living) should remarry elsewhere than in church. After which, the Church would in time readmit them, if they wished it, into its fold. I believe this attitude was close to Christ's in his moving encounter with the Samaritan woman and the adulteress.

But in his cabin that day the Archbishop had apparently, for the moment, brushed Christ aside in order to take sides with the Establishment. His attitude was typically, fundamentally and – it might even be said – wonderfully British. As in 1940: the British were beaten, but they refused to admit it. So they were not beaten. And so now: Margaret and Peter are in love, but we refuse to admit it, so they are not in love. The whole thing, as the Archbishop said, was purely a stunt – 'and a most offensive one at that' he emphasised.

Meanwhile I rode, with a fair share of wins, in amateur races all over Europe. Little did the public realise the 'combines' which go on off the race-course and the dirty little tricks which were practised on it. Neither interested me. I did not bet; I rode to win.

My first win in France was at Maisons-Laffitte on Nemrod, trained by Maurice d'Ockhuysen. While we all manoeuvred nervously at the starting-gate the whip-man winked at me and said reassuringly, 'Don't worry, I'm English. I'll see that you get a good start', and crack went his long-Tom whip. Nemrod whipped round and by the time I had got him straight again, the field were ten lengths ahead. But Nemrod could not bear seeing another horse in front of him; he caught them up and went clean through the lot to win by a short head. Afterwards, in the dressing room, one of the 'gentlemen', a young Frenchman, who had put his shirt on another horse, sat wailing and gnashing his teeth and calling me rude names.

Some time later, at Le Tremblay, again on Nemrod, I rode a bad race, finishing fifth. Nemrod, however decided to show what he was made of. He took a firm hold and, despite all my efforts, careered on past the finishing post to complete another one and a half circuits before I could stop him. The only consolation I got from this spectacular incident was the remark of a jockey who met me as I staggered to the dressing room. 'He did the same with me last week,' he chuckled, 'only when I finally stopped him, he whipped round and did another circuit in the opposite direction.'

Shortly afterwards I fell while riding and received a kick on the calf-muscle of my right leg. It swelled and hardened. When I rode at Neuss in Germany it was so painful that I was given an injection. The German doctor, with a fiendish grin, slid the six inch needle into my leg till it seemed to be grating on the bone. Two weeks later, at Malmö, in Sweden, the leg was so swollen that I had to borrow some bigger boots. They enabled me to ride a great race on Rock, a beautiful English-bred horse, who pulled off a splendid win.

Back in Brussels, I called Dr Adam. He came to my apartment, glanced at the leg and snapped. 'Stay where you are. Lie down and don't move' – and was gone. An hour later he was back with a special dressing and a product which he injected into the leg. He had immediately seized the awful truth – a clot had formed and it might have proved fatal.

And so the days passed, as I waited for the denouement of the Princess's and my problem.

CHAPTER 20

The end of the affair

Princess Margaret's twenty-fifth birthday, on 21 August 1955 was approaching. The press – newspapers, TV and radio – were converging on Balmoral in expectation. The Princess was immensely and deservedly popular; she personified the young and the unconventional, the go-ahead side of England. She won admiration, too, by the way she performed her royal duties. She was serene and dignified, as befitted the occasion, but once it was over, radiated warmth and gaiety. People liked her judicious mixture of the formal and the light-hearted. The public felt her happiness was very much their concern and wished her well. They believed that her twenty-fifth birthday would be the turning-point.

But nothing unusual happened. The Princess worshipped, as usual, at the Kirk at Crathie, where the Reverend Minister John Lamb said a prayer: 'Grant unto her . . . of the fullness of thy blessing so that she may find of thee fulfilment of her heart's desires.'

I, too, went to worship that morning in the English church in Londonstraat at Ostende. I said a small prayer for us both in that dingy little church, with the plaster falling off its walls, and a congregation of five. It was a far cry from Crathie, but that was of no matter. God is omnipresent.

I had come to Ostende the day before, with Giles and Hugo, to ride in a race – which I won, in a photo finish, on Kwenda, a brave little mare. The crowd seemed to catch the spirit of the occasion and cheered warmly – not only because I had won, but because many of them had too. Kwenda was heavily backed.

The following Saturday it was the races at Deauville. My horse, according to its owner, was a certainty. 'You can't help winning, if you get off to a good start and just stay up in front.'

My start was perfect and I settled down just ahead of the field. But, long before the straight, the horse blew up; it finished last but one. I motored back to Paris, caught the 'plane to Brussels, went home and slept for a few hours, then caught a 'plane for Oslo and was whisked from the airport in a helicopter and landed on the race-course.

The English had a good day. Lester Piggott rode a winner, so did I. Embarrassingly, the crowds applauded me as much as the crack English jockey, not so much because of my prowess, as because they took me, despite myself, as a sort of romantic idol.

The same thing happened everywhere. John Heslop, the well-known English amateur rider, had ridden in the Deauville race; he wrote in the *Observer*: '*Leaving the paddock to go out for the race we encountered a seething, highly excitable mass awaiting the appearance of . . . the star attraction . . . Peter Townsend (who) had to have protective police. Townsend was unplaced, but from the applause he might have won.*'

This adulation was embarrassing, not least because it invariably put my horse into a state of wild alarm, so that I, the undeserving hero of the moment, risked being pitched off into the midst of the crowd who were so deliriously acclaiming me. At Copenhagen, people pressed round my snorting, pawing mount, Nautilus. Just as I was about to leap into the saddle someone grabbed me and said, 'Wait a bit old boy, I'd like you to meet the British ambassador.' I begged His Excellency to excuse me.

Popularity is an extremely brittle thing and anyone who seeks it for its own sake is a fool. Should I have given up racing and stayed at home? No, I decided. I did not see why the irrelevant plaudits of the crowds should rob me of my favourite pastime. I simply could not be bothered with the crowds. I raced for the fun of it and accepted the glorious uncertainty of the sport. If the crowds came to look at me, that was their business.

And so I travelled all over Europe in pursuit of my racing career: Vienna, Madrid, Frankfurt, Saarbrucken, Merano in Italy and Aarau in Switzerland. There I rode the most beautiful horse I have ever seen. It finished last.

One morning in September, I was summoned by the *chef de cabinet* of the Belgian Minister of the Interior. He told me that he had received a letter warning that the I.R.A. had decided 'to put me away'. The writer wanted no hand in the murder, so he had decided 'to tell the holy truth'.

I had not the faintest involvement in the Irish question, but I was in the headlines and the I.R.A., apparently, wanted to be there too – over my dead body. So I was provided with a body-guard in the person of Commandant Etienne de Spot. We had a lot of fun together and, luckily, Etienne never had to draw on a terrorist.

At this time, one London Sunday newspaper described me as the unhappiest suitor of our age; another informed its 10 million-odd readers that the romance which had kept the world waiting two years was over. Yet the portents tended to suggest the contrary.

My plea to the Princess, to find out whether marriage was feasible, had been answered. At Balmoral, the clans were gathering. The Queen and Princess Margaret had arrived there. On 1 October, Sir Anthony Eden, now prime minister, arrived.

Eden could not fail to sympathise with the Princess, all the more so that while his own second marriage had incurred no penalty, either for him or his wife, he had to warn the Princess that my second marriage – to her – would bring her the most grievous penalties: she would have to renounce her royal rights, functions and income.

The Princess now had confirmation, for the first time, of the consequences of a marriage with me. If only she had known before the approaching drama might have been avoided. But now it was too late.

We had arranged to meet in London on 13 October. Everything was set for the grand finale. I should once more have to enter the arena; I knew that I was going like a sheep to the slaughter. But I went willingly, for her.

Despite the continuing public clamour, neither Michael Adeane nor Richard Colville invited me to discuss with them how to face a situation which had the entire world watching and waiting. I was given no up-to-date information about the political or religious issues, nor about the views of Eden and his cabinet colleagues. I knew nothing. I braced myself for the ordeal, as I had done when, as a small boy, I had to face a beating. That experience helped; I would try to keep my cool, my eyes fixed ahead.

On 12 October I crossed over, with my car, in the air ferry from Le Touquet to Lydd. I do not know what Marshal Ney and his men felt like when they charged the British squares at Waterloo – about the same, I imagine, as I felt when confronted by the phalanx of photographers at Lydd. Their salvos of flashes left me groping blindly through the customs towards my car.

Followed by a cortège of reporters in their cars, with others on motor-cycles in close escort, I drove on into London, to the flat in Lowndes Square, Knightsbridge, which the Marquess of Abergavenny, a friend of the Queen and Prince Philip and brother of my own faithful friend, Rupert Nevill, had most kindly lent me. A two weeks' siege now began.

That evening, Princess Margaret left Balmoral by train for London. Everyone remarked how lovely and happy she looked, which was not surprising, for we were to meet next day for the first time in a year. As she travelled south, I was being bombarded with questions; a statement, the reporters insisted, would end the speculation which had surrounded us for two years. I was sorry, I told them, I could honestly tell them nothing of what the future held for me. I knew nothing, other than that I should return to my post in Brussels early in November. I knew of no vital decision, no impending announcement.

Princess Margaret arrived in London early on the morning of the 13th. We spoke on the telephone and fixed a meeting for that evening at Clarence House. That day the Princess gave a sitting to the painter, Denis Fildes, who declared that he had never seen her look more beautiful.

That was how she seemed to me when, that evening, I saw her in her sitting-room at Clarence House. There we at last found ourselves once more in our own, exclusive world, which had remained so empty since our separation two years earlier.

As we rediscovered one another, we realised that nothing had changed. Time had not staled our accustomed, sweet familiarity.

Our meeting was the signal for the world's press to take off. There was not a civilised capital in the world where Princess Margaret and myself were not being discussed, often surrounded by the wildest travesties of fact. In France all the papers, except the communist *l'Humanité*, announced that an engagement was imminent. The U.S. press concentrated more on us than on President Eisenhower: 'Meg, Peter in London and all ask is it yes?', 'London agog as Margaret hails captain'.

The London press hailed the Princess warmly, too; popular feeling was roused and there was an outburst, perhaps not always in the best taste, but nonetheless genuine, of public sympathy. The public admired the charm and dignity with which the Princess had carried out her recent Caribbean tour. They loved her because she enjoyed her fun, was witty and sparkling, yet never allowed these things to diminish her royal stature. Never had the Princess been more popular.

The Queen's press secretary, Commander Colville, asked three simple questions about that dramatic meeting, replied 'No comment' to each of them. Next day he issued a tight-lipped, delphic statement '. . . the Press Secretary to the Queen is authorised to say that no announcement concerning Princess Margaret's personal future is at present contemplated. The Princess has asked the Press Secretary to express the hope that the press and public will extend to Her Royal Highness their customary courtesy and co-operation in respecting her privacy.' The press secretary was asking a lot.

I was besieged inside No. 19 Lowndes Square without any hope of relief from the commander, or anyone else. My every sortie provoked a scene suggestive of the start of the 24-hours Le Mans race, as pressmen and photographers sprinted to their cars, engines were started and revved up, and the chase began. It was impossible to evade them, dangerous even to try, for fear of causing an accident (some did occur).

The reporters followed me everywhere; they were decent to me, full of apologies and not a little ashamed for making my life nearly unbearable. But, as in Brussels, they clung to me; their reputations and their jobs depended on their reporting my every movement, expression and word. I could only tell them, 'I have nothing to say,' and at the end of the day, 'That's all till to-morrow.' They quickly came to trust my words, sparse as they were. Unrewarding as their vigil was, there grew up between hunters and hunted the traditional, mutual regard.

Colville's only reaction to the mounting tide of speculation was his single utterance: 'No statement is at present contemplated.' Never, protested the *Daily Mirror*, had the Crown been given such appalling advice. Indeed, if not 'at present', then when? The answer would only come – from the Princess herself – after more than two weeks of wild, world-wide conjecture.

While it dinned about us, the Princess and I met on every day save two. As the hubbub intensified, we tried to keep our heads. As a private citizen, besieged, or pursued, by the press every minute of the day and night, I did not find it easy. Behind my polite and placid countenance, I was being demolished by the physical and mental strain. I could only parry the volley of questions with non-committal answers. It was not for me, out in the street, to give a day-by-day commentary, all the more so as I was not in possession of any of the facts.

The sensationalism which had been generated around our two quiet selves met with severe criticism. The Berlin *Morgenpost* complained: 'The basic error was the unbelievably amateurish fashion in which public opinion was led by the nose.' The Johannesburg *Rand Daily Mail* commented 'The handling of the business was maladroit.' Of the scores of newspapers who criticised the mismanagement of the affair, only one, the *Economist*, gave Colville and his colleagues any reason to preen themselves. 'The Queen's advisers were quite correct' it said, not without a trace of sadistic relish, 'in making Her Royal Highness struggle past every obstacle before she made her decision.' If it were necessary to apply such an exercise in mental cruelty – in public – to a girl hesitating on the verge of marriage, was it necessary to prolong it for over two years? As the *News Chronicle* remarked, 'The continuing mystery and

efforts of the court, two years after the Group Captain's demo-
tion and banishment, to make it appear that no question of
marriage exists, intensifies speculation and creates annoyance.'

On Friday 14 October Princess Margaret and I headed
separately for Allanbay Park, a Georgian residence near Bin-
field in a tranquil, rustic corner of Berkshire, the home of John
and Jean Wills. Jean was daughter of the Queen Mother's sister,
Lady Elphinstone; she and her husband were delightful,
straightforward people, of whom I was very fond.

For three days their quiet home was under siege by the press
as aircraft and helicopters circled overhead. Berkshire's Chief
Constable, Mr J. W. Waldron, himself directed the vigilant
police patrols. Neither the Princess nor I dared venture beyond
the precincts, except under escort. So together we spent the
week-end in virtual custody, surrounded by the press, to whose
numbers were added police guards and dogs and motorised
patrols – conditions which did not make for romance.

During the following week, the world was kept on tenter-
hooks while the flat at No. 19 Lowndes Square, more than
Buckingham Palace, Clarence House or 10 Downing Street,
remained the cynosure of millions of eyes. Each time the
Princess and I saw one another or dined with friends, the
suspense and the speculation mounted. Some said, kindly, 'they
have not seen each other for two years; give them time to
consider the problems and make up their minds.' Others remarked less kindly, perhaps, but more logically: 'The problems
have been known for the last two years. Why, then, can't they
decide?'

The answer was that Mr Eden had only recently brought
home fully to the Princess the consequences of her marrying me.
The brave Princess had a huge load on her mind.

Adding to the suspense came the Queen's return from Scotland; then, on Tuesday 18 October, a cabinet meeting at which
the Princess's eventual marriage was discussed. On from the
meeting with his cabinet colleagues, went Eden to Buckingham
Palace for an audience with the Queen. It lasted ninety minutes
instead of the usual thirty. The Queen and her prime minister
dwelt long on the problem of her sister.

Meanwhile, that afternoon, at Clarence House, the Princess and I, more personally, were weighing the pros and cons. Queen Elizabeth joined us for tea and, in the midst of this appallingly serious situation, an American headline next day gave us a welcome laugh: 'Meg sips tea with Peter. Mom makes it a crowd.'

On Wednesday the 19th, for the first time, the Princess and I did not meet. I kept my distance before the important engagement she had that evening: dinner with the archbishop and bishops at Lambeth Palace.

When I saw her next day at Clarence House she was in fine form, quite unperturbed after junketing with the bishops who, admirably it must be said, refrained from allowing the rigours of the canon law to spoil the party. Some observers commented, somewhat irrelevantly, that the Princess could not now flout the archbishop after dining at his table.

The day after the party, Thursday the 20th, world excitement reached its peak. That morning the cabinet met at Downing Street with the clear impression that nothing, not even the episcopal feast the night before, had dissuaded the Princess from her intention to marry me. The cabinet meeting had hardly started when the Attorney General, Sir Reginald Manningham-Buller, was sent for. He was in the middle of pleading a case in the Queen's Bench Division and, excusing himself to the Lord Chief Justice, left the court and hurried to Downing Street.

I have not the faintest idea what those eminent gentlemen discussed, any more than I had of anything else that was going on behind the scenes. My place was down in the street, among the crowd, while the Government and Buckingham Palace palavered. But it is likely that the cabinet, that morning, came to terms on a Bill of Renunciation, to be placed before Parliament, freeing the Princess of her responsibilities under the Royal Marriages Act, and thus – at crushing cost to herself – enabling her to marry me. It was contended by observers that, while abdication was as old as the monarchy itself, renunciation of royal rights was unknown.

That afternoon, Hugh Gaitskell, as chairman of the Opposition 'shadow cabinet', informed his colleagues that the Princess intended to marry me – his cousin, whom he had, long ago, taken for hair-raising rides on the step of his bicycle. How widely our paths had diverged since those days at Bideford, to cross again now in the heat of this crisis. Hugh's intellectual achievements and his politics did not touch me. I knew him only as a good and a warm-hearted person.

The Opposition apparently saw no objection to the marriage – their party conference had recently adopted a resolution, admittedly rather a frivolous one, that a member of the proletariat had a right to marry a member of the Royal Family.

Friday the 21st was, for the Princess and her family, a day of remembrance. That morning, they all attended the unveiling by the Queen of the National Memorial to her father, King George VI, in Carlton Gardens.

The King, before he died, must have noticed that between his younger daughter and me there was a particular attachment. He adored her. I felt the warmth of his affection. Both of us could have done with his fatherly advice.

For the past week, the world around us had loudly and passionately discussed two concrete questions, one posed by the law, the other by the Church. The legal situation could be solved, but only by exacting big sacrifices from the Princess. Being twenty-five years old, she was free of the Queen's absolute veto under the Royal Marriages Act. But the act did not leave her free to marry whom and when she liked. It required her to give notice of her intentions to the Privy Council, whose three hundred-odd members were drawn from the political, aristocratic and military leaders of the land.

The Privy Council was the hard-core of the Establishment. It could not prevent the Princess's marriage, but its members could strongly influence Parliament to whom the veto, relinquished by the sovereign, had now passed. The Princess would have to wait up to twelve months more before the British Parliament and those of the seven dominions – Canada, Australia, New Zealand, South Africa, India, Pakistan and Ceylon – gave their consent.

If they did not, her last chance was to contract a marriage abroad. It would be illegal, and its offspring considered, in Britain and the Commonwealth, illegitimate.

However, it was practically certain that the British and Dominions parliaments would agree – but on condition that Princess Margaret was stripped of her royal rights and prerogatives, which included accession to the throne, her royal functions and a £15,000 government stipend due on marriage – conditions which, frankly, would have ruined her.

There would be nothing left – except me, and I hardly possessed the weight to compensate for the loss of her privy purse and prestige. It was too much to ask of her, too much for her to give. We should be left with nothing but our devotion to face the world.

Besides, there was an important political aspect to the situation. It was difficult for the prime minister, Anthony Eden, to oppose the marriage, because of his own position as a divorced husband, remarried. But the Marquis of Salisbury, an influential member of Eden's government and leader of the House of Lords, was, as a high Anglican, flatly opposed – to the point where, rather than introduce into the upper house a bill enabling the marriage he would probably resign.

Salisbury's resignation might have seriously weakened Eden's government. Even if it did not, it would come as a bombshell. 'Bobbety' Salisbury was a close friend of the Royal Family. His ancestor, the first Lord Burghley had served Elizabeth I as Chief Minister; it was he who sent Mary Queen of Scots to the block. His descendant could well send Margaret, Princess of England, virtually in the same direction.

The Church of England's 'establishment' – its subordination to the state – was itself founded on a divorce, that of King Henry VIII with his Spanish wife, Catherine of Aragon. His marriage with Anne Boleyn, according to the Church of England's teaching in 1955, was invalid. That being so, Anne Boleyn's daughter, Elizabeth I of England, was illegitimate. Not that this proved, in the end, of any detriment to the glory of England. What it did prove was that, in this year of grace

1955, the Church of England's teaching on divorce was on uncertain ground.

Some of the Church's most devout and erudite prelates had contested the validity of the laws on divorce and remarriage. In this atmosphere of doubt, the Church of England had frequently remarried the 'innocent' or 'wronged' party of a divorce. The Church preached the principle of the indissolubility of marriage but did not universally practise it. After deep and lengthy heart-searchings, in the light of the scriptures, of various learned texts and of talks with Roman and Anglican priests, I was unable to feel that I should be doing wrong to marry again. In this I had the support of no less an authority than the Archbishop of Canterbury himself, who stated publicly: 'I do not feel able to forbid good people who come to me for advice to embark on a second marriage.'

I had never asked the archbishop's advice. Perhaps I should have done. He was at this time being fiercely and, I think, unjustly criticised. His view was that the Church's duty was to bear witness to Christ's word, which was that marriage was meant to be life-long. A divorced person whose former spouse was living must get married elsewhere than in church.

Canon Kirtland, honorary canon of Canterbury Cathedral, was the first of the clerics to raise his voice. Only three days after the Princess and I had been reunited, his Reverence announced: 'Princess Margaret contemplates doing something which is an affront to religion. Any person who marries a divorced person is unmarried in the eyes of the Church.' I, for one agreed. But the Church *had* remarried such people, among them well-known ones. As someone rudely put it, in the sphere of sexual morality the Church turned a blind eye to the exploits of royalty and aristocracy.

Clergy and laity hit back at this minor canon. The Reverend Charles Rhodes, editor of the Church of England newspaper, called him cruel and unjust. But soon another cleric raised his harsh voice, this time from Edinburgh. The Reverend Mr Lockhart, declared, 'If Princess Margaret were to decide to marry . . . she would be taking a step which she is perfectly well aware is contrary to the law of Christ and his Church.'

Confrontation. An interview while the press siege was at its height

Two aspects of an Air Attaché's life. *above:* At a diplomatic soirée in Brussels. *below:* In the Belgian Congo

The world tour. *above:* Crossing the Irrawaddy at Myitkyina.
below: On the old Inca route in the Andes

At the start of a race

Here was an obscure priest contradicting not only the opinion of some of the saintlier divines of the Church of England, but the doctrine of his own Church. His words were quickly countered by Provost Goodenough, of Saint Mary's Cathedral, Edinburgh: it was Lockhart's own interpretation, not an official pronouncement of the Episcopal Church of Scotland.

Unlike the Church, the government took no moral stand, but merely fussed over the legal and constitutional considerations. How, then, did the Church, whose stand on divorce was not supported by the law of the land, come to wield such a mighty influence on the problem of Princess Margaret? The Church of England stood behind the Queen, its Head, for a decent, Christian way of life in a world of rapidly declining moral standards. The Law operated from motives of reason and common justice. The Church's appeal went deeper than the legalistic, material level; it penetrated right down to the conscience.

The Church, like the Law, was fighting a stern, and apparently losing battle against change and decay and the rot in human values, of which a marriage between the Princess and myself would, in its view, have been an outrageous example. I cannot refrain from mentioning that my present marriage (now eighteen years old) hardly supports this view. My children, whose comeliness, decency and happiness have, I suppose, been partly inspired by their once-divorced father, are as good examples as any of the christian way of life.

The Law and the Church were the bones and the sinew of the Establishment. Both had allies. *The Times* was one of the most powerful among them. On 24 October, in a lengthy leading article, lucidly argued in splendid, sweeping phrases, *The Times* gave its views on Princess Margaret's intention to marry me. The heart of the matter, it said, did not lie in legal or theological argument. The real crux was that the Queen was a symbol for her subjects throughout the Commonwealth. These millions of people saw their better selves reflected in the Queen and, since part of their ideal was family life, the Queen's own family was involved. In this context, *The Times* argued, Princess Margaret's marriage with me could not be regarded as a marriage at all by vast numbers of her sister's people.

No one could possibly contest *The Times*' sentiments concerning the Queen and the Royal Family. But who were these vast numbers? Certainly, they were not as vast as those even vaster numbers of Christians whose elected representatives had legislated in parliament for divorce and the remarriage of divorced people. Nor was the Commonwealth composed entirely of Christians. They were, in fact, a 'vast' minority, compared to the hundreds of millions of Buddhists, Moslems and Hindus, all of whom acknowledged the right of a divorced person to remarry.

The Times's arguments, so superbly couched, were specious and based on false premises. They did not, however, lessen its impact. The article has been taken as the turning-point in our story. That may well be so for the readers of *The Times*, but not for us. *The Times*' magisterial leader never swayed me. My mind was made up before I read it.

Where were we then, the Princess and I? The previous week had ended with our feeling hardly able to endure any longer the solemn pontifications, the debates which raged, at home and the world over, for and against our marriage.

The painful facts of the situation were only too clear: the country, the Commonwealth, the entire world, was in an uproar over us. The laity was divided among itself, and from the Church, over the Church's stand on divorce. There were loud cries from the public for the disestablishment of the Church, for the abolition of the Royal Marriages Act. The press was in a turmoil: while the *Daily Sketch* and the *Daily Mirror* spat abuse at each other, the *Daily Mirror* had savagely attacked *The Times* and the Press Council had censured the *Daily Mirror*, concluding that the British press had disgraced itself before the world. Buckingham Palace, the government and the Church all caught the blast. Everyone was by now impatient, and critical of a situation which was fast becoming ridiculous.

On Saturday evening, the 22 October, the Princess and I had met at Clarence House. We were both exhausted, mentally, emotionally, physically. We felt mute and numbed at the centre of this maelstrom. Later, the Princess had left London to spend the week-end with the Queen and the Duke of Edinburgh at Windsor Castle.

Next day, Sunday, we had spoken on the telephone. The Princess was in great distress. She did not say what had passed between herself and her sister and brother-in-law. But, doubtless, the stern truth was dawning on her. One is at a loss to comfort people over the telephone, and above all people one loves. I felt helpless, unable to reassure her, but when we spoke again later she seemed calmer; we promised to meet on the morrow.

That Sunday night I had hardly slept. My mind had turned incessantly on the sadness of the Princess. In just over a week the smile had vanished from her face, her happiness and confidence had evaporated. Events had put us to a rude test and the clamour, louder than ever, still continued about us. It was time to put an end to an unendurable situation.

During the morning of Monday the 24th, the day *The Times* article appeared, I had sat mechanically dictating thanks to the scores of letters pouring into No. 19 Lowndes Square. With rare exceptions, they were simple, touching expressions of sympathy; whether 'for' or 'against' I felt they all deserved acknowledgements.

I felt so played out that I tried to snatch a few winks before leaving to see the Princess at 4 p.m. But sleep evaded me. I was obsessed by the thought that the Princess must tell the world that there would be no marriage. Words, broken phrases turned in my head.

Of a sudden, I rolled off the bed, grabbed a piece of paper and a pencil. The words now came to me with clarity and fluency and I began to write.

'*I have decided not to marry Group Captain Townsend . . . It may have been possible to contract a civil marriage. But mindful of the Church's teaching . . . conscious of my duty to the Commonwealth . . .*'

Less than an hour later I was with the Princess at Clarence House. She looked very tired, but was as composed and affectionate as ever. I told her quietly, 'I have been thinking so much about us during the last two days, and I've written down my thoughts, for you to say if you wish to.'

I gave her the rough piece of paper and she read. Then she looked at me and very quietly, too, said, 'That's exactly how I feel.' Our love story had started with those words. Now, with the same sweet phrase, we wrote *finis* to it.

For a few moments we looked at each other; there was a wonderful tenderness in her eyes which reflected, I suppose, the look in mine. We had reached the end of the road. Our feelings for one another were unchanged, but they had incurred for us a burden so great that we decided, together, to lay it down. As we did so, we both had a feeling of unimaginable relief. We were liberated at last from this monstrous problem.

The Princess was resolved to declare publicly what was on her mind and what she had decided. The message could have been put out within twenty-four hours and the wondering world would have been relieved of the suspense. But the royal advisers were against a statement, which meant that its publication was delayed for one more week, while speculation rose to a fiercer crescendo.

In the hubbub, the Royal Family, the Church and the nation, not least the Princess and myself, were forced into an increasingly humiliating situation, for which the Queen's advisers and the government were blamed. From Sydney, the *Morning Sun* opined: 'Whatever the reasons have been for the government and the Palace to keep silent, the results have been disastrous.' Another comment, one of the most succinct, came from the South African *Die Burger*. Republican and therefore anti-monarchist, *Die Burger* still spoke sympathetically. It was intolerable, it said, that the affairs of the British Royal Family should become the object of offensive cartoons on the Continent, prizes for competitions in the U.S.A. and texts for busybodies in the pulpit. The present situation was creating tensions against which British self-control was not geared. The newspaper had no doubt where the blame belonged. 'The advisers to the Palace who have allowed the situation to reach its present critical phase have a lot to answer for'.

Meanwhile, in the street, I continued, as well as I could, to play out my role in this lamentable drama. There was, however, no hope of going about my life like any other man in the street.

Wherever I went, there crowded behind me my escort of reporters.

I badly wanted to see my mother. She was seventy-two and taking things quite calmly. But after the press – in force – had confronted her on her own front-doorstep, she wisely decided to disappear. She drove off early one morning and two hours later found a safe refuge with that personable godmother of mine, Cousin Addie, not far from Liphook in Hampshire. Could I get to her, let alone to any other member of my family, without bringing my posse of pressmen along too?

No solution appeared until, on the evening of Wednesday the 26th, I drove out of the front gates of Clarence House after seeing Princess Margaret. To my amazement there was not a single reporter in sight. I turned into the Mall, glanced into the rear mirror. No one was following me. Within an hour or so I was with my mother. All I needed to tell her was that there was to be no marriage and that I was still surviving – just. I returned to London early next day, grateful, as she was, for my God-sent escapade.

That Thursday afternoon Princess Margaret called at Lambeth Palace to tell the Archbishop of her decision.

The drama was moving to its close, but still the *coup de théâtre* had to come.

The Princess and I spent the week-end with Rupert and Micky Nevill at Uckfield in Sussex. They, and John and Patricia Abergavenny, whose home, Eridge Castle, was nearby, were the staunchest and most hospitable of friends; without their help I could never have survived those eighteen days of attrition. It was a goodbye week-end for the Princess and me.

At last we could talk without that crushing weight of world opinion – the sympathy, the criticism, the pity and the anger – all the mass of emotion which had weighed so heavily on our minds. Uckfield House was a haven, though one which was blockaded and besieged by the press and the public.

As at Allanbay Park, at the beginning of this tempestuous period, police and their dogs patrolled, reporters perched in trees or hid in ditches; the Princess and I could neither come

nor go. We could only walk in the grounds, sniped at occasionally by long-range lenses. Meanwhile, the world still waited for
the decision, made days ago.

On Monday 31 October, we returned separately to London.
The Princess's statement was to be issued that evening at 7 p.m.
About an hour earlier, I called to say a last farewell at Clarence
House.

It was there, in the Princess's sitting room, that we had met,
so recently (but it seemed like an age), after our long, enforced
separation. We had held out for more than two years to experience, not the unmitigated joys of a lovers' reunion, but a
miserable trial by ordeal, held in public. The hard facts had
prevailed and now that we were released, to be separated,
sentimentally, at least, for ever, we felt as if we needed a stiff
drink.

We did not feel unhappy. Without dishonour, we had played
out our destiny. We were back where we started, that evening,
long ago, at Windsor Castle. The story was ended, the book was
closed. There remained only the glow, once shared, of tenderness, constancy and singleness of heart.

Then we, who had been so close, parted.

As I drove back, under a friendly moon, to Uckfield, the
Princess's statement was broadcast to the world:

'I would like it to be known that I have decided not to
marry Group Captain Townsend. I have been aware that,
subject to my renouncing my rights of succession, it might
have been possible for me to contract a civil marriage. But
mindful of the Church's teaching that Christian marriage is
indissoluble, and conscious of my duty to the Commonwealth, I have resolved to put these considerations before
others. I have reached this decision entirely alone, and in
doing so I have been strengthened by the unfailing support
and devotion of Group Captain Townsend. I am deeply
grateful for the concern of all those who have constantly
prayed for my happiness.

(Signed) Margaret.

Monday, October 31, 1955.'

Churchmen, the Reverend Lockhart in the lead, chortled with satisfaction – as they had every right to do. The Church had scored a resounding victory. Princess Margaret's renunciation was applauded the world over for its courage, for its sacrifice of love for duty. Never was the Princess held in higher esteem or affection. She had rendered sovereign service to the monarchy, to the Church and to the divine institution of marriage. She had shown a shining example in the realm of public morals and everyone – most of all myself – prayed for her ultimate happiness.

None of this, alas, proved of any avail. In Britain, public morality continued to decline, with the drug traffic, sexual delinquency and juvenile crime. The process of divorce, moreover, was in time considerably facilitated.

As for the Princess, who of those who prayed for her happiness would have dared to believe that twenty years hence her own marriage would break up? Her decision was undoubtedly right. But the example it set seems to have been in vain, and one with the sacrifice of all of that youth to which we both belonged, who fought – in vain – for a cleaner, better world.

For people who like fairy tales, our story had a sad ending. As with all fairy tales, no one, at least at the beginning, would believe it was true. When they did, they shouted it from the house-tops. Then, when it ended, people still would not believe it was over.

CHAPTER 21

Escape to adventure:
by road round the world

I drove back to Brussels. Outside my apartment there waited a crowd of reporters, so I veered away. Previously, the new ambassador, Sir George Labouchere, had offered me shelter, if need be, at his residence in the Rue Ducale. It was there that I headed. I rang the bell and stepped inside. The reporters were at my heels but the heavy door slammed in the face of the first one.

The sanctuary provided by Sir George and Lady Labouchere saved me. The last three weeks had brought me to breaking point. I was all in. Now, in the quiet of the Laboucheres' home, I was able to sleep on and off throughout the weekend. On Monday, feeling better, I drove in the borrowed splendour of Sir George's Rolls Royce to the embassy.

Now that the critical time in England was over, the press, amid its universal praise of the Princess, was good enough to put in a sympathetic word for me. Considering the 'cruel ordeal' (as one distinguished observer called it) that we had both endured, I had apparently behaved with restraint and dignity and come through with my reputation unscathed. Those prefects' beatings at Haileybury had left their mark in more ways than one.

But it was predicted that I should have much to endure in the future. And how much – from the press who were now so well-disposed towards me!

People showed sympathetic interest in my future. Some pitied me, which was kind of them, but it was not the moment for me to feel sorry for myself; they saw my career shattered, with me painfully picking up the remnants and beginning again. Others claimed that my career in the R.A.F. qualified me for greater responsibilities; they saw me going on to the top of that great service.

There was much realism in both of these points of view. It was true, the R.A.F. still wanted me; I spent an hour in the Air

Ministry with a high ranking officer who used every persuasion to make me stay on, promising me an important command.

On the face of it, this was the simplest solution. But, when, over ten years before, I had virtually left the R.A.F. to join the King's Household, I was not in a particularly happy frame of mind. Practically all my friends had been killed. I missed them and the happy times we had spent. The haunts and the habits we had known had been grossly changed by the war. Nine years in the Royal Household had isolated me from the R.A.F.; the events of the last two years, despite my many loyal friends in the service, had further separated me from it. I could not again face donning my blue uniform, the shining buttons, the gleaming medals, and all the spit and polish that is part of service life.

I felt unable to face the new generation of pilots. We should, I believe, have bored one another. For my own flying career had ended a decade ago, on propeller aircraft. I belonged to the air equivalent of the age of windjammers, with its artisanal techniques. Modern scientific skills, if they had taken much of the danger out of flying, had taken the fun out of it, too.

The other choice was to start again. But at what? Recent events had marked me too much, whether as the hero or the villain, to make me fit for any official post outside the R.A.F., or, for that matter, any other responsible post. Nor did I notice any particular rush to offer me one, though I turned down a number of enticing offers from more questionable sources. In my own mind the answer lay with neither one choice nor the other.

For in truth I was seized by a huge wave of revolt against society, fed as it was by the newspapers with gossip and scandal, rumour and sensation; against the hierarchy, the 'old-boy network', which thrived on privilege, and fortune and tradition, often outmoded. I may sound hypocritical, for I was, after all, a product of that society and had enjoyed its benefits. But I believe this revolt had its origins long ago, during the air battles, with their perils and joys shared – at the same level – with young men of all sorts and conditions.

That experience had deeply affected my thinking. Ever since, for me, the air-fighting was over, I had felt a bit of a misfit in that society; now, I felt like a throw-out from it. I longed to break clean away from the environment for which my education and my training had filled me. My professional experience was another thing; if it had not made me a specialist in anything, it had fortunately taught me to be extremely adaptable.

In March 1956 I flew off from Brussels with a party of foreign air and military attachés, on a *'voyage d'information'* to the Belgian Congo. One evening, sitting on my bed in the hotel at Elizabethville, I was flipping over the pages of my pocket diary. I came to the tiny world map at the end; I looked at it idly, when suddenly an idea struck me. The world! I carried it in my pocket; I had flown halfway across it to the Congo, looked down on it – yet I hardly knew it. I had found the answer to my quest. There and then I decided that I would make a journey round the world, by road, alone.

The basic reason for this decision was the best reason anyone can have for doing anything worth-while. I wanted with all my heart to do it; there was nothing I wanted to do more. It was like the decision I had made years before to fly; I knew it was the only course to take to liberate my restless, fettered spirit. I wanted to break out beyond the little world which held me prisoner and take the whole world into the compass of my mind. But not superficially, as does the traveller who goes from port to port, airport to airport. I wanted to see the world as it really was, the world of mountains, deserts and jungle, of peaks and plains, rivers and floods and drought. I wanted to get closer to the real world and the people who inhabited it, in their great cities and their mud-hut villages, as they scratched away with primitive tools at the parched infertile soil or sent their tractors ploughing into the rich loam of the valleys. I wanted to see the world in all its incredible variety of people and places, of landscape and climate, and poverty and wealth.

It did not occur to me to wonder whether such a venture had ever been undertaken before – probably not, by the route I intended to take, but that did not matter. I had no wish to break any records. I would just buy a suitable car and drive away into the blue. When the Rover Company offered to provide me with a Land Rover, I turned the offer down and bought the car myself. I would pay my own way.

In order to do so I would have to write a travelogue, a series of articles. It seemed a perfectly legitimate thing to do. It was nine years since, during the South African tour, I felt the first kindlings of a desire to write, and even longer since, at the Staff College, I had learnt the proper way to write reports and appreciations. I had since written many. My training as a writer may well have been better than that of many so-called writers who had written – often the most abominable trash – about me. So I decided to have a go myself.

How, it might well be asked, could I possibly reconcile writing for the press with my burning desire to escape from the society which it fed? It did not seem all that complicated to me. Millions of words had been written about me and much of what they said was quite untrue. I thought it fair enough to give a true account of myself.

I had a 'name', I knew. A writer with a name – above all one that has not been made by writing – is especially vulnerable to criticism. I accepted the risk. As an apprentice, I would at least try to turn out a worthwhile product, free from scandal and sensation.

It was at this juncture that I met Norman Barrymaine. I had first heard of him early in 1955 when Sir Christopher Warner had called me to his office to tell me that Barrymaine had been to see him with a fantastic offer from a well-known American magazine for my memoirs. The ambassador added, 'I know Barrymaine well. He worked in my department of the Foreign Office during the war. You may have complete confidence in him.'

I did not accept Barrymaine's offer then nor, some months later, when he repeated it. The world journey, however, was in a different category, and Barrymaine, in view of his credentials, seemed to be my man. I wrote to him and proposed a series of articles.

Within forty eight hours he presented himself in my office. He was a small man with a big nose, large horn-rimmed glasses and no chin. His sensual lips gave a slight lisp to his speech. I quickly discovered that Norman Barrymaine was highly congenial; an experienced political correspondent, he was full of stories, grim, tragic, hilarious, ranging from Whitehall to China, where he had reported the civil war. Norman negotiated with the *Daily Mail* a contract in which I insisted on a clause agreeing that there should be no reference, in the promotion and presentation of my articles, to the Royal Family or to my personal affairs. To make double sure, I engaged him, for a consideration, (not a large one, it is true) to supervise the editing and presentation of my articles and photos.

My daily stint in the office over, I worked late into the night on my plans for the world journey. I had to obtain dozens of visas. This took time; the one for Communist China took the longest, but it arrived after three months, with a letter saying that, rather than enter China with my car, I should take advantage of the excellent rail and air communications. From that I gathered that road communications, at least excellent ones, did not exist.

But I did collect a mass of information on roads across the five continents, on climatic and political conditions. My chief problem was to reach the right place at the right time. The roads in eastern Iran and Afghanistan became difficult by the end of the year, in India and Burma practically impassable during the monsoons in the first half of the following year. I had to arrive at Singapore in time to catch a boat, in Western Australia, before the arid wastes of the Nullarbor Plain were turned by the rains into a morass. I could not cross the Canadian Rockies before the snow had melted in May; in South America the road over the Andes between Chile and Argentina was blocked by snow until November, when it is spring in the southern hemisphere. In central Africa rain, and in the Sahara, heat, made the route impracticable at certain seasons. I do not exactly know how, but I worked out an itinerary to meet, more or less, all these variations. The political problems, in Middle Europe, Greece, the Middle East, the Far East, in Burma and in parts of South America – I left to settle on the spot.

Finally, I was injected in my right arm and my left, and in every other available part of my body, with vaccines and serums to protect me from every known plague, pest and pox. One problem yet remained: whether or not to carry a gun. I thought long about it, and decided to go unarmed. I had not the slightest desire to shoot anyone.

I had bid farewell to Giles and Hugo during a brief visit to England. In Brussels the valedictory process was a long one, for I had made many friends. It came to a head with a huge party in the Palace Hotel. A week later I drove to Antwerp to say a last farewell to *la famille Jamagne*, who had been so kind to me. Marie-Luce was then seventeen, an adorable girl who made me laugh and touched me, as did her brother and her parents, by her affection. I felt something of a pang on leaving them, perhaps even a little more on leaving her. She scratched her initial M-L on the back door of my Land Rover. M-L; it was the only insignia my little car carried, and it was almost invisible.

Then I was gone.

It was the 21 October 1956, Trafalgar Day, when I drove out of Brussels into dense fog and gathering darkness, along the road which, with only one short sea crossing, the Bosphorus, led all the way to Singapore. The past closed in behind me and I headed towards the mists of the future. I had cut adrift from England, and from all that society which had judged me, be it kindly or harshly, without my being able to give an account of myself. Now I was bent on escaping into the unknown world which lay beyond the confines of conventional society. My friends, who were so good to me, will, I hope, forgive me. I held no grudge against anyone; it was the system, the rules, the style which I could no longer abide.

As I journeyed on between Brussels and Istanbul, I became comfortably aware that the moral gap between myself and the world I had left behind me was widening even more than the physical distance. On the road through Yugoslavia, Greece and Turkey, I met little traffic, only peasants, who often waved at me, as if I were one of them. Then, near Istanbul, I found the road barred – literally. And, signalling me to stop, not the police, but the press.

My heart sank. I had believed that I was free to continue my travels in peace but here they came again, the press boys, to the assault. Only when I left Istanbul and struck out across the wilds of the Anatolian plateau, did I feel free again. At Ankara I passed unnoticed; the Suez crisis, now approaching its climax, made the headline news.

South of Ankara lay a deserted, windy plateau, sparsely dotted with squalid villages where wretched, but not unfriendly peasants scratched the earth. Such poverty, such abject misery is rare. Yet it attracted rather than repelled me. In all their filth and squalor, those peasants seemed to represent, spiritually, something more sublime than I had found in the sophisticated salons of Mayfair and Belgravia.

I was glad to be shot of that high society. As I drove south across Turkey, there came back to me, with immense force, the call of the open, arid spaces, like the deserted spaces of the air. Then, as if my wheels had touched earth again. I found myself in the passes of the Taurus, with the delicious reek of pine-wood smoke in my nostrils. I ran down through the Cilician Gates to the Mediterranean.

I now had to swerve north-east, away from the Arab countries where, with Suez always the pretext, British consulates – and cars – were being burnt. One evening, as I came through a dusty, deserted region to the Iranian border, I sighted, to the north, Mount Ararat – alone, like me, in that wilderness.

It was perhaps the fact of being alone that accentuated my irresistible, almost insane desire to keep moving on. The distance behind me was territory conquered; each and every mile of the thousands of miles onwards to my ultimate destination was an invitation to further conquest. Obsessed by this idea, I forged on through the broiling heat of the day into the biting cold of the night, fighting the winding, atrocious road and the deadening weight of sleep.

At Teheran my course eastwards came to a sudden halt. The British ambassador, Sir Roger Stevens, informed me that Pakistan, as a member of the Muslim Brotherhood, joint plaintiffs in the Suez affair, was threatening to quit the Commonwealth. Karachi had protested by burning down the British Consulate; Peshawar had followed with violent anti-British riots. Sir Roger warned me that if I went to Pakistan, I would be going to certain death.

A week later the crisis eased and I was given the green light. I passed through Isfahan, the ancient capital. What struck me there, more than the slender minarets, the gorgeous blue domes of the mosques and the dazzling splendour of the Shah mosque was the abject poverty which sullied the city's streets.

Hundreds of miles southwards, a row of solitary columns rose unexpectedly from the barren wilderness: they were the monumental ruins of Persepolis, the fabulous capital of Darius the Great. In the silence of the night the ruins of Persepolis stood out in a flood of moonlight, mutely telling that, twenty-five centuries earlier, the minds and the hands of men had been at work in this place. Their souls, and the souls of millions had since passed out of this world, but these ancient stones remained.

We living creatures are the ones who wither and perish and suffer in the process. Where are they now, those upon whose ground at Persepolis I now stood? And where shall I be two thousand years hence when others come to tread this site? Can anyone tell why men are born, to live but a few fleeting years, and die, leaving only monuments of ageless stone? Not until we are lost in the eternal can we hope to see the truth face to face.

Shiraz was not on my way but I went there because it is a city of roses and jasmine and of the poets Hafiz and Sa'di. At the tomb of the latter a *mullah*, turbaned, bearded and wearing a *burnous*, accosted me rudely, calling me a dirty imperialist. Dirty perhaps – that was inevitable, travelling the dusty roads; but this ill-mannered clergyman, incensed as he may have been by Suez, was hardly justified in calling me an imperialist in a land which had once been the empire of the Medes and Persians and whose present ruler, the Shah-in-shah, still boasted the title 'Imperial Majesty' – which the British sovereign had dropped years before.

It is a pity that politics make men so bitter and bloody-minded when, left to themselves, they can be human, decent and generous.

At Nok Kundi, at the frontier of Pakistan where, a week before, I should have gone in danger of my life; the immigration officer greeted me warmly, introduced me to his charming family and invited me to drink tea with them. The same again

at Quetta. There, at the Staff College, with the élite of the
Pakistani army (all ready, a couple of weeks earlier, to fight the
British), I celebrated my 42nd birthday, while past British
commandants of the college glared down austerely from their
picture frames at our revelling.

As I headed for Kandahar, the sun was going down in a blaze
of crimson. In the half-light I passed a shepherd bowed low in
prayer, and beside him a group of men, prostrate, their faces
turned towards the sunset. After Kabul the road, crowded with
nomads driving their encumbered beasts, led up to the 9,000 ft.
Laterband Pass. There, prostrate in the road, lay an old grey
horse. It had borne its rider and all his bulky merchandise up
that arduous climb for the last time. Now its load lay scattered
in the road, revealing on its back a hideous sore, bigger than a
man's hand. In its eyes was the look of death, the look which
sees, not far away, the end of suffering. For the first time I
regretted not having a gun with me.

A mile below, the road ran through the little town of
Jallalabad, then climbed imperceptibly across the barren Loi
Dakka plain to the foot of the Khyber Pass.

The Khyber! No pass in the world has such a ring to its name,
such strategic importance. Darius the Great and his conquering
armies passed that way in their thrust to the Indus. After them
came the armies of Alexander the Great, of the Tatars and
Afghans, of the Mogul invaders of India. After the invaders
came the British, from the opposite direction. For them the
Khyber was the key to India's defence against further invasion
from the north-west.

I had the feeling, in the Khyber's narrowest defiles, that a
shot might ring out or a well-directed boulder come crashing
down. Men, and boys, too, with a rifle slung over their shoulder,
were a reminder that blood feuds still burnt fiercely among the
tribesmen. But the British, in fortifying and pacifying the
Khyber, robbed it of some of its old romance and gave it quite
a civilised look. The asphalt road was as smooth as any you
might find roaming through the hills of an English shire, with
signs that warned 'Keep left', 'Go slow' or 'Please blow your

horn'. They reflected nothing of the conquering spirit of Darius and Alexander, of Genghis Khan and the Moguls – who might, all the same, have been thankful for the sign-posts pointing the way to Peshawar.

On the way there, a chance meeting led to my dining that night with an Afridi chief, Malik Ashraf Khan. Night had fallen when I banged on the massive doors of the Malik's fortress home, and gave the password to the sentinel pacing the crenellated battlements. The Malik, his brothers and their sons all wore a bandolier and a pistol at their hip. Carpets covered the floor of the Malik's quarters, on whose walls there hung photographs – family portraits and a group in which ferocious, bearded tribal chiefs, all wearing the most amiable expression, were ranged about the political officer, a rather small Englishman.

After a meal of stewed mutton and rice, which we ate, seated on the ground, I took leave of Ashraf Khan and his family – fine-looking men, lean, dour and gentle-mannered. There was great warmth in their farewell: perhaps it struck them as odd that I, a stranger, went out into the darkness, unarmed, while they retired to sleep, a revolver by their side.

In the garrison towns of the north-west, Peshawar and Pindi (Rawalpindi), Jullundur, Gujrat – nostalgic names to generations of British sahibs – there still lingered the ghosts of Kipling and the Indian Army. I reached Lahore, and felt elated at having driven there all the way from Brussels. I had shaken the dust of Europe off my feet, changed it for the dust of the Iranian desert and the Indian plains. Europe's drabness had faded before the rich colours of the east.

Colour, like curves and music, has, for me, an almost aphrodisiac power. The Punjab glowed with colour: pink and blue and saffron turbans, orange and crimson saris, the vivid green of the paddy fields, temples of dazzling white marble and a sunset that flooded the sky and earth with gold and purple. That evening, I thrust my way through teeming traffic into Delhi. I was now half way to Singapore.

New Delhi is the symbol of the old British Raj, of India's past and present wealth. But beyond the viceroy's palace, the parks and the polo grounds, the misery of India still lay, ten years after the British had departed, prostrate before her splendour. Before the Old Fort, its battlements patterned against the stippled gold of the sunrise, people were asleep – not, as I had been, secure in bed, but stretched out on the hard pavement with a blanket like a winding sheet wrapped about their bodies. They might have been shrouded corpses, but now and then one would stir; a thin hand would emerge and draw the blanket away from the eyes and uncover the head. Slowly, stiffly, the corpse would sit up, rub its eyes and shudder a little in the chilly air. The day of the Resurrection seemed to be at hand. More corpses were rising and walking over to join others, which squatted round a flickering fire, warming life into their numb bodies.

At Agra, the moonlit dome and minarets of the Taj Mahal rose up, ineffably beautiful, above the scene of human misery and seemed to float on the silence of the night. At Benares, beside the holy waters of the Ganges, life and death touched hands. While the living bathed themselves, praying with up-stretched arms for life's blessings, the dead, wrapped in linen cloth, were borne to the burning ghats, to be reduced to ash and scattered on the same waters. The smoke of the ghats rose into the sky, the sun shone down and the holy river flowed on, cleansing the living and carrying the dead upon their way.

I returned to the Ganges at Bhagalpur, there to ferry the car downstream to a road-head on the opposite bank. But parts of the Ganges being infested at night by pirates, I could not leave until 2 a.m., when the danger zone would be in daylight. So I retired to the club at Bhagalpur – how often it must have been recalled by reminiscing British sahibs. But now they had gone, polo was no longer played on the smooth lawn in front and the cries of Boy! *Qua Hai*! and the sound of tinkling ice in *chota pegs*, drunk at sundown, had all died away in the receding echoes of India's past.

The little boat drifted listlessly on the current under the wan light of the moon. Then the sun came up, a raging red, and melted the moon from the sky. A sail was hoisted, but hung limply in the torrid air. So the crew rowed on, occasionally breaking into a thin, haunting little song, until, in the evening, we reached Karagola Road. It had taken fourteen hours to cover forty-five miles.

The snow-clad Himalayas appeared in the misty distance; then I climbed up to Darjeeling, a once gay but now forlorn little town, with its trim villas clinging to the hillside, looking out vacantly across the valley to the snowy massif of Kanchenjunga and Everest beyond.

On Christmas Day 1956 I reached Digboi, an oil-town in the extreme north-east corner of India – a corner, at least in the sartorial sense, that had remained for ever England. That evening dinner jackets were worn. It was there that I met Fred Warner, first secretary in the British Embassy in Rangoon. My long expedition from Europe to Singapore by road was the second ever attempted. The first was made by six Oxford and Cambridge undergraduates in two Land Rovers. They had warned me that I should meet redoubtable problems in Burma, much of which was infested by bandits. Fred, confirming these warnings, convinced me that I could never make the journey alone. So I gladly accepted his proposal to accompany me. I did well.

From the Indo-Burmese frontier at the 4,000 ft. Pangsau Pass – 'Hell Gate', through which, in 1942, thousands of sick, half-starved refugees, fleeing the Japanese army, came to safety – we had to negotiate twenty-four miles of what the map called 'very dense jungle', a dark, silent crushing mass of vegetation, before again reaching the fringe of civilisation.

It took us seven days to do those twenty-four miles, following the war-time Stilwell road, now reduced by the monsoon rains and the voracious vegetation to a narrow, crumbling track, strewn with boulders and overgrown in places by elephant grass over six feet high. The car was badly damaged – the engine sump, the chassis, the steering and worst of all, the hydraulic brake system – which, thanks to my training when a budding airman, I was able to repair.

We were guided through this green, clammy hell by a Burman, Mynt Wai, who enlisted help from Naga villages hidden in the jungle. We had to hack out new sections of track from the hillside, repair bridges, ford rivers. We passed one night in a bamboo shelter, its floor covered with rotting mule-dung, its roof of leaves bare shelter against the pouring rain, which drenched us as we slept.

New Year's Eve 1956–1957, found us, six days after that elegant evening in dinner jackets at Digboi, in another rickety, evil-smelling bamboo hut. We were a curious company: Fred and I, Mynt Wai, three Chinese muleteers and five Nagas. The Nagas were all opium addicts.

The elder of the party, a wizened old man with a mild, stupid expression, prepared the narcotic mixture. There was a slothful finesse about all his movements – they were deft, unhurried and purposeful. When everything was ready, the old man took his pipe, a length of bamboo with a little bowl fitted two inches from the end. Into the bowl he stuffed a plug of doped banana-leaf fibre. Then he carefully lit it and, with a gurgling noise, drew the smoke over the water in the bamboo stem, holding the pipe against his lips and sucking the smoke straight into his lungs. After a few inhalations a look of sublime stupefaction spread across his flat, ugly little face and remained there, fixed, while his dilated eyes gazed unseeingly through the flickering fire and into the shadows beyond. Then he sat back, deeply satisfied and, turning to us, proffered the pipe. We politely declined, so it was handed to one of the old man's friends. Fred and I, feeling rather left out, borrowed from the Chinese some green Burma cheroots. We felt contented in our peculiar surroundings. I had every reason to be – I was in the midst of a great adventure, a far cry from the elegant *soirées* at Brussels, or the household dining room at Buckingham Palace. I had put behind me the plush salons, the gossip, the rumours. I felt, at last, master of my own destiny. For how long, I dared not think, for liberty is so hard to win, so easy to lose. But here I was, in that abominable little hovel, happy as could be. I was discovering life at its humblest, at its lowest ebb. I was discovering myself too.

The light of the fire had died to a glow, and we were all asleep by the time the old year had given way to the new.

1957, in our little corner of the world, dawned heavy and silent, but full of hope. We spent the next three nights, at the village of Nam Gru, in a bamboo hut standing with two others in a clearing by the river.

Putting up next door was a Naga lady. In front of her hut stood a high platform, and on it the mortal remains of her late, lamented husband. He had been there some time and little of him was now left beyond his hat, shirt and trousers. His widow had come to fetch his skull and the best of his bones and to carry them back home, where she would set them up, ornamented with flowers. It was an old Naga custom.

Though none of that was my concern, the swarms of flies buzzing round me next morning, as I tinkered with the car, most definitely were. They bit viciously and soon my arms and legs were covered with ugly weals, which itched excruciatingly. Then the horrible truth dawned on me. The flies, done with feeding off the dead Naga, had turned on me for a fresher diet.

It took us another day to cover the eight miles to Nam Lip, where we found civilisation again. The village nurse, Lamung Htaing, and her cousin, the school teacher, both Kachin girls and Christians, looked after us. That evening, in their house, the village children came to look at us – strange apparitions, they must have found us. Then came the village elders, dignified, solemn old men who sat round in complete silence, as courtesy demanded.

After negotiating the swampy Hukawng valley to Myitkyina, the only real hazard we faced was bandits, which we could only hope to avoid by praying the Almighty to spare us a meeting with them and by trusting in the armed escorts provided by the local authorities.

By the time I reached Mandalay I was running a high fever. The bumps and potholes were torture to my wretched, aching body as we pushed on, with our escort, across beautiful but bandit-ridden country, through Kalaw, Taunggyi and Takaw, across the swift, shimmering Salween river, on to Kengtung.

That day, however, the escort quit at 3 p.m., so we went on alone. We knew that the next seventeen miles were dangerous for bandits; Fred remarked 'Mile 90 from Kengtung is supposed to be hell's corner'. In an atmosphere of high suspense, I drove on, while we made corny jokes and counted down to mile 90.

Suddenly, a station-wagon appeared and its driver signalled us to stop. 'This is it', Fred and I murmured simultaneously. But the driver simply handed me a note which said, 'An escort is waiting in the next village'. It took us to Kengtung.

The Burmese venture was ending. The hardships of the jungle, the hazards of bandits, far from lessening my love for Burma, made me feel more deeply for the country of my birth. Half a century earlier, at Myitkyina and in the Shan hills, where I now was, my father had been one of a small band of Englishmen who had tried to bring justice and order to this country. Their presence in Burma may not have been appreciated by all the Burmese, but their efforts seem to have borne some fruit. There was that little Christian community, peaceful and organised, at Nam Lip on the fringe of the jungle; there was Kengtung, to which the Sawbwa ruler, 'Shorty' Long, with his British education, had brought the benefits (without the disadvantages) of western civilisation. And there was the road, built by the British, which, though it had deteriorated since they left, had brought me all the way from Nam Lip. Imperialism was not entirely without its blessings.

It was doubtless because of the rigours of the trip through Burma that, beautiful as Burmese women are reputed to be, I hardly noticed one. Now, on the road to Bangkok, when the peasant girls at work in the paddy fields looked up at the passing car, I was often struck by their loveliness. After weeks in the wilds, I began to react once more to the enchantments of civilised life. The rehabilitation process was continued in Bangkok, thanks to the hospitality of the British Ambassador, Sir Berkeley Gage and of my long-lost Thai friend, Dawee Chalasapya. It was twenty years since I had seen Dawee, who was now an affluent air marshal and one of Thailand's leading men.

Leaving Bangkok, I drove on through the breezy sea-side town of Hua-Hin, through the jungle, and then, beneath a fiery sun, along a road, red and dusty, where pairs of little doves flapped just in front of the car and huge butterflies fluttered about, beating their gorgeously coloured wings on the heavy air.

In Malaya, British forces and Chinese terrorists were locked in a pitiless guerrilla war. At the frontier, a Scots police officer reassured me: 'As long as ye stick to the road, ye'll hae nae bother at all.' So I stuck to the road, which led across this beautiful land that I had known twenty years before. Driving through the green paddy fields, down roads lined with shady palm trees and sweet-scented frangipani, through sleepy kampongs where adorable Malay children waved, I felt once more, as strong as ever, the spell of Malaya. It was the Chinese New Year. Every family was dressed up for the occasion, the girls in the pretty high-collared jacket and trousers which so become their willowy figures, the children with bows in their hair.

From Johore Bahru, at the tip of the Malay peninsula, it only remained to cross the causeway to my destination, Singapore. But first I had to call on my brother Philip, then commanding a brigade of Gurkhas. I drove into his garden and found him, immaculately dressed in jungle green. As handsome as ever, he stood, microphone in hand, beside a wireless truck. I had not seen him for years. 'What on earth are you doing?' I asked him. 'Fighting bandits', he replied abruptly. 'I must rush off in a moment.' I asked, 'Can I come with you?' He eyed my dusty shirt and jeans and replied, 'All right, but first change into something more respectable.'

It was hard to believe that, two decades ago, I had sailed away from Singapore and now had driven back there – a 14,000 mile drive. It was one of those enjoyable moments in life when the wheel has turned full circle and everything that has happened in between is forgotten. Suddenly you rediscover the good times that were. I was forty-two, but felt only half my age.

CHAPTER 22

Oriental journey

About a third of the way across Australia, from Perth to Sydney, lay through a semi-desert, the Nullarbor Plain. This suited me. Though I passed through Adelaide, Melbourne and Canberra, I was glad to keep away from towns and the exigencies of bourgeois life. I had by now acquired a taste, if not a hunger, for the open spaces. I never felt lonely in a desert; it was like being in the air – the emptiness left me the room and the calm in which to think and to look myself straight in the face.

So I felt elated as I set off into the Nullarbor, trailing a long cloud of dust, with a thousand miles to go before hitting the asphalt again near Adelaide. The wide blue skies and far-off horizons helped me to find peace of mind – though I could not have borne that changeless scene for ever. I was glad when, beyond Adelaide, I came to rolling grasslands and blue gum-trees – horse country. Australia was a land of horses; the wild 'Brumbies' I had seen on the Nullarbor, the swift thoroughbreds I rode at work in the early morning and the sure-footed station horses.

Horses and the men who rode them, lean, hard men with a drawl and a dust-dry sense of humour – it was they who had much to do with making me, a simple Pommie, feel at home in Australia. Diggers, I found, were extroverts, open-hearted and down to earth. They brought me out of my shell.

New Zealand led to nowhere, but I could not resist pushing on to the furthest antipodes. So I shipped the car to Auckland and circuited first the South Island, then the North. In New Zealand, my self-chosen solitude began, for the first time, to weigh on me – above all in the South Island, whose grandiose, romantic scenery left me with an acute feeling of loneliness and a longing to behold all that beauty with someone – I knew not whom.

Since the Red Chinese authorities had insisted that I 'make use of the excellent rail and air communications' I had to send the car by boat from Sydney, via Honolulu, to Vancouver. I flew to Hong Kong, and from there entered China, carrying my bags across a bridge straight towards the muzzles of two Chinese machine-guns. I then boarded a train which puffed off, to the deafening strains of popular music, to Canton.

There I stayed in a hotel called Love of the Masses. The Chinese masses are doubtless ardent lovers, considering the number of little Chinese born each year, but there was no hint of eroticism about the Love of the Masses hotel; it was dowdy, though impeccably clean. Tinkers and tradesmen and passers-by regarded me, a long-nosed foreigner, with curiosity and good-humour. A band of urchins followed me everywhere; they were bright, receptive and enjoyable company – the marvellous thing about the Chinese is that you can get through to them, and they to you, without a common language.

I flew, in a Russian-built Ilyushin, to Peking. At Hengyang airport, a scheduled stop, the trilling of larks and the haunting cry of wildfowl more than compensated for the ugly, deadly-looking Migs lined up on the tarmac. They had no place in the melancholic beauty of the Chinese countryside, where the misty outline of the hills, the peasants wading, bent, in the paddy fields, among watery reflections and shades of vivid green, were details subtly woven into an exquisite tapestry.

At Peking, Spring had come, and the elusive fragrance of blossom, the budding green and the morning song of birds awoke in me an overwhelming nostalgia. Spring is the time I live for, the time of birth and perennial rebirth. It is faith and youth and the mounting of the sap, the desire to love and create and go crazy. It is the return of the graceful swallow and the cuckoo to their old, well-known haunts. Spring is the resurrection of the dead, a hint of eternity. It tells us, as we emerge from the tenebrous hell of winter: 'Believe it, the sun does shine'. That is what I need most to know.

Of all the cities I visited, Peking was the most remarkable. I felt at home among the Pekingese, courteous, hardy, good-humoured people with a taste for life. At the foot of the White

Pagoda an old lady beckoned me over and handed me a hard-boiled egg from her lunch-basket. If she and those adorable children who followed everywhere, are the Yellow Peril, then let's have the Yellow Peril. The Chinese call it Love of the Masses.

On the way back, via Shanghai, to Canton, bad weather forced the Ilyushin down at Nanchang. The passengers were driven into town in an open truck, sitting under orange umbrellas in the drizzling rain. We returned to the airfield at 4.30 next morning. Already, China was beginning to stir; men, women and children were trudging down the road into another day, carrying or pushing a variety of loads. They were desperately poor yet in their mild eyes there showed no desire.

From communist China, I returned to capitalist Hong Kong where wealth sat on a pinnacle and poverty had its habitation in the darkest hovels. On the steep slopes of the island stood the white apartment blocks and modern villas of prosperous English and Chinese businessmen – this was the bright side. The tarnished side you could see on the pavement outside the very offices where all that wealth was made, where the poorest of the poor huddled together to sleep.

Yet in Hong Kong, Dives and Lazarus did not regard one another from opposite sides of a fixed gulf. They rubbed shoulders and seemed to take one another for granted, the gulf between them being filled by the intense and complex currents of trade, in which even the most destitute played an active role. Toil and trade were the warp and weft which held together both the golden and the tarnished threads of Hong Kong's fabric.

It had been my good fortune in Hong Kong to meet Mr Eugene Black, president of the World Bank, which explains why I came to be staying in the house of Mr Yamamura, a friend of Eugene Black, in Kiso Fukushima, three hours by train from Tokyo. Mr Sen Matsuda came along as interpreter.

From the moment I took off my shoes at the front door I began to live Japanese-style. I stupidly held out my hand to shake that of Mr Aoki, the caretaker; he just as stupidly took it in his left hand. The point is that in Japan you do not shake hands – you bow. Aoki knelt in the living room and bowed his head to the floor in welcome. I did likewise, feeling rather silly. Then we drank green tea.

Tea over, Sen Matsuda and I decided to take a bath, in Japan no light thing, but a ritual. I felt like the victim in a game of strip poker. I was not sure how far or how fast the undressing business was meant to go, so I lagged about half an arm-hole behind my Japanese friend until at last we both stood stark naked. Mr Matsuda and I then entered the bath-room.

In Japan it is unthinkable to wash *in* your bath. Having soaked for a few minutes you step out, sit on a little stool and scrub yourself, splashing water over yourself from a hand basin to wash off the lather. The conversation runs on in nonchalant fashion. After drying, you gather the ample folds of your kimono about you, then stretch out on the floor to relax. Japanese floors are not meant only to be walked on. That night I slept on the floor.

The Japanese countryside was at its loveliest. Rambling wistarias by the river-bank cast a purple shadow on the water and on the slopes above, red azaleas looked like spurts of flame upon the mountainside. Cherry-blossom time was over, but apple and peach, apricot and plum were blooming wild; violets grew by the roadside and young ferns thrust up their pale green shoots towards the sunlight. The air was still and golden and somewhere down the valley a cuckoo called. I found it hard to believe that I was in the orient; Japan seemed to be beyond the orient, a link between east and west.

In the school at Kaida, a village smothered in wistaria, children were performing, somewhat erratically, an English folk dance – Shepherd's Hay, I think. Over the hill from Kaida, I walked, through woods of glistening silver birch, to Higesawa, a lovely hamlet with a stream tumbling through it and turning a dozen groaning waterwheels. Azalea, peony and violet were strewn along the footpaths which wandered between the timber cottages. The people of Higesawa were very poor, but laughter kindled quickly in their open, handsome faces. Higesawa pleased me. There was great peace there, and I would gladly have stayed.

Instead, I flew away out over the Pacific and by way of Wake Island, came to Honolulu. It seemed hardly conceivable that the bikini-clad bathers, whose bodies littered the fashionable beach at Waikiki, were of the same flesh and blood as the toiling peasants of Cathay and Nippon. A whole ocean, literally, lay between them.

The boat arrived, bringing my car from Sydney. We had been separated for six weeks and I longed for the open road. On 14 June the boat docked at Vancouver. The Far East lay behind me; before me, the Far West.

CHAPTER 23

Across the Americas

From Vancouver to Rio de Janeiro was the best part of 15,000 miles – at least by the road I intended to follow, across Canada and the United States, down through Mexico, Central America and South America as far as Santiago in Chile, then across the Andes to Buenos Aires and on, up to the Brazilian capital.

Originally, I meant Calgary to be the limit of my eastward run across Canada. Then I would turn southwards into the United States. But the call of the mountains, forests and prairies, was too much for me. It drew me on across the Monashee Mountains up over the Kicking Horse Pass into the Rockies, to Lake Louise. Then I turned north to Jasper, following for 150 miles, a chain of monumental peaks. Gigantic and aloof, they seemed to frown contemptuously on my puniness.

For three days I drove among pines and balsam poplars, millions and millions of them, until I was almost intoxicated by their heady scent. Then the road led into the prairies, into emptiness and nothingness, except for the pools of mirage, which themselves evaporated into nothing, leaving more road and more shimmering pools beyond.

The absence of human company made me deliberately shun any, yet I found myself heading, inescapably, it seemed, for Winnipeg and civilisation. I was only saved by one of those chatty Canadian road-signs: 'Look out folks – road up for the next fifty miles'. It jerked me out of my numbed senses; I turned right at the next crossroads and entered the United States.

One thing now worried me: the American press. As it turned out, I managed, despite my British number plates, to drive four thousand miles across the States without attracting attention. It was at the customs post at Noyes, Minnesota that I had my nearest escape. Looking at my passport, then at me, the immigration officer said, 'Funny, I got a kinda feeling I've seen you some place.' At that I dived into the car and, before the penny dropped, drove away.

One evening, along a road sparkling with fireflies, I approached Charleston, South Carolina. In the past ten days I had driven across half Canada and America, from the Pacific to the Atlantic. I now made a detour through the deep south, through Georgia and Alabama, through charming country towns where white timber houses shaded demurely beneath the trees and pink mimosa grew down the streets. The dead, as if they still belonged in the land of the living, slept, in unfenced graveyards, beneath the green turf, their graves marked by simple headstones, so much more in keeping with the passing event of death than those ornate travesties, festooned with plastic flowers, of the Cross of Calvary. When the southern evening fell, the air was warm and velvety and smelt of camellias.

I kept on westwards, and crossed two great rivers, the Alabama and the Tombigbee. The heat was overpowering and birds and butterflies beat their wings lethargically on the leaden air. It was not only the climate that I found oppressive. All the way across the United States I had been subjected to the crushing weight of American publicity. It came across ceaselessly over the radio, interrupting even the religious services. It shrieked from the road-side in vulgar, blatant language.

Towards New Orleans, the road ran, like an avenue, miles long, lined with advertisement boardings; so closely serried were they that they were barely readable. Then their frenzied, and apparently futile, messages faded for a while and New Orleans appeared, luxuriant and indolent in the humid heat.

In the teeth of a scorching wind I crossed Texas, a corner of Oklahoma and Kansas, and came to Colorado and – at last – fair, fresh country, unmarred by bill-boards. The ranch-lands rolled on westwards until they ended beneath a great bank of cloud piled high up into the sky. Beneath it stretched the Rockies, north and south, across my path.

I followed the Navajo trail over the Rockies, softer in outline than the austere massifs of the Canadian Rockies, but as pleasingly sensual, with the delicious smell of wood-smoke, of pines and poplars. There came back to my mind the talk I had years ago with Jan Smuts, when he told me how mountains gave him a sense of permanence and eternity.

After crossing the Continental Divide at 11,000 feet I ran down off the western slopes of the Rockies. The road flattened out and entered a vast amphitheatre. Tall, pink pillars of rock, carved out of the cliffs by millions of years of erosion, rose up and seemed to shout at me:

'Where wast thou when I laid the foundations of the earth?
When the morning stars sang together,
And all the sons of God shouted for joy.'

Away to the south-west, at Los Alamos, lay the research station of the United States Atomic Commission. By co-incidence, I passed that way on 16 July, the very day, twelve years earlier, that the world's first atomic bomb was exploded, experimentally, at nearby Trinity site. Within a few weeks, over a hundred thousand people had been liquidated in the holo-causts of Hiroshima and Nagasaki. It was claimed that this massacre of the innocent was committed to spare an even greater number of other lives. A better plan to save the innocent might be to immolate the wretched men – they are relatively few in number – who envisage crimes, including war, against humanity.

I reached El Paso, Texas, at night, half blinded – mercifully, for the last time – by an electric storm of neon signs. A bridge led across the Rio Grande into Mexico and I passed from the New World back into the Old. Centuries separated the two towns; down the road southwards, no sumptuous, soft-sprung limousines were to be seen, but lean horses carrying swarthy, leather-faced *rancheros*, and donkeys, some of them labouring under the weight of two passengers.

At Aguascalientes, Senor Dosmantes – he rejoiced in his name, which means 'two lovers' – took me to his *hacienda*. At the private chapel, *el padre*, who was teaching the *doctrina* to a score of children, greeted me kindly. Not so the poster he had nailed to the door. '*Cuidado*! Beware!' it said 'of Communists and Protestants'.

Perhaps it was the altitude – 8,000 feet – of Mexico City

which made me feel so light-hearted. But I sobered up in the early hours of 28 July when an earthquake began to rock my bed. As in the London air raids, the initial reflex was to get under something, so I crawled in the dark under a table and there waited for the building to collapse or, more hopefully, the tremors to cease – which, after what seemed an eternity, they did.

I was spared the fate of scores of others who were crushed beneath collapsed masonry, of the girl who, in a panic, leapt from the twelfth floor of the Hilton Hotel (which was split from top to bottom), of the golden angel which crashed from atop the Peace monument in the Paseo de la Reforma.

I had come to a part of the world where earthquakes and volcanoes were current phenomena, where human emotions, too, were wont to flare up into revolution. This explosive scene was overlaid with a crushing, hideous poverty, relieved with scenes of sublime beauty. The volcano Popacatepetl was a symbol. Its dark, misshapen form was no longer, its furious energies were spent. Now its outlines, concave, snowcapped, swept gracefully upwards into the hazy blue. Further south, climbing into the hills above Oaxaca, I felt that I was flying, suspended, motionless, in the air, looking down upon towns and villages still wreathed in mist.

On the way to the Guatemalan border, I stopped in Tehuantepec. The town, that day, was suffering from a hangover. The *fiesta* ended, townsmen lay as if dead, sprawled in the gutter or across the pavement. An old lady spread a blanket over the inert body of her portly husband, and beside the senseless form of her father there stood, on guard, a young girl. It was the women of Tehuantepec who gave distinction to the town, with their skins of polished mahogany, their hair done up in long pigtails, plaited with coloured ribbons. In long, flowing skirts of vivid orange and dazzling blue, they walked, erect, with a stately allure.

President Armas of Guatemala, had just been assassinated, so I had to load the car on a train, nicknamed *El Pollo*, the chicken, and bound for the only frontier post still open. *El Pollo* puffed and jolted past dilapidated villages – untidy slums among the wild luxuriant vegetation – whose poverty-stricken inhabitants nevertheless waved or whistled cheerfully at our passing.

In the towns of Guatemala, bells tolled and blue and white flags fluttered at half-mast in mourning for the murdered president. But in the highlands, the air sparkled and grassy banks were splashed with flowers, yellow and purple, and only the bleating of sheep or the whistle of a shepherd boy broke the silence. No one would dream of mourning a murdered president in that airy paradise, where politics had no meaning.

On the steep run down from the highlands, I met American Indians, '*Indios*' as they are called locally, trudging up-hill in the opposite direction, bent under huge loads. One old lady put down hers and mopped her brow; it would be another hour before she reached the top. A girl of fifteen followed, carrying a heavy load of wood; in her face was a naive loveliness, all the more poignant for the distress written in her staring eyes and dilated nostrils.

Another hour, and she too would reach the top. Another lifetime, and she would still be carrying loads up that cruel slope, her beauty withering away until she looked worn and shrivelled like the old lady ahead of her. Could I not stop the car, relieve them of their burdens and in five minutes drive them to the top? I am ashamed to say that I dismissed the idea, afraid that, being born to suffering and unused to the slightest charity, they would rudely refuse any help.

During an overnight stop in San Salvador, capital of El Salvador, I asked a man, 'Why do you have so many revolutions?' 'Why', he retorted, 'do you have so many football matches in England?' 'They're a popular recreation,' I answered. 'It's the same here with revolutions,' my friend explained. 'People just love them.' At Tegucigalpa, capital of neighbouring Honduras, I learnt that, during their last revolution, aircraft had bombed the insurgents, who shook their heads in dismay: bombs and aircraft had taken the fun out of revolutions.

Nicaragua's president, Anastasia Samoza, had been assassinated a few months earlier. In Managua, the capital, where I spent the night, a series of deafening explosions awoke me. Another revolution, I thought, but it turned out that they were celebrating a saint's day. Again, at San José, Costa Rica, I was awoken by gunfire, accompanied, incidentally, by an earth tremor. Again I was mistaken, it was another saint's day.

The road ended abruptly forty miles beyond Panama City. Between it and South America, lay hundreds of miles of swamp and jungle – 'the Darien Gap', which I went off to explore with Tommy Guardia, the engineer in charge of the projected road link with South America.

In a tiny aeroplane, we skimmed the tree-tops for 250 miles and landed at El Real. Then we sailed, in a dug-out canoe up the Tuira river into the country of the Choco tribe. Vampire bats were wheeling overhead when we and the four negro boatmen arrived to spend the night with a Choco family in their hut, built on stilts beside the river.

Tommy and I sat before a flickering fire and talked, over a bottle of whisky, late into the night. A Panamanian, he held broad racist views and thought that the mixture of blood, black, white and yellow, of which his countrymen were compounded, was a logical process in the integration of the human race. Tommy may have been right, but marriage is one thing (and a chancy one at that), breeding another. As with the rest of animal and plant life some cross-breeds give happier results than others. Some give none at all.

I felt very closely integrated myself that night with the negro, the *indio* and the animal world. All of us, animals included, slept together on the raised floor, and below it. Two feet from my head a little pig snorted away comfortably. Dozing fitfully at ground level were half a dozen middle-aged pigs and a fat sow with her implacable litter. In the early hours there came an eerie whistling noise from the jungle. It woke up the *Indio* children who began to cry. They in turn awoke the little pigs below, who wisely seized the chance of an impromptu meal. At this their long-suffering mother uttered a furious, piercing squeal and awoke the middle-aged pigs who protested with ill-concealed bad temper. Before I had time to doze off again I was brought violently awake by a loud beating of wings and the clarion tones of the household rooster announcing the break of day.

Some days later, from Colon at the north end of the Panama canal, I sailed away with my car, in a Japanese cargo boat, to La Guaira, the port of Caracas, Venezuela. Venezuela, in 1957, was a dictator state. The servants of the government were the masters of the people, the mastership being imposed by an efficient, if corrupt, National Guard. Foreigners were evidently not welcome, though the local press made an exception in my case, pursuing me hot-foot through Caracas.

I quickly fled this loathsome atmosphere of insolent wealth and *paperazzi*. Turning off the magnificent highway leading south, I sought refuge in the mountains, among country people who barely scratched a living from the ungenerous earth.

A rough, tortuous road climbed into the Andes, where the air struck clean and cool, a relief after the clammy atmosphere of Caracas. But soon I was down on the floor of the Mucuchies valley where the wind blew in hot gusts. And so I began, switch-backing from alpine to tropical climates and back, my journey down the Andes – one that was memorable, both for the wealth and the splendour of the scenery and the poverty of those who lived in its midst.

In the thin, chilly, but deliciously exhilarating atmosphere of the high plateau in Colombia, peasants huddled disconsolately behind walls, or in hollows in the ground, their *ponchos* gathered about them. On the low ground, the *campesinos* looked so destitute that it was hard to see what hope, if any, life in their wretched world could hold for them.

Beyond Cali, long, massive slopes, ablaze with flame trees, slanted down to the sandy floor of a parched, stifling valley where only negroes lived and blazing yellow flamboyants were as dazzling as the sunlight. Out of that arid garden of Eden the road climbed again and was lost in the dank clouds. Then it ran down once more, into Ecuador and the land of the Incas. The road I took, southwards from Quito, the capital, was once a highway in their extensive road system.

South of Quito is the country of the Coltas, a primitive *Indio* tribe, timid creatures whose greasy hair hung down in rat-tails over their faces. On the outskirts of a dilapidated village, *Indios*, with their hands, were smoothing the sand over the last resting place of one of their brethren; others stood around bareheaded, their red ponchos lapping in the wind about their broad shoulders. The widow crouched apart from the mourners, and the sound of her wailing followed her man to his long home. Inexpressibly lugubrious it all seemed to me, alone in that strange land, when I thought of all the souls which had entered this world and, leaving their frail bodies, had departed into the next.

Suddenly the gloom dispersed and I came to a sunny plateau where shepherd boys and girls were driving their flocks of sheep and goats. Then, just as suddenly, the road was empty again; dusk fell and I came to Cuenca.

Leaving Cuenca at day break, I started up a green valley where willows and eucalyptus grew. Girls, some with their husbands, were leaving for the fields. Their long, full skirts and jackets of scarlet matched the colour of the roses in their gardens, and the sight of them made me long for company and colour, for laughter and conversation.

But without hope; the road I had chosen was a lonely and a long one. It now climbed up over the high sierras, where the solitude was almost unbearable. Not a living soul could I see, nor did any sound disturb the silence, save the murmur of the wind and the muffled roar of the river far below. That afternoon, at Huaquilla, I crossed a bridge into Peru, and into the desert – a strip of desert between the Andes and the coast, which stretched southwards for 2,000 miles until it petered out near Santiago, in Chile.

In Tumbes, in the middle of a sleepless night, I got up, dressed and drove out into the desert, southwards towards Lima, 800 miles away. In that Peruvian desert, I heard on the Australian news that the Russians had launched their first satellite, Sputnik, into space. Above, the heavens were ablaze with a million stars. 'One star differeth from another in glory.' I wondered what Saint Paul would have thought of this Russian star.

At dawn I was among sand dunes with the murmur of the sea

in my ears. All day long I drove across the desert. That night, the moon, nearly full, rode up high into the sky and in its light the desert looked as white as snow.

South of Lima, the desert was never more inviting, with the air crisp and clear and the horizon lost in a blue-gold haze. I felt as if I were in another world, where the sand was coloured pink and yellow and grey, and moulded into crescent-shaped dunes upon which the wind had traced exquisite, wavy patterns. Far away, snow-capped mountains rose up out of the sand and pierced the blue sky. One of them, the volcano Misti, marked the city of Arequipa.

I turned my back on Misti and climbed up to the *altiplano*, an airy wilderness devoid of any sign of life, save a few flocks of llama, tended by slovenly *Indios*, and where, at nearly 16,000 feet (over 5,000 metres) the lungs labour for oxygen. Suddenly, in the midst of that desolation, there appeared the unimaginable blue of Lake Titicaca, fringed with yellow flowers and, wading among them, pink flamingoes.

It was quite unexpectedly that I happened upon La Paz, which, though it lies in a deep hollow, is the world's highest capital. Returning from there, I retraced my steps, past the mysterious waters of Titicaca, on which darkness had fallen, while the new moon, holding the old moon in her arms, looked terribly frail among the galaxy of fiercely blazing stars. With the dawn, there appeared the faint outline of Misti, beckoning me down off that bleak plateau.

By now the thousands of solitary miles in the mountains and barren deserts had given me a sensation of total insignificance. I felt as much of a nonentity as any one of those tatterdemalion, anonymous *Indios* of the *altiplano*, preoccupied only by my simple, immediate needs. At the same time my mind reached out and dwelt on far-off, intangible things; they had no place in this world, in which I myself had no particular interest – any more, I believed, than it had in me.

Three days in Arequipa brought me sharply down to earth. The town was *en fête* for Miss Universe, Gladys Zender, a Peruvian girl, charming, natural and intelligent, apart from her striking beauty. It was enough that we should meet for the world press to start wondering whether we were, as they say, 'romantically linked'. So – for her convenience and for mine – I disappeared once again, into the peace and oblivion of the desert. A day's run brought me to the Chilean frontier at Arica.

In the evening, I drove to the end of the last dusty street in Arica and out into the desert – a thousand miles of it. Along a track bulldozed out of the sand, I sat through a night of brutal, solitary torture until, at dawn, I reached Antofagasta.

Southwards, there was, about the desert, an unearthly, enchanting loneliness, with the pink sands sweeping up into a range of purple hills, bathed in yellow sunlight. I stopped and lay down on the sand to rest. No life existed within sight or earshot of where I lay; no bird, nor beast, nor reptile moved in the desert or in the air above it. The desert was absolutely still, sterile, a lifeless vacuum painted in heavenly colours.

In the evening I came to Taltal, where I found a club – an English one. That little English community, attracted to this remote spot by mining interests, had long since dispersed. But the club bar still felt – and smelt – very English.

With some sandwiches and a bottle of wine I headed out once more into the desert and the dark, with only the moon and the stars for company. A cheerless dawn revealed the desert in grim mood, with the going atrocious. Then, at long last, I reached the calm of La Serena, and more hospitable country.

I had had my fill of the desert, of its solitude and silence, and its sterile emptiness. I longed for comfort, for warmth and human company. The latter appeared immediately. No sooner clear of the desert, I found, to my infinite dismay, some reporters waiting by the roadside. They could not have been kinder, but, after more than forty-eight hours of non-stop driving, they were not the company I desired. They dogged me all the way to Santiago, where I arrived after midnight.

From Santiago I turned north-east, crossed the Andes, and ran down among the foothills into Argentina and the pleasant town of Mendoza. From there the *pampa*, fair and flat and featureless, stretched, all of 700 miles, to Buenos Aires where, to avoid the press, I aimed to arrive at dawn. This meant an early start.

Under a sky of pale blue and white, the colour of Argentina's flag, I once more felt the lure of the open spaces. It was as if I had left the ground and soared into the heavens; there I would stay until I reached my destination. I drove on all day across the *pampa*, until the sun set, and the moon stepped up demurely over the horizon. Like a huge balloon, pale gold and gloriously radiant, it floated up into the grey-blue sky.

After Buenos Aires, Montevideo and the *pampa* of Uruguay, where I rode out all day with the *gauchos*. Then, in my car, I rode on across more *pampa*, over the Brazilian border, through the rolling grasslands of the Rio Grande del Sul, where all was peace and pleasant.

The towns got bigger, the skyscrapers higher – Puerto Allegro, Curitiba, Sao Paulo – where once again I fell foul of the press, headed by a wretched little man called Tico, who, armed with a microphone, practically assaulted me on behalf, as he kept repeating, of the people of Sao Paulo. I was thankful when, next day, I drove unnoticed into Rio de Janeiro.

Rio was my South American journey's end. Only one thing marred my arrival – a letter from Norman Barrymaine, the man to whom I had entrusted the editing and handling of my articles. Since Singapore, ten months earlier, no word had come from him. Now I learned the reason for his silence: he had been writing my 'life story'. That book, which would make him a fortune, was to be a load of trouble for me.

Otherwise, Rio was all sun and colour and music. After the rigours of desert, mountain and *pampa*, I willingly surrendered to its charms. I could not imagine one extreme without the other.

And so, after basking for some days in the sybaritic atmosphere of Rio, I felt it was time to turn and face the sterner prospect of crossing the fifth continent in my path, Africa.

CHAPTER 24

Homeward through Africa

Viewed from Cape Town, the African continent looked even vaster than usual. At the nether end of that formidable land-mass, I felt microscopic and lacked the courage to start north-wards towards the Mediterranean. My route would take me on a nostalgic jaunt up through South Africa, then into Rhodesia, on through Nyasaland (now Zambia) and Tanganyika (Tan-zania) into Kenya. From there I would turn westwards across the continent, through Uganda and the Belgian Congo (Zaire) to Léopoldville (Kinshasa). After crossing the River Congo into French Equatorial Africa, I would aim for the forest hospital of Doctor Schweitzer at Lambaréné. Then I would head north-wards through the Cameroons and Nigeria to Kano, the jumping-off place for the 2,000 mile Sahara crossing to Algiers.

At last I pulled myself together and, at dawn on 21 December 1957, left Cape Town and started on the great drive north. Two years later, to the day, I remarried, yet on this home stretch, marriage was the last thing I dreamed of. On the contrary, having driven out into the world and found my independence, I meant to keep it. As if to put a seal on my intentions I per-formed, for my sole benefit, an odd little rite.

Somewhere in the middle of the veldt, miles from anywhere, I took the few letters that I had kept as souvenirs – those from Marie-Luce, enthusiastic, newsy, funny, touched me most – and tore them up, scattering them in the hot wind, watching the pieces blow away until they disappeared. It hurt slightly, cutting those sentimental, if simple, ties, rejecting the affection and the sympathy of others; but this little private ceremony was meant to prove to myself that my freedom was real, that I was the sole master of my destiny. I felt very sure of myself – unusual for me – as I continued on my solitary way.

It was ten years ago that South Africa had first enchanted

me, since that night, up in the Drakenbergs, when Smuts had said to me 'What we are working out, between blacks and whites, in South Africa may serve as a guide to the world'. But that was before apartheid, which has since proved to the world that Smuts was over-confident. However, South Africans, blacks, whites and coloureds, are still trying to work something out. Thirty years after Smuts said those words, I talked to one of the leading protagonists in the black-white conflict, Chief Gatsha Buthelezi, the Christian prime minister of Zululand, and a descendant of Cetewayo, the Zulu king whom the British, in 1879, had defeated at Ulundi. His view was that, since the whites, Boer and British, had fought as hard for this fair land as the blacks did, it belonged equally to both.

Standing on the banks of Blood River, where, more than a century ago, 16,000 Zulus were defeated by 450 determined Boers, I wondered when, if ever, the conflict between human beings would cease. Perhaps, like the river, it will go on for ever. But there was a hopeful sign to the contrary at Rorke's Drift, where, in 1879, Zulus, having just massacred 1,000 British at nearby Isandlhwana, were repulsed. Today, at Rorke's Drift, there stands a Christian mission; it gives hope that, if Buthelezi's view prevails, the bloody path of South Africa's black-white conflict may one day lead to peace.

I came to the Rhodesian frontier, at Beit Bridge. That night I slept in the bush, feeling very close to the heart of Africa. The night air throbbed with the rasping of a million insects and the throaty croaking of frogs; the dark purple night, vibrating with the light of myriads of stars, further energised the teeming life around me. In this electrified atmosphere, my own senses became too alive for sleep; I could only listen, waiting for the stars to fade from the sky, and the break of day.

Then I crossed the Limpopo, 'the great, green, greasy Limpopo', into Rhodesia, and made my way through the Matopo Hills, gigantic, rounded mounds of granite with massive outcrops of rock, perched one upon the other. Alone, amid this grotesque but not unlovely decor, sleeps Rhodes.

Three hundred miles down stream from the astonishing Victoria Falls, at that point on the river Zambesi, where the

Kariba dam was being built, I marvelled at the white man's technology, which enabled him to harness the Zambesi's mighty energy. At Zimbabwe, I explored the crumbling ruins, which tell of an earlier civilisation – between 500 and 700 A.D., it is thought – when the Bantu, in their southward migration, reached the Rhodesian area.

Black men had peopled the country, white men had forged it into a civilised nation. When the blacks claim Rhodesia and all that the whites have created as their own, it is enough to make Rhodes turn in his lonely grave. For he was the first to insist that civilisation, not colour, should be the criterion of responsible citizenship.

It is a pity that politics have to poison relations between men. In Nyasaland, children raced down to the roadside waving and shouting '*Bwana, Bwana*!' which gave me huge pleasure, not because I felt in the least like a *bwana* (master), but because to me, a long-nosed white, those black, flat-nosed children seemed so happy and friendly. What a perfect place the world would be if it were only full of children.

A long run across Tanganyika brought me to the country of the Masai, lean, virile, aristocratic people. Then, after a steep climb out of the Rift Valley, I came to the Ngorongoro crater, and beyond, the Serengeti Plain.

Wild game were thick on the ground – eland, gazelle and antelope, zebra, wildebeeste and wart-hog. It was remarkable how all that diverse multitude of animals, in contrast to human society, managed to live in peace – no doubt because they had enough to fill their bellies. Even the lion, leopard and cheetah who stalked their prey among those calmly grazing animals, killed only for one reason – to feed. It is an odd paradox that the life of one creature requires the death of another. Life is sustained by death and death by life.

Wheel tracks over the grassy hills were all I could find as a road to lead me into Kenya. After Nairobi, I followed the equator westwards into Uganda. At Entebbe, aircraft kept coming and going in the night. In one of them I could be home within twenty-four hours; by car it would take another two months.

Entebbe, with its small holdings and gardens full of flowers and, here and there, a wheelbarrow or the garden tools propped up against the wall, had a noticeably contented feel. Children, fat and well-dressed in their school uniforms, waved at the car. Among these stolid, home-loving people of Uganda, civilisation seemed to be firmly rooted. Nobody had then heard of Idi Amin Dada.

Nor could anyone then foretell that soon blacks would be slaughtering whites in the Belgian Congo. From Bukavu, in the east, a primitive track led 2,000 miles to Léopoldville, in the west. Driving that road was prolonged torture – which I soon forgot. What I shall never forget was the warmth, unstinted and natural, with which black Africa, at its very heart, greeted an anonymous white.

At my approach to each village a little rush would develop, led by small naked figures and followed at a more leisurely pace by their elders. From the roadside came a lively ovation, with cries of *bonjour m'sieur*, a frantic waving of hands and warm brown eyes peering into the car for a glimpse of the stranger. In villages and at river crossings – there were fifteen of the latter – the locals gathered round and we talked and laughed together. The rich laughter of those blacks still rings in my ears, their *joie de vivre* will for ever remind me how good life can be in this world. And how bad: two years later the Congo was aflame, as the blacks turned against the whites and massacred them. To-day no white – or black – would venture alone and unarmed, as I did, across that once fair and hospitable country.

Beyond the River Congo, a couple of days on from Brazza-ville, is the isle of Lambaréné, deep in the primaeval forest, where Doctor Albert Schweitzer had (mostly with his own hands) built his hospital. I sent a note to *le grand docteur*, asking if I might see him. His invitation to do so was signed 'with my kind thoughts, yours devotedly, Albert Schweitzer'.

The extraordinary thing about Albert Schweitzer was that, from the moment I met him, he made me feel that we had known each other for years, and that we were equals – although he was one of the greatest thinkers of our times and I, by his side, an ignorant child. Well into his eighties, he came walking briskly down the path, a striking, sympathetic figure in sun helmet, loose white shirt and grey drill slacks.

It was not his drooping moustache nor his long grey hair, which he scooped back now and then with one hand from his temples, which were his most arresting features, but his eyes, their steadiness, their burning clarity, their look of certainty. They were the eyes of one who knew the truth, who saw you, as you saw him, with nothing added and nothing taken away. We were down to brass tacks immediately.

All morning we talked, and when I left Doctor Schweitzer I had an overwhelming feeling of not wanting to go. He was so true to himself – and to me – that I felt I had been talking to a trusted friend. He opened my eyes and unlocked my mind, so that my strange destiny and all the things I had seen and felt during my journey round the world began to fall into place. He encouraged me to feel no regrets for the past, only a bouyant hope for the future.

It was in high spirits that I headed north from Lambaréné, through the Cameroons. Five days later I at last disentangled myself from the forbidding, claustrophobic forest and crossed Nigeria to Kano, where there was already a feel of the desert. Then, a long run through a wilderness of sand and thorn bushes brought me to Agades and the land of the Touaregs.

At Agades the Sahara really began. I drove the whole of next day across a hazy ocean of sand, tensely anxious, never for a minute certain that I was on the right track, for the wind had all but swept away the traces of previous vehicles and the oil drums and posts, intended to mark the track, instead floated somewhere above it in the shimmering mirage. When, once, I lost the track altogether it was only by climbing on the roof of the car and scanning the sands through my binoculars that I could faintly pick it out again. Recently, three other travellers lost at the same spot, had died.

That night, in the little oasis of In Geuzzam, my mud-walled room in the *bordj* remained empty. I walked out some way into the desert and there, on the bare sands, lay down to sleep. For some time I looked up into the glittering, star-filled vault of the sky. Directly above me was the constellation of the Twins and for some time I mused on the theme of two and one: 'Two are better than one'. It was months since I had last thought of those lines, in the midst of another starry night in Persia, right at the outset of my journey round the world. 'Two are better than one. If two lie together then they shall have heat: but how can one be warm alone?'

As I dröve on deeper into the desert, my sense of freedom and contentment increased. The Sahara was hard going and had its dangers. But in its midst, I experienced the most exhilarating moments of the whole of my long journey.

I loved the Sahara; in its calm, its silence and its immense space I felt very safe – completely free. I would gladly have stayed there, for I had a feeling that the milieu from which I had freed myself was about to close in on me once more.

Reluctantly I continued northwards. Then, at Ghardaia and, again, at Laghouat, as I neared the troubled area of the Algerian rebellion, the military insisted on my having an armed escort. Back to civilisation under escort! It was symbolic; the nearer I got to civilisation the faster my hard-won freedom seemed to be ebbing away.

Suddenly, in the Atlas Mountains I was robbed of it. Reporters picked me up, followed me and watched my every movement. I became once more a hunted animal. At the hotel in Algiers, I was brought to bay – and there was Barrymaine waiting for me.

He was the last person I wished to see but, in my disarray, I was putty in his hands. He persuaded me that he could help me affront the press. He became my self-appointed, unwanted counsellor. He stuck to me like a leech, and followed me everywhere. I longed to turn round and drive back into the Sahara, but I had to reach Brussels without provoking a blaze of publicity. I arranged for my car, covered with a tarpaulin, to be loaded after dark aboard the *Ville de Bougie*, bound for Sète. I was the sole passenger.

Despite these precautions, on my arrival at Sète, the reporters were waiting. For a year and a half, apart from occasional skirmishes, I had avoided contact with the press. Now they had once more fastened on to me. During the thousands of miles that I had driven around the world, I had only rarely needed to glance in the mirror to see if I was being followed. It had been an unspeakable relief to be free of that complex, bordering on paranoia. Now it once more possessed me, forcing me to use ruses and stratagems to outwit my pursuers.

In Arles I bought a loaf of bread and a bottle of wine and took on enough petrol to cover the remaining 1,000 odd kilometres to Brussels. Thus provided, I intended to sit it out until the reporters left me.

In the event, they disappeared from my rear mirror sooner than expected. So I made for Baix. In that small village in the Ardèche, an *agent* stopped me right in front of the sign indicating La Cardinale, the inn where I meant to lie up for a day or two. I protested, but the *agent* explained. 'There is a madman with a gun in the house next door. He has already fired at the *Commissaire* and he will certainly fire on you if you go that way.'

So, having survived, unarmed, a journey round the world, there I was, back in France, within a day of my destination, to find that my life was threatened! I was finally smuggled into La Cardinale through the kitchen door.

I suspected (rightly) that the press would be lying in wait for me on the main road to Brussels so, for this final lap of the journey, I took to the byways, aiming to arrive after midnight, when all would be quiet.

France, that Sunday, 23 March 1958, was at her most ravishing; the trees were burgeoning into life and the pale blue waters of the Rhône and the Saône reflected a cloudless sky.

It was 1.30 a.m. on Monday morning when I reached Brussels. The streets, brilliantly lit, were all but deserted, and I could hardly realise that my extraordinary adventure was over. Nearly a year and a half had gone by since I had driven out of Brussels along a road, 60,000 miles long, round the world and back again.

It had been a rich and rewarding experience. But its principal object, to shake off the past – and the press – had apparently ended in failure.

CHAPTER 25

Back to 'civilisation'

Needless to say, Eric Kennedy called next day to record, in his own peculiar style, the 'irony' of my return: 'There was not one friend to welcome him – except me.' His presence, really, was the only irony; the rest I had carefully planned. Friend Kennedy went on to recall how three years ago, he had watched crowds clustering round my car, which now stood 'battered' (it was hardly scratched) and unnoticed in the street. If only Kennedy's impression of the public disinterest in me had been true! For if there was one thing that I wished above all, it was to remain unnoticed.

I called Princess Margaret from Brussels to say hullo and tell her I was back. We were thrilled by the possibility of seeing one another again – though, for us, there was nothing more in it than a meeting between two old and devoted friends. Neither of us had the slightest *arrière-pensée*. Apart from a brief farewell at Clarence House before my world journey, we had not met for two and a half years, since that evening, in London, when the Princess had put a definitive end to our story with her public statement. It should have seemed inconceivable to any right-minded person that she would now go back on her decision. Yet, as we approached one another again, after so much time and distance, we were to find, to our great surprise, that there were people – with powerful voices – who, incredibly, believed we might still be contemplating marriage.

The Princess had to go to Germany on Friday, 28 March; I to Spain the following week for a fortnight's holiday with my sons. We agreed to meet in London on Wednesday the 26th. The Queen Mother very kindly invited us to do so at Clarence House, and the Princess naturally informed her sister, the Queen, who would that day be away on a state visit in Holland.

Everything, then, was set for a happy reunion; and so it

turned out to be. But wonderful as it was to be together again, we recognised in each other two people who, despite their sentimental past, had decided to go their own way. We brought each other up to date with our latest news and arranged to meet next day.

Unfortunately, the press read into that first meeting more than was really there. It was blown up into sensational news: 'They're together again . . .' And why not, for God's sake? After all, as Princess Margaret was reported to have said: 'We are not criminals.' Surely we had the right to see one another?

More unfortunately, the *brouhaha* over our meeting eclipsed, in the newspapers, the news of the Queen's visit to Holland. This immediately provoked a spate of tut-tutting; some British papers, inspired, so they said, by remarks from 'those close to court circles', accused the Princess of being 'headstrong', etc. and me of 'barging in behind the Queen's back'. Suggestions were even made that I was trying to 'force' the Princess into reconsidering the question of marriage, which, I need hardly say, was not mentioned by either of us.

In an attempt to put things straight I stated publicly: 'There are no grounds whatever for supposing that my seeing Princess Margaret in any way alters the situation declared specifically in the Princess's statement in the autumn of 1955.' The statement may have sounded a bit pompous, but it said exactly what it was meant to say.

Meanwhile, we dropped the idea of a second meeting; we had no wish to add to the excitement caused by the first, particularly as it was blamed on us – though Hannen Swaffer, the well-known columnist, wrote sarcastically in the *World Press News*: 'It's all very well for court officials, incensed by the fact that the Townsend-Princess Margaret meeting made the royal visit to Holland a mere second-rate performance, to complain "It's just what Townsend would do". But the Queen Mother, in whose home the frustrated lovers met, must have known. Was she, as well as Margaret, put on the carpet?'

Princess Margaret left, on Friday, the 28th, for Germany. I went to Somerset to see my mother who was staying in Bicknoller with my sister, Stephanie, whose lovely house I found closely guarded by the press. My mother was seventy-five and I had not seen her for eighteen months. I was determined that the reporters and photographers should not disturb our privacy. So, unnoticed, I drove on up into Bicknoller combe, and from there, through my binoculars, surveyed the scene, village and pressmen, and worked out a way to avoid them. Down through the narrow lanes I went again, through the orchards, finally to scale a six-foot wall and drop into my sister's garden. For two days, the press boys were unaware that I was inside her house, watching them through the window.

When, on Sunday, the Princess returned from Germany, we spoke on the telephone; both of us were confident that the present excitement would blow over and we looked forward to seeing each other again after her forthcoming Caribbean tour. Next day, I flew back to Belgium and went off to Spain with my sons.

I brought them back to England early in May; the Princess was still away, in the Caribbean, and the press left me alone. I returned to Somerset. So beautiful and peaceful was the countryside, those lovely rolling Quantock Hills where, in my youth, I had lain in the heather swotting for my exams and watching the buzzards soaring overhead, that I longed to stay there; it seemed an ideal place to write my first book.

Princess Margaret came back from her triumphal tour of the Caribbean and called me in Somerset. She told me that the Queen Mother had invited me to luncheon at her home, Royal Lodge, near Windsor, with the Princess and a few friends. That day, the Princess and I planned to meet again at Clarence House. We did so twice during the following week. But our hopes, that our meetings would no longer be news, were dashed; they only fed the rumour that marriage was again in the air.

The rumourmongers were still avid for news. This time Buckingham Palace, breaking with tradition, issued a denial, on 21 May, to a report, in the *Tribune de Genève*, that our engagement was imminent. That, stated Commander Colville firmly, was 'entirely untrue'.

The denial, though timely, was, in the event, a parting shot. Continually watched, reproached for 'forcing' the Princess's hand, I felt decidedly *de trop*; my only wish was to clear out, once and for all.

The reporters were naturally on watch when, on 20 May, I had called on the Princess at Clarence House. There and then, we resigned ourselves to the fact that, as long as we could not meet without provoking speculation, it would be better not to meet at all. Public curiosity killed our long and faithful attachment. That evening, Princess Margaret and I, warmly, affectionately, said adieu. We have never seen each other since.

As for my plan to settle in the west-country, to write, I put it out of my mind. I said goodbye to my mother, only to see her a few more times before her death. Then I turned my back on England and returned to Belgium, to sure friends and the quiet charm of the Flemish countryside.

I rented a cottage made of stone and thatched, surrounded by corn-fields and meadows where cows grazed peacefully, swishing their tails. There I sat down, like so many budding authors have done, to write what I imagined would be the most beautiful book that ever was. Three days later I was ready to shoot myself, so lonely and depressed did I feel.

Away from the solitude of my cottage the company of Marie-Luce was my main consolation. She had matured, during my absence, into a delightful girl, now nineteen, tall, straight and alluring. She had a passion for French literature, the theatre and the open air. She was a talented, if amateur, actress, and a champion in the show-jumping ring; her most spectacular success to date being to win an international event in front of Pat Smythe, England's best rider. But although she was a great success, Marie-Luce never changed from her good-natured self – simple, straight, generous, and pleasingly witty. She was a girl with a taste for life and a mind of her own. She had always been a good and loyal friend whose disarming naturalness to me, a man twice her age, touched me especially. Of all my friends, it was Marie-Luce for whom I felt most tenderly. Yet away from her, back in my cottage, my solitude weighed unbearably.

This was one of the reasons that motivated my future actions. The other, far stronger, was the despair and disillusionment I felt, after that exhilarating sensation, in the Sahara, with the world behind me, of having gained my freedom, of being master of my fate. This hard-won illusion had vanished overnight. Once again, and so quickly, I was shackled to a conventional mode of life, caught up in the stifling atmosphere of publicity, drifting uncertainly on a tide of rumour and speculation, incapable of taking any decision which did not have its repercussions in the world press.

Ironically, it was my desperate longing to escape once more from the clutches of that publicity which drove me, through a thoughtless, foolish impulse, to a disastrous decision that was to land me further, right up to my eyes and over my head, in a morass of cheap sensationalism.

One evening in June 1958, after watching 'Carousel' in the American pavilion at the Brussels Exhibition, Marie-Luce and I were invited to join a group of Americans, most of whom were in show business. Someone suggested that I should make a film of my journey. The idea was to make another world tour, this time by air, and film at various locations I had previously visited. Innocently, enthusiastically, I imagined a serious documentary which would rediscover some of the more extraordinary places and people that I had encountered during the journey.

But that was not what made me leap at the film project. It was because I believed that another world journey would offer the chance, heaven-sent, of escape from the solitude of my cottage and from publicity. What a naïve hope, the latter!

So I accepted and, in doing so, made a capital error.

Victor Stoloff, a dynamic and voluble American who had made a number of travel films, was the director. The film unit was composed of Frenchmen, including André Bac, one of the best cameramen in the country. Believing we were in for a pleasant round-the-world jaunt, I persuaded Marie-Luce, with her parents' permission, to come along. A photographer was needed – what for, I did not quite know, having never worked with a film unit. Marie-Luce had the eye and agility of a good amateur photographer, so that could be her role.

However, a regular photographer, a real pro., was later attached to the unit. Had I realised what he was up to, I would have walked out. But until I did, I naïvely imagined that he was just taking photographs. Then it was too late.

Though I had no notions whatever of film-making, I had brought back with me some useful material, shot with my 16 mm camera, in Peking, the Burmese jungle and other inaccessible places. The documentary, I now envisaged, would incorporate some of my original film (recopied in 35 mm). Victor Stoloff had far more ambitious ideas: he went out to make a Hollywood version of my world odyssey. He tried to turn me into a movie star, to make me act in the most ghastly travesties of the scenes that I had lived or observed.

For instance, to interpret my getting lost in the Sahara, he hired a score of camels (and a score of camel-drivers) and drove out into the desert near Ouargla to shoot them against the sunrise (or sunset, I forget which). Then he decided that it was not me who was lost, but an unfortunate Bedouin whom I, staggering, half-blinded, through a searing sandstorm would discover, as he lay, groaning and writhing in the sand, at his last gasp. Then I, the good Samaritan, would load the Bedouin into my Land Rover and drive him off to the nearest oasis.

'I'm sorry,' I said to Victor, 'but I just can't do it your way.' And so it went on during our four-months' film-making. Victor kept reminding me of the money I could make, I replying that I was more interested in making a sincere – not sensational – documentary. We had, after all, a lot of rich, original material at our disposal.

In the upshot, I succeeded in winning my argument, but not in making my fortune. Though I did not earn a penny from the film, I had the satisfaction of seeing it warmly acclaimed in the provincial capitals of France and the takings from each première handed over to charity. This, I know, would not exactly enchant a Hollywood mogul or an actor struggling for stardom. But it delighted me.

That was the end-result. Before then, the film had had consequences disastrous for me and for Marie-Luce. The tour, far from being the pleasant jaunt I had imagined, became an appalling publicity stunt. Unknown to me, Victor Stoloff had it all worked out, to the point where he had signed up with a London magazine for women, to report each lap of the tour, in an emetic series of articles, of which I, with Marie-Luce in the supporting role, was to be the central attraction. Our photographer, meanwhile, was feeding the world press with photos, as well as culling material for his own series, published in a London Sunday newspaper, of slushy articles, featuring Marie-Luce as the heroine, with me playing the 'heavy'.

On top of this came the publication, in September 1958, of Barrymaine's book. It was about my 'story', and no book about me could fail to be about Princess Margaret, also. Considering what had been written already, the material was not all that dramatic but the bore about Barrymaine was that he claimed to be an almost life-long friend of mine. This immediately suggested that I had collaborated with him in writing his book – which, needless to say, was untrue.

When Barrymaine appeared, without warning, in Algiers, I had felt like telling him to go to hell. Indeed, I would have done so had I not received counsel's advice to accept Barrymaine's offer to let me read his manuscript. My hope was that I would be able to remove from it any suggestion that I had conspired with its author. It took three days of haggling; my 'friend' tore his hair, strode from the room, slammed the door and even cried, but I finally agreed with him a relatively harmless version, which his publisher and my lawyer agreed upon. He had, however, no hesitation in adding an epilogue, compromising enough for me, which he did not allow me to read. By the time I was able to do so the book was already in print.

The newspapers naturally imagined that I was revelling in the ceaseless spate of publicity and (while revelling in it themselves) gave me a frightful lambasting. I may be forgiven, I hope, for remarking that few of them have survived to this day as I have.

The nightmare film tour ended, in December 1958, in Paris. By then, I had become an object of public entertainment; it would need time to play myself out of my unwanted rôle and regain my self-respect. 1958 had been a year of purgatory. 1959 was to bring its rewards.

In Paris, I was at last able to get down again to serious work, on my book *Earth my Friend* and the commentary for the film. I believed in both; they were my first ventures into creative art and, whatever their faults, they were sincere and free of the scandal and sensation which had surrounded their making. For some weeks, all was quiet, until there came a particularly offensive attack, first by a weekly, then by an evening paper, both French, on the grounds that I had traded to Barrymaine secrets of my '*idylle*' with the Princess. The court awarded me a symbolic 1 franc's damages against one of them. It was more than enough; I had at last turned the tables, if only slightly. The other publication acknowledged my right of reply and printed my denial.

These were passing hazards, unpleasant but successfully negotiated, in the long climb out of the mire. The next was the appearance, in May, of the film, and in June of the book. Asked by the producers, the Pathé company, to present the film in a dozen or so of the provincial capitals of France, I agreed – on condition that the proceeds of each première be given to a local children's charity. This was another small blow struck for respect and decency.

An unforgettable tour followed; from Lille to Marseilles, from Strasbourg to Bordeaux, to Lyons, Limoges and Nancy, Rennes and Vichy I went, and the mayor or his deputy did me the honour of receiving me at the town hall, beneath mingled tricolors and union jacks. My welcome was moving, above all, because it was given to me not as celebrity or author but as citizen of the country to which the French, remembering 1940, felt moved to express their gratitude. The tears of the deputy mayor of Strasbourg as he made the point, were but one of many similar expressions of the feelings of those who so kindly received me. The only jarring note which marred this demonstration of Franco-British *entente* was a letter from the British Embassy objecting that I had no right to such civic receptions. That may well have been true on the basis of protocol. But the

British Embassy should have known that when French hearts are stirred, protocol is no bar.

That *tour de France* has left a lasting impression. More immediately, it encouraged me to feel that there were people who took me as they found me and not as the notorious character they had heard about in the media. The sympathy I met during my travels in France gave me new confidence and eventually influenced me to make France my home.

But I was not yet out of the wood – or rather, the jungle.

CHAPTER 26

Marie-Luce: a new life begins

Since that day, about a year ago, out on the South African veldt, when I had felt so inebriated with my freedom, events had changed me. I longed to end the speculation. I longed for a home and someone with whom to share it. 'Two are better than one.'

The only conceivable one was Marie-Luce. We had known each other for years and through the turbulent events which had wrenched my life apart she had remained an unchanging, loyal and ever more endearing friend. I greatly loved her, but serious obstacles lay in the way of our marriage.

As Eve Perrick, in the *Daily Mirror* – on the morrow of our engagement – asked with such charming candour: could I be considered a matrimonial catch? I was forty-four, twice the age of Marie-Luce, divorced and the father of two sons. My financial background, Miss Perrick confided to her millions of readers, was not impressive, and my future uncertain. Marie-Luce of course was a catholic, I a protestànt; few marriages can have looked less likely to succeed than ours.

None of these considerations, redoubtable as they were to a lovely young woman, exercised Marie-Luce so much as the fear that she might always be, for me, the substitute, the second best. Her anxiety, so understandable, saddened me. For she was no substitute, but the ultimate, and has been ever since. The fact that, despite all the doubts and disparities, she accepted me, increased a thousand-fold my gratitude and esteem for her.

We announced our engagement in October 1959. Naturally, the press, which had been prying around us for some time, now closed in. As usual, the men – and the women – on the spot were generally sympathetic, though some did not write such kind and congratulatory words as is normal on such occasions. And there was the usual rubbish. It was said that Marie-Luce, thanks to an exploding V2 years ago, still found difficulty in reading and writing. This little handicap was however compensated for by her being the rich heiress of a Belgian tobacco king – it was highly probable that we would settle on one of his many estates in the Congo. Alas, tobacco had not brought a fortune to my father-in-law, who derived his richest rewards from literature, fine art and the theatre. His revenue may have sprung from diverse sources, but that from tobacco was limited to his fees as a director of a firm of tobacco manufacturers. On the other hand, he could recite, chapter and verse, from Balzac, Racine or Rousseau, from Molière and Labiche. He was, above all, an intellectual and a *bon vivant*.

Marie-Luce and I consoled ourselves that we should be through the worst after our wedding-day. When would that be? was the eager question, and because we wished to be married discreetly we declined to answer. It was sad that our wedding ceremony had to be such a hole-in-the-corner affair, but the alternative was to offer a picnic to the media.

In the event, the operation was executed in the best traditions of the Resistance. On the morning of 21 December, we fore-gathered in the private residence of Maître Jacques Wiener, Burgomaster of Boitsfort, on the outskirts of Brussels. Word came through that the Hôtel de Ville was being watched by a couple of reporters – a 100–1 chance had given them the tip. So we waited till midday, when the main doors of the Hôtel de Ville were closed for the luncheon interval. At this point the hungry reporters pushed off to lunch. We then slipped into the Hôtel de Ville by a back entrance and stood before the silk-sashed burgomaster – who had given orders for the main doors to be re-opened, as the law required, during the ceremony. Twenty minutes later, when it was over, they were closed again.

Thus were we joined together in matrimony.

Marie-Luce and I have been together for nearly eighteen years. To judge by our happy and close-knit family, our state of matri-mony seems to be quite as holy as, if not holier than any cele-brated to the sound of church bells – which is ironical since, for the Church, our marriage, as I was divorced, is not a marriage at all.

Ironically too, but infinitely sad, is that the Princess's marriage, consecrated by the Church, is itself now no marriage at all.

The ultimate irony will be when our marriage before the worthy burgomaster fulfils the Church's ideal of christian marriage: 'to have and to hold till death us do part'. I hope we yet have some way to go. So far, eighteen years of conjugal life have provided us with a fair share of storms and shoals and more than a fair share of sunshine.

Having got ourselves married without undue fuss, our object was to fade out. We spent our honeymoon in an unfashionable resort in Switzerland; the Balearics or the Bahamas would have been more romantic, certainly, but the need for discretion left us with no choice. Then, early in 1960, we settled in Paris, in an apartment on the Quai Louis-Blériot and there, in the shadow of the great aviator, before a panorama which stretched from the double-decker Pont d'Auteuil to Montmartre, we lived contentedly our *vie parisienne*. Beyond our circle of friends, nobody noticed us.

We felt at home in Paris. For a year I had been working there and still was; researching and writing, in collaboration with Pierre Kast, the French *metteur-en-scène*, a series of documentary films. I enjoyed the rigours of writing. My first book, though no gem of literature, had got by in Britain and the U.S., though the absence of any allusion to the Princess disappointed some. Possibly for that reason it did better in France than elsewhere. The French have generally behaved in an adult, honourable and discreet way over that much-discussed aspect of my life which – for those who think about it – means less than the fact that I happened to be leading a fighter squadron over London in 1940.

This has not always been the case in England. In April 1960 I took Marie-Luce there for the first time. After a peaceful week in the country, we stopped over, on our way back to France, for a night in London, where I had urgent family business. Though I had known for some time, thanks to Princess Margaret's consideration, that she was going to marry Tony Armstrong-Jones on 6 May, it seemed absurd that, with the wedding still over two weeks away, I should consider London, for a single night, out of bounds. Yet one London newspaper, with tight-lipped reproof, sniffed 'What a time to arrive'; and one or two other prudish busybodies wrote in the same vein.

In Paris, that brilliant spring of 1960, we savoured to the full *la belle vie*. Yet the lure of the country has always been stronger for us both than that of the city, even Paris, so in August we moved out into a small and rather dilapidated hamlet, Sainte-Gemme, in the parish of Feucherolles, west of Paris. The Clos Sainte-Gemme was our first home, a *maison bourgeoise* with no pretentions but unquestionable charm. The previous owner had been told by an old inhabitant that he remembered, as a boy, playing with his friends, when they heard the clatter of hooves of Uhlan cavalry in the street. So they took to their heels and hid in the foundations of our house; that would put its date around 1870.

Sainte-Gemme, eighteen miles from Paris, slumbered in the past, with its single shop, an *épicerie-café-tabac*, and its *garde-champêtre* who came, ringing his bell, to announce the village news, ending with *'qu'on se le dise'*, 'pass it on, everybody'. Its drainage system had surely been conceived well before the Revolution; fortunately our house was at the entry to the village, towards the centre of which our and everybody else's sewage ran sluggishly down an open gutter, to disappear mysteriously I don't know where. Whenever it rained hard, our long, vaulted cellar became flooded. Only after a Sherlock Holmesian investigation did I discover the cause; our neighbour, Monsieur B., had contrived an ingenious system of piping to empty *his* rainwater into *our* sewer, which thereupon overflowed into the cellar. Monsieur B. found that quite natural.

We made a garden, an English garden, with the labour of our own hands and those of Pierrot, the gentle-spoken, herculean son of Monsieur and Madame Vaidis, whose farm was across the road.

Soldiers, they say, dislike returning to old battlefields. It is as bad, I think, for gardeners when they revisit their old gardens. We made that garden; with Pierrot's help we ploughed up the earth and planted a hedge all around. We dug flower-beds and filled them with shrubs and flowers, with roses, hydrangeas and daffodils; we built a wall of stone, levelled and sowed a lawn. People admired our *gazon anglais* though, with the weeds and the mole-hills included, I thought it more appropriate to call it a *gazon anglo-français*.

I planted trees. Long ago I had talked with Princess Mary, the King's sister, about trees; she loved them and opened my eyes to their beauty. Trees are very close to us. In our youth we climb them, we rest beneath their shade and are finally carried to our long home encased in wood hewn from the forest. In planting a tree you commit an act of faith in the future – far beyond your own.

I planted dozens of trees, small ones four feet high and one which was but a cutting from a balsam poplar growing in my mother's garden in England. But before my hopes could be realised, fate intervened. We sold the Clos Sainte-Gemme, leaving behind something of ourselves. Now, years later, the garden has matured and become beautiful, the trees tall – and the tallest and stateliest is the one from my mother's garden. The only consolation is that we have given a garden, a *jardin anglais*, to France. (It was at the Close Sainte-Gemme that Henry Kissinger, U.S. Secretary of State, in 1975, held some of his peace talks with the North-Vietnamese delegates.)

Not for a moment did we believe that we should ever leave the Clos. Our souls had entered into its stones. Three times, at the final signal from Marie-Luce, I drove her from the house to the nursing home in Paris where, between 1961 and 1964, Marie-Isabelle, Marie-Françoise and Pierre were born. The Clos Sainte-Gemme was their first home, as it was ours. We believed that it was there, in the soil of France, that we had sunk our roots. Alas, they were too shallow to survive the upheavals that followed.

Already, about the time we moved to Sainte-Gemme, there occurred a fateful change in my life. Before Pierre Kast and I could complete our documentary film project, the producers, frightened by the cost, backed out – but were so nice about it that I told them to keep what they still owed me, reflecting that, after this further frustration, I was destined never to make documentary films.

So, as I longed to continue writing, it would have to be a book. My agent was begging me for one on the Battle of Britain. My idea, an original one, was to do it from both the British and German sides, but in spite of my agent's enthusiasm, I hesitated. Marie-Luce wondered whether we should ever survive on my author's royalties – only a score of authors in France do. But she had a stronger point too: book-writing is inseparable from publicity. As a business it is like any other, requiring a considerable investment by publisher and author, and, finally publicity to sell the 'product'. Of publicity we had had enough.

So I decided, reluctantly, against writing – the thing I most wanted to do. A writer, particularly the inexperienced one that I was, has to learn the hard way, on the job. By giving up then, I was to lose five years' experience, at least two books. It was a hard decision which I have always regretted, but it was probably the right one. We had been bedevilled by publicity; it was necessary to retire for a season.

The last thing I wrote at this time – an article in a series, 'Why I believe in God', run by a London newspaper, earned me enough to buy my son Giles a new suit.

Having just paid for the house I was down to my last franc. The question now was how to earn my living; the answer, thanks to a discreet hint dropped by a French friend, fell out of the sky. A cable from New York arrived at Sainte-Gemme and in mid-October I found myself in the big city, cloistered with the directors of a firm of wine-shippers.

Would I, they asked, form a subsidiary in France and ship French wines to them in New York? I knew nothing about the wine business (or for that matter any other), but this did not worry them. The essential was that I lived in France and spoke the language. Further, and here the prospect brightened, would I, once settled, write a monthly wine-letter for their clients? By the end of 1960 I was in business.

CHAPTER 27

American adventure

Short of pursuing my ambition to write, I could not have asked for a more congenial pursuit, despite the horrendous logistic problems of assembling, in the hold of a given ship, at a given time and place, hundreds of cases of different wines from suppliers scattered all over France – particularly when, with wine, you are dealing with something which reacts more or less as we do, hating to be knocked about, left out on a wind-swept quay or dumped next to the ship's boiler room. When, as sometimes happened, a shipment arrived in sorry condition, I found myself acting as intermediary in an international dispute, between the French wine-grower, an unhurried artisan, and the American businessman, a quick-thinking, hard-headed realist. My sympathies were with the French; my loyalties with my American colleagues. That was the seamy side of my job, and the experience was edifying.

Fortunately there was more to it than that. Wine, being as old as civilisation, is surrounded with folklore and history, and being a product of the earth, with mystery, love and toil. Someone said that wine was the noblest reward of man's immemorial struggle with soil and weather. This was the atmosphere I loved and in which, despite my ignorance, I felt at home – the vineyards and valleys of France and the men who toiled there. I often heard Americans say 'You gotta romance wine' and I responded gladly when I wrote about it. I revelled in my subject and the people and places which enriched it.

There was Pierre Quiot and his Mas de Maucoil, the *mauvais coin* where many a brave Gaulish resistant suffered at the hands of the Roman invader. Courage was needed still – to cultivate the orange-coloured soil, covered with a layer of pebbles, some bigger than a man's head and burning hot under the Midi sun, from which the red-purple wine of Châteauneuf-du-Pape gets its formidable savour and strength.

The wine-growers I best remember were peasants, craftsmen, sons of the soil. There was Monsieur Courbin whom I first met in his cellar, on one side of a shady courtyard at Pouilly, in the Mâconnais. He had just finished pressing; after a year's labour a new vintage had been born. Night had fallen on Fuissé, the adjoining village, when later on I called on Monsieur Cambier. On the floor lay a bundle of wispy *sarments* which would keep *le père* Cambier and his family busy all evening, splitting each one full length with their teeth, for use the following spring in tying up the new vine shoots.

Touring with Monsieur Barbet the villages of the Beaujolais – Morgon, Moulin à Vent, Fleurie, Chenas, Saint-Amour – he recalled how in his youth the grapes were trodden out by men, waist-deep in the must. In the Chablis vineyard Monsieur Raveneau led me to the top of the Montée de Tonnerre, to the spot where, during the late frosts, he camped out each night, ready to light the smoke-pots and cover the tender vine-shoots with a protective cloud.

In Burgundy, one crisp February morning, at the ancient Champ de Bertin – more familiarly Chambertin – I came upon Monsieur Louis Trappé tending his vines. Did he, I asked innocently, stick rigidly to the official pruning regulations? 'In general, yes' he replied, then glancing up towards the *coteau* with its serried rows of vines, thousands upon thousands of them, he added 'but you must never forget that each vine is an entirely separate individual.' Such is the art – and the love – of the *vigneron*.

The wine and the pretty villages of Alsace enchanted me, but my great love was the Loire, bubbling out of the earth where the Mistral grazes the foothills of the Cévennes and, without ever losing its placid charm, traversing France to meet the Atlantic rollers. From there, in the Pays nantais, upstream to Pouilly, I wrote of the *vignerons* and the vineyards of the Val de Loire, of Anjou, Saumur and Touraine where, in the shadow of those great masters, Rabelais and Balzac, I felt but a feeble imposter. But I had to keep on writing, about Vouvray's dark caves wherein is stored that delicious, heady wine; about the subtle Blanc Fumé of Pouilly and the succulent wine of Sancerre.

And so the vines, the *vignerons* and the vineyards of France became the joy and the inspiration of my life. Through them I came to know, and to love, *la belle France*.

Another, if only occasional, preoccupation was to visit, twice or thrice a year, the United States. I travelled the length and breadth of the land, from New York to Los Angeles and San Francisco, from Houston, Texas, and Miami to Milwaukee in the north, and all points in between.

I never fancied myself, nor did my colleagues, as a business-man. My job was to inform and persuade, to get French wines across to the Americans, whose ideas on the subject were generally rudimentary. On entering a wine-store, the first thing an American might do with the wine of his choice was to grab the bottle by the neck and hold it upside down against the light, expecting it to be as still and as limpid as Coca Cola. The merest speck of sediment, and the bottle was rejected.

I travelled far and wide, explaining, demystifying, romancing. Often I would find myself confronting a mass of flowered hats, a human herbaceous border. But the ladies beneath that array of flowers were attentive listeners. Reactions were some-times unexpected. At Albany, N.Y., a lady gushed at me 'Oh Mr Townsend, whatever you do, *don't lose your English ac-cent*.' At Saint Louis, Missouri, an attractive young woman asked what wine she should offer her husband. 'Why not a Saint-Amour?' I asked, 'there's the name – Amour, you know.' She laughed. 'Oh I'm past all that now. I've got five children!' Men were less receptive. 'Gee, I guess all I need is a couple of shots of scotch to set me up!' *La civilisation du vin* had yet to make an impact on such intrepid drinkers.

Another target for my talks were our distributors and their sales force – the military ring in that term is appropriate, for American salesmen, like Baring Gould's Christian Soldiers, are forever marching onward, as to war. Never can they afford to relax, for hiring and firing is a rapidly alternating process in the American business world. Leaving the office one evening I called goodbye to our national sales manager. 'See you to-

Marie-Luce on a station north of Sydney, Australia

above : With Hein Riess as Goering during the filming of
The Battle of Britain

opposite page : above : With Marie-Luce at the première of the film of
The Battle of Britain. below : At Malmö in July, 1955. The author, in the
centre of the leading horses, is winning on Rock

With Marie-Luce and the children, left to right: Marie-Françoise,
Marie-Luce, Marie-Isabelle, Pierre and the author

morrow, Al!' But next morning Al was missing. Overnight he had been fired.

If the British (according to Bonaparte) are a nation of shop-keepers, the Americans are a nation of salesmen. A salesman's survival depends on his sales. I admired those men as they struggled to grasp the complex appellations of French wines. Pouilly Fuissé was transformed into Pooly Fousse; Châteauneuf du Pape was explained away as the nine châteaux of the Pope. Then there were Coats de Provence, Mon-rashay and Ho-medock. How those brave salesmen must have cursed such outlandish names. Some reached a point of despair where they looked as if they would shoot someone, preferably themselves. Others became intoxicated with a wild enthusiasm – like Max Woontner, who must have sold hundreds of cases on the strength of a quote from Saint Paul: 'Take a little wine for thy stomach's sake'.

I liked Max because, while sincere, he laughed at his own extravaganzas, his favourite of which was a plastic fountain in the form of a Venus, from whose navel there flowed a stream of (bogus) Beaujolais. This monstrosity brought Max some excellent business. *In vino veritas* so inspired our Las Vegas distributor that he built himself a swimming pool in the shape of a champagne bottle – filled, alas, with chlorinated water.

My efforts at propagating French wines had earned me the approbation of my colleagues, and not least of Frank H. Bartholomew, owner of the Californian Buena Vista vineyards. Frank's main preoccupation, however, was as the distinguished president of Associated Press. It was encouraging to be complimented by this giant of the newspaper world on my 'interesting, informative and physically attractive' news-letters. More so when he asked me to go back to China and do some articles for A.P.

I jumped at the idea, but the Chinese were less enthusiastic. After sipping innumerable cups of jasmine tea while we parleyed in their legation in Berne, I was politely told that my visa was refused. Times had changed since 1957, when I had wandered unimpeded in China. But now a very different voyage was contemplated. Paul – the young president of my company – came all the way to Sainte-Gemme to persuade me to leave my home and settle with my family, at least for some years, in the United States. Marie-Luce and I were aware of the upheaval it would mean after the years we had spent making a home and a family in France. But when you are on the band-wagon the strongest urge is to stay there, not stop and get off. I know now that this was the moment to do so. I should have stepped down, picked up my pen and begun writing again. Instead, I agreed to emigrate, with my family, to the U.S.

Up to then I considered myself, and was considered by my American friends, as a foreigner. I could say and do what I liked in my peculiar foreign way, joke with impunity about American gangsters and the American way of life. I was, after all, a Limey. But once settled in the U.S. as an immigrant and integrated into the company, I was expected to play it the company way.

Having not the slightest intention of doing so, I made a number of fatal *gaffes*. First, since Marie-Luce was 'waiting a baby', as she rather nicely puts it – in the event our third, Pierre – she adamantly refused to have it elsewhere than in the Paris clinic where our two daughters had been born – Marie-Isabelle looking like a ripe strawberry, Marie-Françoise like Queen Victoria, not the least amused at having arrived on this planet.

So I left Marie-Luce waiting her baby and for the last three months of 1964 lived in a little house, built and smelling deliciously of wood, in the back-woods of Connecticut, forty miles from New York.

I should, I know, have played it the company way and lived in Long Island, but I chose Connecticut because it was horse country and some of the fairest I had ever seen. Moreover, I had a perfect arrangement with the owners, Doris and Arthur Hibbard. When the family arrived, we would move into the big house, a delightful early-nineteenth century New-England farmhouse. As it happened I had settled in a 'WASP' – white anglo-saxon protestant – area, though this need not have offended my company friends, most of them Jewish, since none of my own family was a full-blooded anglo-saxon nor a protestant.

Then I had trouble over my company car. My allowance as a vice-president would have enabled me to rent a fat Pontiac or a sleek Buick Riviera. I wanted a Mustang. Eyebrows were raised – why, even on a salesman's allowance, I could get something with a better status symbol than that. But 'I wanna Mustang' I kept repeating, like a petulant child who covets a toy. If, I told Paul, you insist on my spending my full car allowance, then why don't I pocket the difference between it and the Mustang's rent? That ended the argument. I got my Mustang.

Pierre was born in December. This time Professeur Musset allowed me, white-coated like him, to remain by Marie-Luce's side, to hold her hand throughout her ordeal of 'painless' childbirth. As an enthralled spectator of this stupendous event, the dawn of a human life, above all that of my own son, bold, beautiful and bellowing a greeting to the world, I bow in reverence to every mother, reflecting humbly that one of life's strange paradoxes is that man, the creator of life, should make such a minimal, if essential, contribution to its creation. Yet such is man's relentless urge to create and procreate that, hardly delivered from the womb of one woman, he is back, thrusting himself into the womb of another. Incorrigible is man as a creator – and, another paradox, as a destroyer, too.

With Pierre's arrival, his christening, Christmas and the closing up of the Clos Sainte-Gemme, with the dragging hours queuing with the family (including Pierre) in the U.S. Consulate for forms, photos and finger-prints, this was a hard time for Marie-Luce. Our departure for the U.S. was set for early February 1965, and my company friends, with characteristic hospitality, had laid on a reception for us at Idlewild airport. But as the day approached, it was obvious that Marie-Luce needed a breather.

So, once more, I resolved to play it my way and not the company's. I cancelled the air passage and booked in the *Queen Elizabeth*. We docked at New York in snow and — 15° centigrade. There was no one to meet us, no dockers either – they were on strike. I humped the family baggage out of the ship, loaded it and my half-frozen children into a station-wagon and drove to our new home in Connecticut.

Next morning, when I entered the New York office, the reception was as cold as the weather outside. Clearly, I had boobed again. At that moment, I – a day-old-immigrant – vowed that I would never stay in the U.S., at least with those people. They had given me a rude shock. America was a land of dreams, exciting, free. The feel of challenge in the American air stimulated me, and still does. Undeniably, my colleagues and I were made of different stuff, but it had never struck me until that moment how fundamental the difference was. It had been tolerable, fun, even – for both sides – during my brief visits, as a foreigner. But the moment I became one of the gang, our different personalities clashed.

Marie-Luce and I had good friends and absorbing interests in New York and around, but this intensified the clash. Thanks to kind friends, I became a member of the Dutch Treat Club – the basic qualification was to have practised one of the six arts, or the seventh. On Tuesday I would slip out of the office to attend the club's weekly luncheon, a welcome change from the daily picnic in the boardroom, supplied by a passing vendor and eaten off cardboard plates with plastic knives and forks. At the Dutch Treat Club, there were always lively, interesting people, and one Tuesday I had the unimaginable pleasure of hearing the guest, the celebrated Hoagy Carmichael, singing, to his own accompaniment, that sublime echo from the past 'I get along without you very well, indeed I do . . .'

It happened to be the theme that was developing, mutually, between the company and myself. My excursions from the company into the outer world seemed to put me more and more at odds with my company friends. I was sorry, for they were good guys and had treated me well. But man being a product of his environment and theirs being different to mine, things were set for a break between us. The crowning calamity, however, occurred not in the social, but the professional area. Now that I, the vice-president (Imports), had myself been imported I was expected to participate in the selling effort of the company. Selling must be a rewarding adventure for those who have the knack. I haven't. I am incapable of selling anything; I would rather give it away.

My disarray was total. It was, I suspect, to boost my morale that Paul arranged for me to lunch with Elmer Leterman, America's No. 1 salesman. Elmer was selling twelve million dollars worth of insurance a year. After reading, in Chapter I of his book, *The New Art of Selling*, 'You are potentially greater than you think', I was convinced that Elmer was right – at least about me. If he was the greatest of guys, I could be as great as him. But when I found him waiting at our table at the chic 'Four Seasons' my heart sank, my appetite failed. Elmer had festooned that table with a variety of gimmicks – flags and emblems and printed dicta, all signed Elmer G. Leterman. One of them said, 'If you see a man without a smile, give him one'. That, I suppose, was why Elmer smiled when he saw me – so broadly that I felt incapable of smiling back. I was crushed by his magnetism, his selling power, his oomph, I knew in an instant that I had not got it in me to be as great as Elmer.

Soon afterwards, I told Paul that I was through and he, quite amiably, confirmed that the company was through with me. From now on, the let-down was gradual, the end inevitable. I remained in Connecticut, at the company's disposal, for three more months – delicious months in which I felt gloriously free from having to play it the company way.

Our home on Riverbank Road was a dream home; the only drawback was that it was not ours. We had, in fact, no home at all. Beguiled by the bright vision of a bonanza in the States, I had burnt my boats, sold the Clos Sainte-Gemme. So far away were we that it did not, for the moment, hurt. Our New England home was our castle and it enchanted us, wooden-built, as it was, with its open fire-places and floors of rough hewn, polished planks. Though nearly two centuries separated us from its original owners, we still felt close to those pioneers, living there, within the bounds of their own stone walls, amidst the energetic comings and goings of chipmunks and squirrels, of woodchucks and gorgeous birds, of croaking frogs and snapping turtles in the lake – and snakes, king-size, like everything else which lived in that over-generous vegetation, but harmless.

All our neighbours either drove a Volkswagen or rode a horse. We stabled ours at the cosy, log-built ranch of Norman Hill, an Englishman who had taken root in New England. We even felt our own roots going down into that warm, friendly soil where you make life-long friends at the first encounter.

The closest of our friends kept their horses at Norman's, and with them we rode out along the trails and through the cool, enchanted woods 'in back' of Greenwich, Connecticut. Vying with each other, we galloped madly and flew the stone walls of the pioneers and laughed a lot. No western sheriff ever had a more gay and daring posse.

But our happy time in Connecticut drew to its close. One evening, in August 1965, our family trooped aboard a Boeing of Sabena at Idlewild. Pierre swung in a basket above my head, Françoise sucked her thumb and Isabelle, gay Isabelle, screamed with delight as she felt the massive surge of the Boeing's engines sweeping us down the runway into the night, away from the new world, back to the old. Being a tightly-knit team, greatly loving each other, we felt happy among ourselves. But on the face of it we were a sorry little band. Only a few months earlier we had emigrated to the United States. Now we were more like refugees.

CHAPTER 28

Back to France:
and they lived happily . . . :

Back in Belgium I found myself homeless and jobless, but not
without an aim, which was at all costs to get back to France and
regraft myself on to the roots I had left there. It took a year,
during which I had to face the fact that people, kind, understanding, generous as they were – out of working hours –
nevertheless regarded me as a man with a past, the man who
nearly married Princess Margaret, not a man who would fit
easily into a responsible post. The fact that I was married to
Marie-Luce, the father of her three children, did not efface the
basic image, which remained indelible.

My salvation, as I had foreseen in 1955, lay not in others'
hands, but in my own. That meant setting up again as a writer.
But my agent had now retired and no one was interested in my
adding one more to the fifty-odd books already written on the
Battle of Britain. The time was to come, but meanwhile anxious
months passed until I was accommodated – out of charity, for
which I felt grateful – in a London public relations firm. There
I pottered about aimlessly, frustrated and uncertain of myself.

All the while, I felt my love for England drawing me further
from my aim to replant my roots in France – to a point where I
nearly bought a charming house in Edwardes Square. Marie-
Luce telephoned an offer, which was accepted. Then, brusquely,
it was rejected for a better one.

Shortly afterwards, the clouds opened and an angel called
Paris-Match descended and spoke soothing words to me. Would
I write an article for a special number on the Battle of Britain?
Certainly I would. Bill Smith, once a brave bomber-pilot and
now on the staff of *Paris-Match*, helped. The article, published
in September 1966, came across well, so well that it ran into
two special numbers. Immediately there came offers from three
Paris publishers for a book – the one I had first thought of six

years ago. It was with Robert Laffont that I decided to stake my future, a decision I have never regretted.

This exciting event, which dispersed the dark clouds over-head, coincided with another which I also took as a sign from heaven, a nudge in the right direction. My P.R. partners in London charged me with the opening of an office in Paris. In October 1966, with the sun shining warmly down on us, my family and I, with Julie, the Labrador puppy, crossed the Channel. That evening we all slept again on French soil, at La Bullière, a coquettish Napoleon III house that I had dis-covered, and rented, in a tiny village, Lévis-Saint-Nom, twenty-five miles south-west of Paris. Our period of migration, trans-Atlantic and cross-channel, was over.

A few months later the City of Paris made me a charming gesture. Summoned to the Hôtel de Ville, I was handed the city's silver medal, engraved with the legend 'Paris à Peter Townsend'. It made me feel at home again.

Thus encouraged, I at once plunged into research for the book. But combining authorship with business was not my ideal, so I resolved to risk all on writing.

The last P.R. project I wrote up was for the Jordan Govern-ment. A few days after delivering it, the Six Day War gave Jordan more pressing things to think about. With that, my star, never a brilliant one, faded from the business firmament.

I find it faintly wounding to be asked, 'What do you do besides writing?' Writing for a living means writing for dear life, from dawn till dusk and sometimes on into the small hours of the morning. There is hardly time for anything else. You do not have to be a literary genius to find yourself forced to endure hours of solitary confinement, torture and despair; no writer is immune. Yet if genius is an infinite capacity for taking pains there must be at least a grain of it in every conscientious writer, however obscure.

In France, where a writer is classified as a *travailleur intel-lectuel*, it is reassuring to be recognised, if not as an intellectual, at least as a *travailleur*. For appearances are deceptive. The brain – anyway, mine – simply will not stand up to the same demands as the body which, like a brave horse, will go on till it drops. The brain is capricious, like a camel. When it has had enough it lies down, leaving you stranded in the desert, far from the wells of inspiration. And inspiration, I should say, is less a child of the brain than a mysterious alchemy of thoughts and sights, sounds and sensations, which the brain decants and moulds into words and phrases. When the brain tires, the process stops and frustration and despair take over.

There is some consolation in that the great ones have suffered as much, probably more. Ernest Hemingway, sitting glumly at dawn before a blank sheet of paper, could only get started by copying out, like any school-boy, what he had written the day before. Somerset Maugham would write pure rubbish until the right words came. And listen to another master, Joseph Conrad: 'I sit down for eight hours every day . . . I write three sentences which I erase before the table in despair . . . I want to howl and foam at the mouth . . .' Even I, who am not Conrad, have had it as bad as that. But the ultimate consolation for all the suffering is that, when at last it is over, you have created something and, in so doing, given your best, however much that may add up to.

Thenceforth, you are in the hands of your publisher, who may make or mar you. In the first category comes Robert Laffont, a master of his trade and an unfailing friend. Robert has seen me through some very dark hours. So have my editors Georges Belmont and Hortense Chabrier. On my school reports it was always noted, 'Needs encouragement'. I still do, every day, as I tell myself, 'You're no good, you worm. Chuck it!' But Georges will not have it. 'Just keep going', he tells me. And Robert is behind him, with his moral – and material – support. The lack of one or the other perpetually haunts most writers.

The research for *Duel of Eagles*, my first big book (*Earth my Friend* was only a starter) took me to Germany, to the Luftwaffe airmen who had fought us in 1940, among them Karl Missy, whom I had shot down and grievously wounded, and Werner Borner, who had tried to kill me before I parachuted into the North Sea. But it was with Frau Emmy Goering, widow of the Luftwaffe chief, and Edda, their only child, that my most poignant interview took place. They received me kindly in their fifth-floor flat in Munich. Edda, a blonde, attractive young woman, bore a striking resemblance, in profile, to Goering and had his eyes, which I had never seen, but which people said drilled you like gimlets.

That meeting with Frau Emmy and Edda has ever since remained on my conscience. Their warm hospitality touched me. I had previously seen the heart-rending photo of Goering embracing ten-year old Edda, his only child, on the day before he was to be hanged (he finally cheated the hangman by committing suicide). I felt sorry for all that Frau Emmy and Edda had suffered in a tragedy which was none of their making. Yet when I came to write about Goering I could not, in all honesty, find a good word to say for him.

The actual writing of *Duel of Eagles* – 700 typed pages – took seven months, and the only explanation I can find for my having gone so much faster than with succeeding books is that my family were so young that I hardly took part in their lives. When Pierre, aged three, came puffing up the circular staircase, bursting into my study in the attic, brandishing a revolver and announcing '*Papa, je vais te tuer*', I could hug him and send him gently packing. Now, ten years later, if the threats to my life are fewer, the demands on it are more exacting.

People believe it must be heaven to work at home in the country. In fact it can be hell, and often is, because of the demoralising paradox that, while working for the daily bread of my family, it is they who impede my efforts – because, loving them so, their presence about me saps my will to work. Times have been when the torment drives me, frustrated and despairing, away from them, to live like a hermit in the mountains, with the eagles and foxes and marmots, or by the sea, alone with the waves and the wind. Alone – that is the imperious, the cruel condition.

At La Bullière, the house I had rented at Lévis-Saint-Nom, I was not distracted by the children's simple routine – the village school was five minutes walk away and they had most of their fun climbing the lofty Wellingtonia and on the swing hanging from one of its massive branches. Life at La Bullière was very pleasant. There was nothing more we could do about our pretty garden, with its lawn sloping down towards a mass of red roses and purple campanula, than maintain it faithfully within its Cartesian dimensions. But as we felt our roots going down again in France, there came a new longing for a home of our own.

One Sunday in the summer of 1968, all of us called at a dilapidated farm near Saint-Léger-en-Yvelines, in the country, thirty miles south-west of Paris. On one of its gables was engraved, perhaps by an illiterate mason: MAR-O-SOISOS 1797. La Mare-aux-Oiseaux – there lived the widow Lecourt, alone, with five cows, a dozen hens and a couple of fierce dogs. Madame Lecourt was getting old and might, we were told, sell.

It happened, that Sunday afternoon, that she was having trouble getting the cows in. Marie-Lucie and I volunteered to help. The ladies, I admit, did most of the herding while I dodged cautiously from tree to tree avoiding the stampede, which ended up in the courtyard where the children, who were playing there, ran screaming for safety. The *corrida* over, that dear, brave old lady insisted on plying us with eggs and butter – which she made in a churn. As if that was not enough, she refused to sell to higher bidders while we made up our minds. This did not take long.

I bought that dear ruin and the meadow around. Next day I wondered if I had gone mad and kept on wondering until in 1971, *Duel of Eagles* began to pay off; the rebuilding of La Mare-aux-Oiseaux began, as well as the building, which took far longer, of the new book, *The Last Emperor*.

Meanwhile, I had been fighting the air war all over again – with my feet firmly on the ground. Harry Saltzman, producer of the epic film, *The Battle of Britain*, asked me to present it to the press and public in Europe and America. Why did such a historic and unforgettable battle need to be put over to the world? Because at least half the world had forgotten it or had never even heard of it. People in the United States thought it was an American victory in the War of Independence. An American girl student, at the mention of my name, remarked, 'Why yes, that's the English guy who won the Battle of Trafalgar'.

So I believed that I should be doing a worthwhile job for
Harry Saltzman and the British nation (in that order) if I took
on the job. My crusade took me round the capitals of Europe,
then I barnstormed the big cities of Canada and of North and
South America.

Back in France, *Duel of Eagles* had just been published. During
the lull between it and the next book came an unexpected
assignment – a talk show on Radio Luxembourg. A London
newspaper spread a silly story that I had become a disc jockey;
I had neither the qualifications nor the inclination. I simply
talked for an hour every afternoon to Pierre Dumayet, then the
best-known literary critic on French TV and radio. Pierre was
a serious, intellectual fellow and no one had ever heard him
laugh; but it so happens that the more serious people are the
more they make me laugh. Pierre half killed me with his grave
expression so that during our (taped) talks I often laughed so
much, and so did he, that the show had to be stopped.

Paris-Match then asked suddenly (as is their way) if I would
do a piece on the Israeli Air Force, an assignment I welcomed.
It was my first essay in reporting. At Tel Aviv, I called on Ezer
Weizmann (nephew of the great Chaim), who had begun his
career as a R.A.F. truck driver, became a crack pilot and air
marshal, and was now, appropriately enough, minister of
transport. It was the Sabbath, and Ezer, in shirt sleeves, invited
me to join the family barbecue. Mordechai Hod, Chief of Air
Staff, came over and we talked a lot about the air. Ezer recalled
a charming moment which occurred during that lamentable
period of terrorism involving Jew and Briton, as Israel struggled
for statehood.

He had flown to Britain to kill a British general. One evening,
as he sipped a drink in a London bar, a man spoke to him.
'Good evening, Mr Weizmann' said the stranger, 'my name is
Inspector B. of Scotland Yard. Please don't do anything rash.'
My meeting with those two ex-R.A.F. types immediately
opened the gates which normally takes the Israeli authorities a
month to refuse. When I thanked General Ezer he snapped: 'I
wouldn't have done it if I didn't like you.' I was allowed to fly
as a passenger in a Skyhawk of the Israeli air-force. As we

overflew Nazareth, I wondered what Jesus would have thought of the fighters patrolling overhead.

Surprisingly, my article in *Paris-Match* incited the Egyptian newspaper *El Ahram* to accuse me of working for the Israeli air force. It took all my powers of persuasion to convince Egypt's ambassador in Paris that I was not. The thing which really mattered to me was the tragic fact that, despite a common passion for flying, the youth of Egypt and Israel could find nothing better to do than to immolate one another in the sky.

That article I wrote, with René Sicart, for *Paris-Match*, was begun at 8 a.m. in Tel Aviv. We finished it at 2 a.m. the following morning. At 7.30 I took off from Tel Aviv and returned to Paris. That evening I gave a lecture in Marseilles. During the dinner which preceded it, the overwhelming desire to sleep sent my head lolling this way and that. Once or twice it may have come to rest on the shoulder of my neighbour, Madame la Préfète.

By November 1971, La Mare-aux-Oiseaux, cowsheds, pigstyes, hayloft and all, had been transformed into a charming human habitation, though at some inconvenience to the swallows which – since the end of the 18th century, I suppose – had nested under the oak beams, and now had to find new accommodation in the outbuildings. Once again, as we had done at Sainte-Gemme, Marie-Luce and I set to and began to make an English garden, this time out of mud and meadow, where cattle had once grazed.

I was already embedded in the new book, *The Last Emperor*, when we moved in. Two years later, in October 1973, still deep in labour and longing once more for a break, I received one of those unexpected calls from *Paris-Match*. Would I leave next day for Israel to report the Yom Kippur war?

It was the first time I had taken part in a land war – and I found it highly dangerous. But more frightening than the bombs and shells, the minefields and the ground-straffing Migs, was the deathly hush up-front in No Man's Land. Never before had I seen a corpse, but on the Golan Heights I looked for the first time in my life into the eyes of a dead man. Very calm and peaceful was their expression, even when they looked out from a horribly burnt or mutilated body. They seemed to be staring straight into the eyes of God.

The following summer, as I finished off *The Last Emperor*, swallows flew in through the window, glided across my room and out through another window. Of all the birds which come to La Mare-aux-Oiseaux – herons, king-fishers, duck and moor-hens, nightingales, woodpeckers and wrens, the swallows are the ones to which I feel the closest. They come from far away, perhaps as far as Africa and the Orient, as I have done, to nest here. They are as familiar with the place as I, the most far-flown bird of all that has come to La Mare-aux-Oiseaux. The swallows come to raise their young, as Marie-Luce and I have done, in this lovely place, which is their home as much as ours.

In the next life I would not mind being a swallow. Which reminds me, sometimes people ask: 'but wouldn't you like to be buried in England?' I really do not care; let the dead bury their dead. If anything, I would rather my ashes be scattered here, where my roots belong. And if the wind, the south wind on which the swallows ride, blows them on towards England, then let it be. I shall never know or care.

This much said, I feel not the slightest rancour on account of the strange fate which brought me to this place. We are all, like the swallows in their passage, tossed hither and thither by the gale of the world. Life might have been otherwise, but wasn't. Here, among the swallows, with my wife and children, I have found my true home. I have done so, I believe, not because it was written in any book, but because, like the swallows, I have out-flown the storm.

Index